This beautifully written and illustrated book has given me the chance to live again the lectures I heard at Ian and Barbara's training sessions. Seeing patients' symptoms as a symbol of their illness and exploring this with them enables the doctor, nurse or therapist to 'get in with the client and listen to their inner and outer reality ... by being with them in the interface we can help them to explore that interface and to take a stance which will allow conversion of energy to take place'. Even with all the wonderful treatments we have today, in the end the 'healing' is done by the patient's own self at many levels. With Transpersonal techniques of imagery, visualisation and the use of symbols in the process of healing, our understanding of the complex and subtle nature of our health is advancing from the current Newtonian thinking into the realms of quantum energy physics.

Dr. Jonathan Meads MB, ChB, DRCOG, MRCGP

I found this book very illuminating and well presented. It is extremely clear and helpful in understanding people's different personalities, including my own. Barbara Somers's work is of enormous interest and relevance to anyone who wishes to understand more about themselves, about parents and children, and about relationships and complexes within the wider community. It is like a multi-faceted jewel added to the sum of our knowledge about and insight into our psyche.

Anne Baring, MA Oxon

Jungian analyst (retired) Co-author of *The Myth of the Goddess: Evolution of an Image*; *The Mystic Vision* and *The Divine Feminine*; and more recently with Scilla Elworthy *Soul Power, an Agenda for a Conscious Humanity*. She is also the author of *The One Work, A Journey Towards the Self*; her current book in progress is called *The Dream of the Cosmos: A Quest for the Soul*.

Hazel Marshall brings us the fourth book in her edited works of Ian Gordon Brown and Barbara Somers. If you are a therapist, health professional, or just wish to know more about how the transpersonal perspective can help enrich your own life, then you can do no better than to read and dip into the wisdom in these books. The current work takes the approach of Symptom as Symbol to explore the different personality types. It will be particularly useful for counsellors and psychotherapists who wish to include the transpersonal perspective in their work. I highly recommend it.

Peter Merriott
Chair, Centre for Transpersonal Psychology

In 'Symptom as Symbol', Barbara Somers makes accessible some significant insights into the relationship between mind and body, *psyche* and *soma*. While this book opens a door for the individual who seeks greater self-awareness, it also enriches the work of psychotherapists and practitioners whose therapeutic fields involve direct contact with the body. Her lightness of touch, while reaching the heart of the matter, is freeing and enabling.

Monica Anthony
Psychotherapist and craniosacral therapist

# Symptom as Symbol

A TRANSPERSONAL LANGUAGE

**The Wisdom of the Transpersonal**

Also in this series:

Journey in Depth: A Transpersonal Perspective
The Fires of Alchemy: A Transpersonal Viewpoint
The Raincloud of Knowable Things:
A Practical Guide to Transpersonal Psychology

For a full list and details of all our titles
please see our website at:

www.transpersonalbooks.com

# Symptom as Symbol

## A TRANSPERSONAL LANGUAGE

BARBARA SOMERS
and
IAN GORDON-BROWN

Edited by
HAZEL MARSHALL

Illustrations
IAN THORP

Original paintings
PAMELA ALLSOP

ARCHIVE
publishing

2010

First published in Great Britain by
**Archive Publishing**
Dorset, England


Designed at Archive Publishing by Ian Thorp MA
Transpersonal Psychotherapist and Workshop Leader


© 2010 Archive Publishing
Text © Hazel Marshall, 2010


Barbara Somers and Ian Gordon-Brown assert the moral right to be
identified as the authors of this work


A CIP Record for this book is available from
The British Cataloguing in Publication data office


ISBN 978-1-906289-10-2  (Hardback)
ISBN 978-1-906289-09-6  (Paperback)

Cover painting 'The Island' and those inside reproduced courtesy of the
artist, Pamela Allsop, Lyme Regis, Dorset. www.pamelaallsop.com


also at www.transpersonalbooks.com


Printed and bound in Paola, Malta
by Melita Press

## PUBLISHER'S NOTE

This book is dedicated to the Editor

Hazel M. Marshall

without whose skill, passion, love and dedication
these books may not have emerged into life

The Ancients

# CONTENTS

# ILLUSTRATIONS

# FOREWORD

Barbara Somers has always been a pioneer, intuitively sensing a new idea whose time had almost, but not quite yet come. Thus she first started talking about the concept of Symptom as Symbol in the late seventies, when even holism as such was only beginning to surface into public awareness. After four hundred years of the Cartesian dictum which separated body from non-body – modern medicine is still largely under its shadow – the idea that body and psyche are inseparably linked and influence each other in sickness and health took a while to become known and begin to be accepted. Barbara, however, immediately went a step further and explored the deep wisdom of the body whose symptoms often, though not invariably, carry a symbolic message from the psyche.

Since then much has happened in the field of body-mind links: for instance, Psycho-Neuro-Immunology has delivered clear evidence of how our prevalent inner states can strengthen or undermine our immune system. There is still so much that we don't know about the miracle of the body-mind, but whatever else will emerge, Barbara's intuitive insights remain valid and valuable.

*Symptom as Symbol* is the fourth and final volume of the series that began in 2002 with *Journey in Depth*, and continued with *The Fires of Alchemy* (2004) and *The Raincloud of Knowable Things* (2008). They add up to a unique treasure-trove of Transpersonal wisdom, theory and practice, teaching and sharing, having the power to stop the reader in mid-sentence, struck by an awe-inspiring 'Aha!' moment, or by a happy chuckle over a witty aside in the text. They preserve the wealth of material created by Barbara and Ian, material that is both strikingly original and also linked to the timeless oral tradition which is either transmitted from one generation to the next – or falls silent forever, unless it is saved and secured in written form.

This is what Hazel Marshall has done, and this is the moment to thank and celebrate her for her major achievement. Starting out with ninety-one audio tapes and a mass of typescripts, which Barbara handed over to her in the late nineties, she turned them into the books we now have, with immense patience, skill, professionalism and perseverance.

And, of course, with love for the work. Thanks to Hazel, these books enable us here and now, and those who follow us, to read, explore, enjoy and learn from the Transpersonal wisdom radiating from them.

Thank you, Hazel, from all of us sharing the journey, for being such a faithful 'keeper of the scrolls' entrusted to you.

Beata Bishop
Transpersonal Psychotherapist
International Speaker and Workshop Leader
London
2010

# INTRODUCTION

I owe Barbara Somers and Ian Gordon-Brown an immense amount. Meeting them changed my life. Attending their first workshop in 1977, I became aware that I must write down everything I heard them say. For the next twenty years, not only I but many other participants did the same. For a short time around 1980 Barbara also tape-recorded some of the sessions they were running and it is those recordings, together with their notes and ours, which make up this series of four books of their work and teaching. The material for *Symptom as Symbol* was presented as part of their two-year counselling training. It was not included in *Journey in Depth* (which also comes straight from their recordings) because there was enough of it to make a book in its own right. This is that book.

I have been extremely fortunate to be able to edit their work – a further gift to me, conferring yet more meaning and fulfilment. Also, I have much enjoyed using this material over the years; these workshops and courses are still being run here at Rock Bank in Leicestershire, for people who wish to experience the work directly.

Barbara and Ian were ahead of their time. They would have said their inspiration came through, rather than from, them. They held as a working hypothesis that *we come from somewhere and we go to somewhere. Birth is not the beginning, death is not the end. Although we have bodies, feelings and thoughts, we are more – our being includes and transcends them all. The body-mind with its symptoms in times of distress is but part of the whole.* Even by 1978 such a working hypothesis still came as a breathtaking revelation to many.

However, they cautioned us against a too rigid approach which would try to tell *other people* that their symptoms had a meaning to be heeded and that they could change their health if they would only try harder. Rather, they encouraged us to listen for our own symptoms speaking to us in a possibly symbolic way. They showed how each person might learn the language of the body and heed its messages for their whole being. This gave much hope: symptoms could confer meaning; redemption lay in working with them until we could move on to the next stage and find within ourselves the *Other*, the Self, the inner friend. Seen in this light, our symptoms became compost for further development, rather than something undesirable that we just wanted to get rid of.

I have loved editing this series. To be granted both the heart and the chance to do it, in collaboration with my own inner world, has been privilege beyond compare. The books are for the present era and for this century. I trust they are also for the future, to be discovered many years hence by those who also speak their language and hear their message.

I hope they will have wings. In this, they will be helped immensely by their artists: Frances Crawford, whose lovely pictures grace the first three books, *Journey in Depth*, *The Fires of Alchemy*, and *The Raincloud of Knowable Things*; and Pamela Allsop, whose wonderful and inspired set of paintings has been created especially for this fourth book, *Symptom as Symbol*. Its pictures, full of energy, *are* its wings.

Hazel Marshall
Director of the Rock Bank Transpersonal Centre
Transpersonal Psychotherapist and Workshop Leader
Leicestershire
2010

hazel@rockbank.co.uk

## ACKNOWLEDGEMENTS

With profound thanks to Barbara Somers and Ian Gordon-Brown,
who were ahead of their time

I owe an immense debt of gratitude to many people, among them:

Dorothy Allen, Monica Anthony, and Peter Merriott
for material help as well as for their friendship and understanding;
Pamela Allsop for the inspiration, beauty and energy of the paintings;
Sacha Abercorn, Anne Baring, Renita Barwell,
Julia Crabtree, Alison Gaffney, Jonathan Meads and Susie Nixon,
all of whom read the manuscript and contributed their responses;
Beata Bishop for tirelessly proofreading the early manuscript,
and for her contribution;
Hossein Farhadi for his generosity over the computer;
Anita Somers for her encouragement and steadfast support; and

My particular thanks to the publisher,
Ian Thorp, for his skill and his tireless enthusiasm for the project.

Care has been taken to protect the identity of the people
whose stories appear in this book

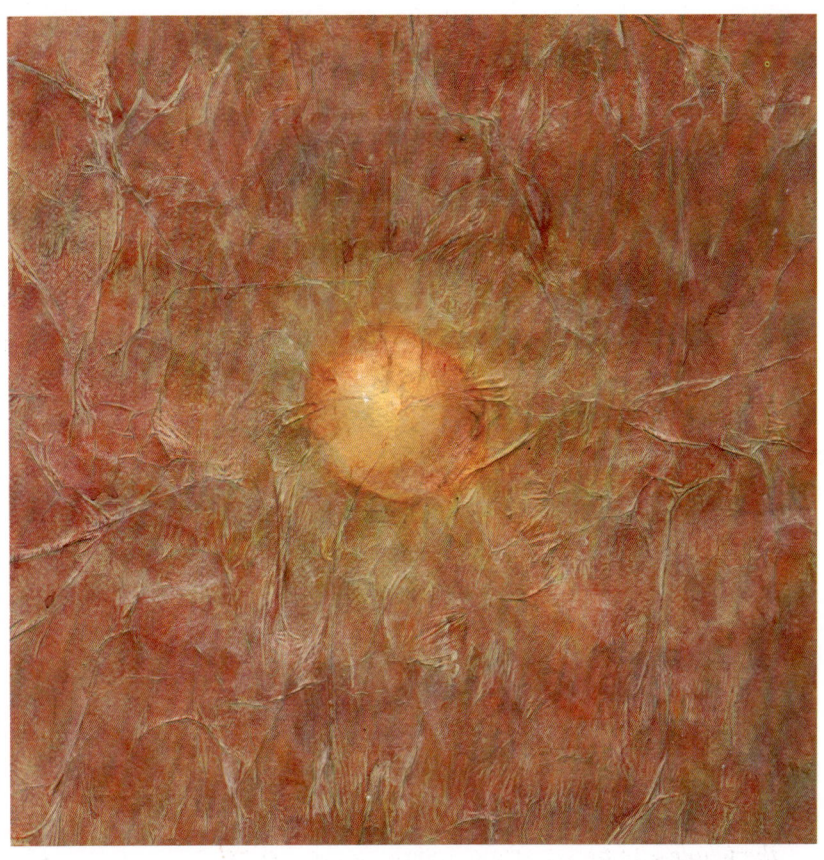

The Seed

# CHAPTER ONE

# Introduction:
# The Psyche and the Symbol

## Barbara Somers

*The Transpersonal is that which transcends the personal
but also includes it*

The psyche speaks in symbols. When we talk about *psyche* and *soma*, we are talking about the interaction of mind and body, spirit and matter. The art of Transpersonal counselling is to help the client and ourselves to listen to the symptoms – and to the symbols. By degrees we learn the language of these symbols, so that we can understand at our end what is being said.

This comment by Jung is very valuable:

*When we attempt to understand symbols, we are not only confronted with the symbol itself but we are brought up against the wholeness of the symbol-producing individual.*

Jung went on to say that this includes a study of the cultural background of the individual, thus filling in many gaps in our own education. He continued:

*I have made it a rule myself to consider every case as an entirely new proposition about which I do not even know the ABC. Routine responses may be practical and useful while one is dealing with the surface, but as soon as one gets in touch with the vital problems life itself takes over, and even the most brilliant theoretical premises become ineffectual words.*[1]

So it's all about the symbol-making individual. Our theories, however valuable, are secondary to that. We need to explore the wholeness of that symbol-producing individual.

---

[1]  Jung, *Man and his Symbols*, pp. 81-2; also in 'The Function of Religious Symbols', para 574.

### *The art is the listening*

Either explicitly or implicitly, we take it that the ego, the personality, the everyday self in the outside world, may in a very real sense be a symbol – even a *symptom* – of the greater Self. (And the Self is probably itself a symbol, or symptom, of something greater still; we are positing the microcosm as symbol of the macrocosm.) So we listen and attend, letting the symbols and images of the person speak, trying increasingly to hear what is being said. Being able to listen is different from actually *hearing*. A lot of people listen, very few can hear.

It is important to look at our own roots: our parents and the images we hold of them; the symbolic meaning behind the triangles of relationships with our brothers and sisters. We consider the child who is also present within the adult. With our clients and with ourselves, it all has to do with the quality of listening. We take the individual to be both a seed of potential and a symbol of the Self, and pay heed to the space and the boundaries he or she has. And through it all, we listen to the symbols speaking to us. There are archetypal patterns within this. Someone tells their story, their myth, and exploring how they do it is to observe the teller, the 'symbol-making individual'. They reveal themselves in the very way they tell the story.[2]

### *It's only psychosomatic!*

In the middle of the twentieth century, people typically used to say, 'Oh, it must be psychosomatic', implying, 'It's only imaginary. Therefore it doesn't have to be heard, so let it be dosed'.[3] After the seventies there was a swing in the opposite direction. People looked at psychosomatic factors and dealt with them more usefully, and many forms of therapy grew up.

However, since then there has been the danger of going too far the other way and falling into the error of seeing *everything* as psychosomatic. That way lies madness. Some people, assuming that all bodily hurts are in their heads, have felt that whatever happens – catching 'flu, falling downstairs, being hit by a tree, struck by lightning – is somehow caused by their minds and is their own fault. But if as counsellors we work with a client from that footing we can burden them with a load of guilt. Not only do they have their physical problem – accident or illness – they now have the load of misery that they are paying someone each

---

2    Somers, *Journey in Depth*, p.17. 'Sooner or later, willy-nilly, from a still deeper level, the gods (the meaning and nature of the Transpersonal Self) begin to rain down the archetypal symbols which, underlying everything, hold that person's own myth and meaning.'

3    See Jung, *Man and his Symbols*, pp.93-94, on the contemporary mistrust of the psyche. Ed.

week to pile onto them. Very frequently they end up worse than they started.

## Accidents do happen

So first, I have to say that I believe that, while everything can have a psychosomatic impact, accidents do happen. We are part of a collective. Things can go wrong. If I don't keep my eyes open, I will be run over. Right, I may have a psychosomatic reason for not keeping my eyes open in that moment; but, again, I may just be being extremely obtuse. Perhaps someone near me falls sideways onto me and I fall down and break my leg. That is not psychosomatic, that is my interaction as part of the collective, the risk I take.

Together with interuterine accidents and predispositions within the individual, inherited traits have to be taken into account. For instance, among my own ancestors, as far back on both sides as I can trace, everybody died from some blood or heart condition. I recognise in myself this weakness of blood and heart, which comes to the surface particularly in times of stress. Of course, it does raise the question, 'Why did the Self choose that time, that society, that family background to be born into, that particular damage?' These collective and family tendencies have to be borne in mind but, when listening to our clients' psychosomatic dysfunctions, we allow for other factors too. It all leads back to mysteries greater than we can account for.

## Check it physically

I underline this caveat: we *check the physiological situation* with our clients before approaching from a psychological, psychosomatic angle. There is a danger of forgetting this terribly important factor and I have seen some dreadful things done. Very early on we need to hear a person's medical history and background and the form their illnesses have taken, and be ready to suggest that they go to see a doctor. Excited though we may be about diagnosing through their images, we still have to be very careful with our clients. Check it out physiologically first. Those anxious to be 'helpers' can do wild things.

For instance, a counsellor was working happily on what he considered to be 'the opening of a higher chakra' in the client, but this 'crown centre opening' turned out to be an incipient brain tumour. I have seen someone working courageously into 'the deprived feminine principle' when the person actually had heart trouble. Of course, this might have emerged *because* of the feminine principle's also being deprived – there might *also* have been a higher chakra opening – but a physical check must run parallel. Again, blurring of vision can be psychological. Impaired eyesight can occur when somebody is in the process of coming to a new perception of something. Nonetheless, I would still have the eyesight checked out.

We have to keep a very sane outlook on this, holding the two in balance, keeping the possibility of the opening of the Self, yet still checking out the personal body. It is a two-handed job. *The body is involved*. The Transpersonal transcends the personal, but also includes it. We are talking to a whole person. Jung said that no deep experience in life, no breakthrough in consciousness, no enlightenment, is complete except that the body is involved in it. The body is the carrier, the grounding, the outward act of the internal Self. If any 'enlightenment' leaves the body behind, then it is only partial. 'I am an enlightened master!' claims the student, and the Zen master comes straight back: 'And what have you *done* with it?'

So we shall explore psychosomatic aspects, taking *symptoms* as *symbols*, hearing it all as a symbolic language related directly to the person creating the symbols, expressing them as they emerge, through their body, or in their words or in their attitude to life. We shall look at physical splits as a prelude to the exploration of splits within the psyche. We shall consider the tendencies to hysteric[4] or depressive or schizoid reactions to anxiety as manifesting these psychological splits, looking briefly at the clinical states of hysteria, depression and schizophrenia and considering their Transpersonal perspectives. We shall look at obsessive and compulsive and phobic tendencies as a symbolic language which is trying to heal splits for the individual. We shall explore the development of sexuality and the way it too can split into variations. All this should give a pretty accurate mapping of ourselves and of our clients.

---

4    Barbara Somers's use of the word *hysteric* is unusual. She did use it as a noun, to mean an hysterical person, so agreeing with the Oxford English Dictionary. However, she also adopted the word less conventionally as an adjective, describing the state itself; so *an hysteric personality*, *an hysteric position* or *reaction*, *hysteric behaviour*. She rarely used the word *hysterical*. I have chosen to keep her original usage throughout. Ed.

Secret Garden

# CHAPTER TWO

# Recoiling the Better to Advance

## Barbara Somers and Ian Gordon-Brown

*Crisis is the unknown – if it's known, then it's not a crisis*

### Crisis

*arbara Somers (BS)*: In any crisis something happens that we cannot handle. Our human reaction is to go back, in order to get space and time to handle the unknown factor. In other words, we regress. This is inevitable. The regressive act pushes us back to earlier stages. The healthy approach is to allow *time*; time to begin to move forward, to take a step into the present, to handle the present in a new and more positive way. Then, from that step forward and from what we learned in the step back, we develop new ways of living, new attitudes. Very often we have to drop some old attitudes. We have learned something. The crisis has become a place from which we can take a step forward.

Naturally, as shown in Figure 1 overleaf, anyone will recoil from the crisis of a trauma. In Tai Chi, the movement back from a hit is a regressive movement. Then there is the pause, the holding of tension; and the next step of the Tai Chi is to move again into the present, to look at it in a new way in order to go forward. In that movement, the possibility of the future opens up. It is exactly that conversion of energy that happens with our own crises. If we have the courage – *if* we have the courage? – to help our client to convert it into the 'now', to stand in the present, then the energy-flow helps them to recognise that there is somewhere else to go. There is an alternative way of using energy. However, this showing up of other possibilities is done not by disregarding what they are doing now – recoiling – but by accepting it. It is the dance of life. Their step back may take a long time, but in the end *they* will have the courage to move forward into the present, handle the crisis, look at it in a new way, and go on. A lot of people are able to do that. It can be long, tedious painful work, but it really is very exciting in its outcome.

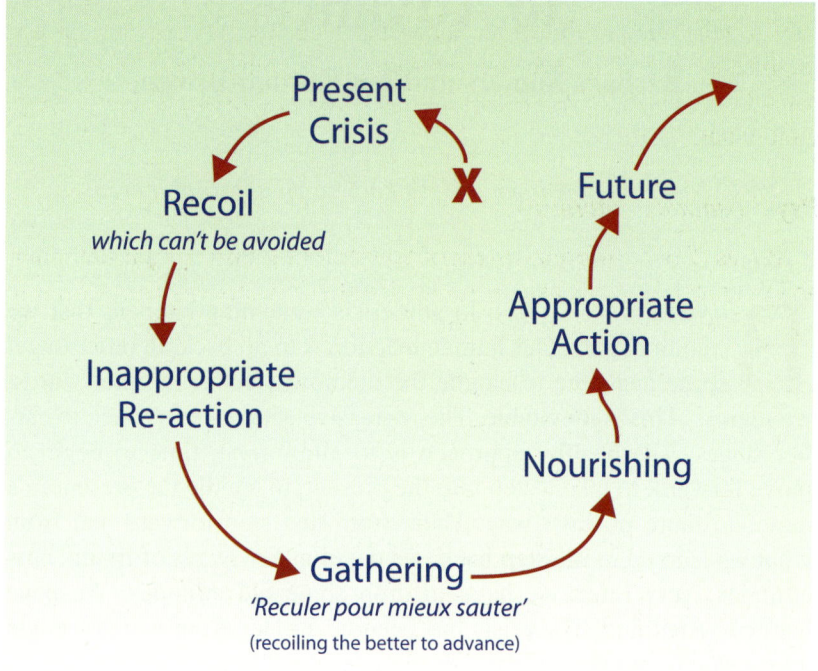

Figure 1. Crisis and Nourishment

So a crisis is where we are challenged by the *unexpected* (if we know about it, it's not really a crisis but a repetition of something we can handle). Any crisis is going to cause us to take a step back to past patterns so that we can assimilate it. And healthily, given due time, that will bring us into the present again to try to deal with this unknown in a new way. It gives us life experience, the opening up of a new potential which we did not know we had, a bit of confidence to go forward into the future.

### *The interface*

This is my attempt to make clear what the inner, and the outer, and the interface are. It may make sense as a map, but we remember that the map is not the country. If our inner world and our outer world are all one reality, which indeed they are, the point of interface is where this one reality, which has been split into two by our consciousness, comes together. The interface is where the total nature of the psyche tries to rebalance itself, where inner and outer seek balance under the impulse of the Self. We are exploring, listening to the interaction between inner and outer at the interface where they meet. It is a very vital pattern.

### *Psychosomatic factors*

It's as if two different levels of tension build up between the inner and the outer. These tensions are held at the interface in terms of *soma* and *psyche*. Firstly, the 'regressive tension' that allows somebody to

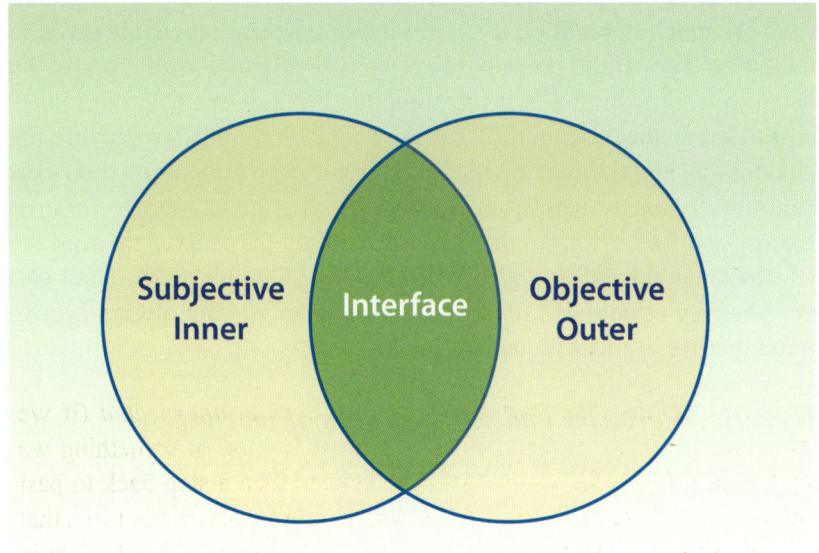

Figure 2. The Inner, the Outer and the Interface

develop *somatic* or physiological factors; secondly, the *psychological* tension that changes a person's approach to life in mainly *hysteric* [5] or *depressive* or *schizoid* ways.

Physiological symptoms will often emerge out of this area of tension in order to communicate to the individual that there is a problem between inner and outer, a need for readjustment. The various psycho-somatic symptoms that emerge may be suggested by earth, water, air and fire motifs, and these can point towards what is required to help balance inner and outer in a new way. At the physical level, this rebalancing is likely to show itself in terms of the person's outward physical posture. The way they stand is a very exact demonstration of their inward psychological stance, and their physical actions are usually reactions to some inner impulse. And dreams can state the need to rebalance inner and outer.

When some disturbance from outside sets up trouble inside, or *vice versa*, a circuit can be set up and go round in a never-ending psycho-somatic loop. So we stand at the interface and listen to the body as it expresses itself in physical symptoms. As we listen to the psychological dysfunctions, we know that the physical and the psychological tend to run very much in parallel. By exploring one we are inevitably taken to the other. The whole point is to set up a dialogue with the body. We listen to it, accepting that it has something to say. We help our clients also to set up that communication. And so, intervening, we can turn the circle into a spiral, breaking the dead circuit from either direction. This can allow what is being said to emerge as a new, creative tension. Energy is released to take them forward. Often they no longer need the psychosomatic trouble, and it is left behind. Though, as we shall see, *the physical symptom is often the last thing to go*. But always bear in mind that we are looking at one reality.

### Hysteric, depressive and schizoid ways of reacting

So we have looked at some *physical* ways of reacting to imbalance and crisis. How may a person respond *psychologically*? Well, we recoil. During the stepping back, however well we may manage to contain it, we become, say, hysteric for a moment – perhaps for quite a period. Or we go into a depressive state for a while, which can give us the breathing-time that we require. Or we split off into what would, if

---

5    See Footnote 4 for use of the word *hysteric*.

extended, be a schizoid state, giving ourselves the space to handle the crisis. It may be a measure of our health that we can express it in these ways. We recoil, the better to advance: *reculer pour mieux sauter*. The healthy, reasonably-adjusted person then moves forward and begins to function again, handling it as it is.

*It is not usually 'clinical'*. Only when the splitting has become an inappropriate reaction to too many circumstances – only when a person does it most of the time, or when the trigger is inappropriate to the degree of their reaction – only if, later, they frequently become hysterical without any particular cause for that degree of response, if they become depressed too long without enough of a trigger, if they are in a schizoid state most of the time – only then could we begin to see that the label 'clinical' might be applied to them.

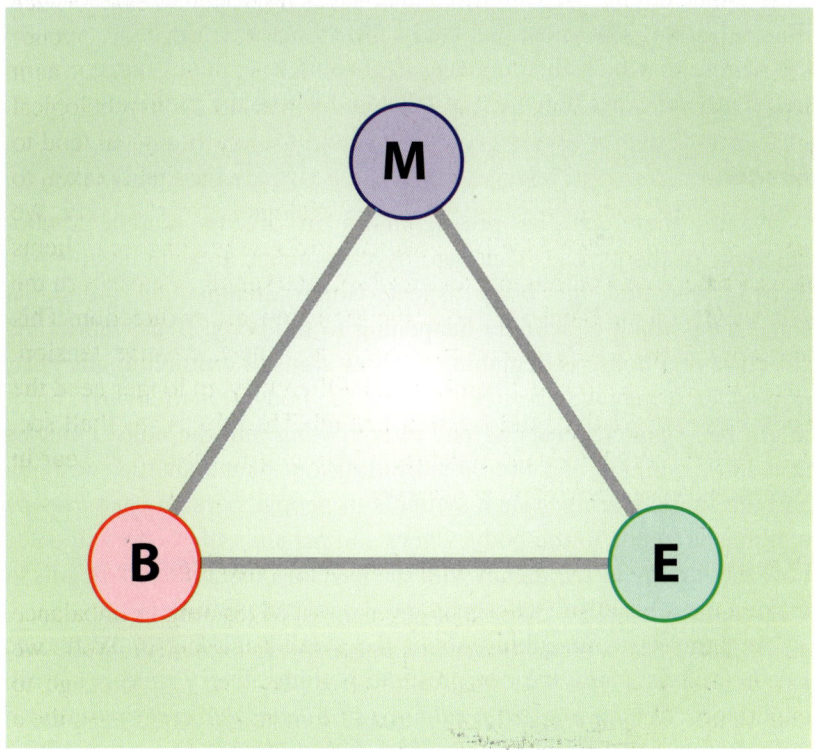

Figure 3. Body, Mind and Emotions

Looking at the interplay of our *minds* with our *bodies* and our *emotions*, we see the three forming a trilogy which normally keeps itself in fair nick. Their interaction is a self-functioning process.[6] However, we tend to intrude into it, perhaps blocking off one part or neglecting another. Then, within that normal, healthy homeostasis, we are going to have trouble and it will probably manifest itself eventually as a psychosomatic factor. Hence the need to have a fourth position, either outside or in the centre of the triangle, from which we can listen to what is being said by any one of these aspects.

A great deal of pre-signalling is given from this circuit of the three of them before actual illness occurs. Aiming for the preventative rather than the remedial, we need to listen to those signals, those early-warning signs. They are messages in a symbolic language advising us to make adjustments and adaptations to help bring back the homeostasis of the circuit. We can then adjust our lifestyle and attitudes before illness occurs. The more we study the symptoms, the more we see the degree to which the language is absolutely explicit, the symptom frequently an exact statement of what and where the problem is.

### Dreams

Again, there can be pre-signalling in dreams, another major language of the psyche. There are psychosomatic areas in dreams too, bearing in mind the *body* aspect. Some dreams can pre-signal something which is actually happening to the body. If the fabric and structure of a house is beginning to show signs of crumbling, disrepair or neglect, it may well be talking about the body. It isn't always, but it might be – gardens erupting and overgrowing into the house, jungles invading; spinning and the thread falling out of the shuttle; weaving and the fabric tearing – such symbols in people's dreams just *may* be making reference to the body. Check the person's life history and see how the linking of the dream with the psychosomatic factors begins to make a most beautiful, awesome and wonderful picture.

As Jung says, in talking about the symbol-making individual as *psyche* and as *soma*, we can presume nothing. Every time is a fresh experience. '*I have made it a rule myself to consider every case as an entirely new proposition about which I do not even know the ABC.*'[7] When we are working in these areas of the interflow of *psyche* and

---

6    Gordon-Brown and Somers, *The Raincloud of Knowable Things*, pp.109-111. 'Mind, Feelings and Body are like a three-pin plug: all in together, and the light comes on.'

7    Jung, *Man and his Symbols*, p.82.

*soma*, we need to listen first to the person's language; and there is nothing more individual than personal experience. Only *after* the event may we lay our own knowing in beside them, putting it side by side and in parallel with theirs where it can amplify and accompany their pain, or their joy. But only at the end do we do that. First, we need to have their own associations, and they may surprise us.

### Word associations

Here are a couple of examples. I was asking for my client's associations to words that had come from him. We came to *love*. Now, I personally associate 'love' with the organ of the heart, the solar plexus and the abdomen. I thought it would probably have quite a lot to do with the feminine principle, the left-hand side. But 'love' for my male client? It is fortunate that, instead of leaping happily in and making all those presumptions, I first asked him what the word *love* meant to *him*.

'Could you just put your hand where for you *love* is?'
'Desire!' he said, immediately.
'Where do you feel that?'
Straight down, in his genitals. 'Also,' he said, 'love means food?' Hand immediately to his stomach.
'What sort of urge goes with love?' I asked.
'An urge to express … '
'Where do you feel that?'
'Bowels, abdomen, throat.'
'Here's another word, then: *joy*,' said I. 'Where's that?'
'Heart,' he responded briefly. 'Oh, and library. Joy's all about the head,' he said.'About love of ideas.'

Now, how many people are going to put *joy* together with 'library'? Only with the word *joy* did he point to his heart but, for him, it was much less important than all those other areas. So all my assumptions went to pieces; they needed that widening by his own image-making process. And I could have blocked off every one of them by over-concentrating on my own associations and bringing the focus continuously to the solar plexus and the heart.

Checking back on this man's medical history, up came 'genitalia, stomach, bowel, throat, heart, head'. A pattern had built up. The life-history of that person's ailments was also the history of his inner development. It took us to the moment of crisis, which for him would be a breakthrough.

Again, the word *loss*. I personally associate loss with eliminatory problems, difficulties with blood clotting, with loss of courage, loss of heart, the recognition that *courage* and *coeur*, 'heart', come from the same root. And so for me to abandonment, to the navel and the lower abdomen and that deep-down instinctual area for loss. My subtle experience over the years led me to look for those possibilities, but also to listen at the back of my head. Because when – sitting there thinking all those useful things – I asked another client what *loss* meant to her, she responded, 'For me, loss means freedom, flying, release, letting go, sunshine, playing, flying a kite.' And that is *loss*? Who would ever have guessed it?

So with words we all share – *rejection*, *bereavement*, *grief*, *redundancy*, *pain*, *acceptance*, *home* – we presume nothing because all these words have sub-tones, half-shades, nuances, which are theirs, not ours. We have no idea of their music until we begin to listen. We presume nothing and let the symptoms and symbols speak. All these words are containers, and the associations we each make to them are of our own personal experience.

Somebody for whom the words *rejection* or *loss* are important, for instance, will carry their personal experience (early or later) locked into both their *psyche* and their *soma*. Over the years they will symbolise it in their physical posture, facial expression, stance, musculature, in the particular organs involved in symptoms. We watch and observe and see it there. We recognise that, over the years, the body has been carrying at a symbolic level much of the experience which has been too painful to be lived out. It has been missed, not seen to be there to *be* lived out. But the person will go on carrying it and carrying it, until they can release it into current living and move on to the future.

### The man with the migraines

Forty-three, in industry, one man had been married for twenty-two years, with daughters of nineteen and sixteen and a younger son.[8] The trouble he had brought was not his own, it was the heavy stutter this boy had developed at the age of seven. Could I suggest a therapist for

---

[8]    This account is also given in Somers and Gordon-Brown, *Journey in Depth*, pp. 51-59.

his son? We know that the problem a person brings in is only partial, the tip of the iceberg. (If they could state the problem they could probably solve it.) This man was seeking the innate nature of his own being.

Together, we worked back to find out who he really was. Gently I said, 'And how about *you*?'

'Well, my marriage is a bit problematic. My wife's a very difficult woman, you know.'

'Anything else?'

'Well, I do have these migraines. I'll talk about them another time. You see, it's my son's stutter … ' Only the migraines would he accept as his own. So we talked about his son.

'Yes, I can recommend a therapist.' (And the therapist worked extremely well with the child in a very short time.) 'Perhaps there are things in your son's environment that need to be looked at?' I said, 'but what gives *you* joy?'

'Music – Mozart – and New Orleans Jazz – oh, and driving at speed...'

Gently, gently I asked, 'When you hit the bottom of your barrel, what keeps you going?'

'Stubbornness!' he said. 'I'm too shit scared to stop grinding on.' (I thought to myself, 'Never presume you know what stubbornness is!') 'Let me say this', he went on, 'I have no imagination, I never dream, and I certainly can't visualise. That's it.'

'Got to work with this man!' I thought.

He'd been born in South Africa of Polish-Jewish parents, not very orthodox, 'a minority within a minority'. His father was a solicitor's clerk. 'Not a very good one,' he said, 'gentle, shy, intellectual, second-rate, unsure, introvert. He was always reading.' Father had been 'silent – the sound of music – Bach and all that intellectual stuff', he said. 'He didn't think much of emotions' (a very typical comment: didn't *think* much of emotions) 'and he had migraines.'

And his mother? 'Emotional, fiery, sentimental, ambitious.' On the other hand, 'She's like a hot oven, sometimes full of goodies, sometimes empty, and totally unpredictable'. (He didn't know he was visualising – he can't visualise!) There had been a double message from her. First, 'Get out there and do something, make a man of yourself' (your weak, wet father never did).' Second, 'Whatever you do, don't make trouble!'

So on the one hand, the silent, withdrawn, introverted father, shy, musical, unsure of the man's role, undervaluing the emotions; on the other, the mother, unpredictable, fiery, sentimental, extravert, wanting to fight for causes, valuing the emotions but fearing their effects, blowing hot and cold. And that just about exactly defined this man's own situation. He'd inherited and carried forth both these things. 'I tend to cool my emotions with my mind. I seek relationship but avoid commitment. I'm ambitious but I always pull out just when I'm going to make it. I go into a state of lethargy. That's when I get migraine.' This was also true sexually, with his wife.

From about seven he'd been aware, through feeling and intuition, of the tension of South Africa. 'It's black and it's white,' he said. 'It's savage and it's beautiful; it's music.' And then, suddenly frightened of going on, 'Oh, it's just Africa.' With his natural sense of justice and fair play, he'd begun battling for the underdog. After all, he was in 'a minority within a minority'. Remembering his mother's double message, at first he kept the battles at the verbal level. Introverted like his father, he was frightened of physical pain and aggression. So the other boys accused him of cowardice. So he got into fights. Then his mother beat him up with her tongue: 'Make no trouble!' A lovely closed circuit. Where do you go from there? You've got to be a man among the boys, so you have to fight. And you're terrified of it. And if you do fight, Mother knocks verbal hell out of you at home.

*'I felt both a coward and the need to be a hero. I was frightened of my own powerful emotions. I went up into my head and became an intellectual good-boy'. His deeper feelings were very passionate, very strong. He would 'cool it' in order to handle them. He began to see everything in extremes. If it wasn't this, it must be that. I asked, 'What did you do to help yourself?' 'I went out and watched the animals.' Up came the voice of the poet he had denied so furiously, 'I lay on the land and drank in the beauty of it all.'*

Migraine often goes with a split between head and heart. Fighting for causes, not being able to follow it through, migraine. The headaches which started then became very apparent later on.

At eight or nine he went to school in England. He hated being sent away from Africa. He felt deeply, he cried at night under the bed-clothes, and he dreaded anybody knowing he was upset. He detested aggression. 'I felt feminine inside and the female inside was stronger than the male outside,' as he eventually said (he didn't use that language at first). He also detested rough games, feeling the whole pack was bearing down on him personally. Boxing he loathed, pretending to be knocked out because he couldn't bear it any longer. However, he was very good at high jump and short races. 'I could turn in a sprint because they were all after me!' He dreaded admitting his love of music and poetry. They'd think him a sissy (they didn't rate music and poetry much at that school). Extremely frightened that they would know he was frightened, he was in quite a bad way.

He couldn't relate to the stereotyped masculinity at the school, having a heterosexual dislike of the homosexuality manifested there. 'I majored up in my head even more,' he said. 'I put poetry, music, feeling and all that stuff underground.' It is much easier for someone to find out what they are not than what they are. 'I worked and worked, too terrified to let up.'

Thus by degrees he was pushed further and further away from his own natural growth. I played back to him his feeling for Africa, his sense of beauty, his love of nature, his deep understanding of people. 'Yes, it's possibly so,' he admitted. I explained that, though he couldn't express his own measure of feeling and there was no place in his environment for intuition, yet he was high on feeling, and he was intuitive. He came to see the conflict between his father's cool intellect and grey absence, and his mother's fiery, blow-hot, blow-cold unpredictability, and he knew he did not want to take on either of those two forms.

We moved together into the period of *adolescence*, and then of *courtship*. He'd been deeply attracted to feminine women – surprise, surprise! – unconsciously searching 'out there' for the feeling and intuition so pushed down in him. However, afraid as he was of the missing factor deeply repressed in his own nature, he was also frightened of such women. He admired them, but at a distance; they were 'out there', untouchable. So instead he had begun consciously to seek 'boyish women' (his words). 'They were adolescent, good at games, with good minds, ready to fight for ideas.' He'd related to them as brother and sister, 'for fun, for sexual play,' he said. 'It didn't go deep, but I felt all right with those women.' Of course he did, they were reflections of the self he'd become in the world, majoring in the two functions he'd developed in himself. He was compromising with his own persona and ego. The bodies of a different kind of woman frightened him, reminding him too much of the aspects he'd lost. He was making an adaptive compromise.

Then at twenty-one he was proposed to. Because he did not like to say no ('Don't make trouble, darling!'), he married. And whom did he marry? A maternal, ambitious woman, who wanted him to be a man while treating him like a child. In other words, he married his mother. She gave him the adaptive set-up he needed. Though not safe in the long run, as history will relate, for the moment he was threatened by nobody he couldn't handle. He stopped playing games with adolescent girls. 'It's time you settled down and became a man.' He was so cut off from what he was really about, that he chose – or happened to stumble into – a career in industry. By the time he was thirty-six, with two daughters and a son, he was still living up in his head, pushing feeling, poetry and music aside. His wife was a woman to guarantee that he wouldn't easily regain touch with them. Good, dutiful, loyal, orderly, well-mannered, discreet, he'd never really been allowed off the leash. But now, because he was such a good negotiator and fighter, his employers let him out and he began to travel. His wife (pushing and ambitious like his mother) was quite happy about that; it left her free, while his success gave her the background she wanted.

But during the next three years, lo and behold he was 'horrified' (the number of times he used that word was fascinating) to find himself seeking out other women on his travels. He had several affairs. 'Is there any connecting link between these women?' I asked.

'Yes, they have a lot of feeling. They all love poetry. We go to concerts.' Duty conflicted with morality. He hated the double life he was leading (his passion for justice again). Initially horrified, he became amused to see that the further he was from home, the more likely an affair, while the nearer home, the more he modified his behaviour.

'Who's keeping an eye on you?' I asked.

'My wife!' Guilty and screwed up with fear of the coming confrontation, he tried very hard, but he 'couldn't help it'. 'All right, so we are incompatible, but it's not as bad as all that,' he said. 'It's just I can't live at home with her.' Terrified she'd find out, he searched the more obsessively for these other women. And he couldn't make love to his wife. It was a good day when he said, 'I suppose if I thought of her as my mother ... you don't make love to your mother, do you?'

I said, 'Well, no, better not ... ' He got on well with his daughters, liking them and his son very much, treating them as people. But around this time his own headaches really came out. We mapped those migraines. 'They come as I go away. I don't have them on the trip back.' He visualised himself leaving home in an aircraft. 'I'm going into an area I love and am fascinated by. *I'm so happy to be there that I feel terrible.* I don't know what to do with it – it all gets cramped up in my head.' Then, coming home, 'I'm a good boy now, it will be all right, *Mother will have me back*'.

Well, as inevitably happens, his wife, alerted by the change in him, found out and there was a confrontation. 'What are you *doing* on these trips?' He made a fine old mess of his reply, and the whole thing came out. She declared, 'If you think *you'll* be allowed around our girls just when they're adolescent, you've got another think coming!' This was the most awful thing she could possibly have said. He told me he was 'absolutely screwed up, shattered, shamed'. Hardly knowing what to say, he stuttered, 'It was monstrous – absolutely monstrous – and unfair, and un – unjust, I – I – I'll n – never forgive her!' And then he told me that that was the time when his son's speech impediment had begun.

Oh the horror of being debarred from his daughters! When his wife cut him off from them (and he felt she might have a point), he was 'horrified in every possible way'. The migraines became crucifying, the boy's speech troubles worsened and for him who 'never dreamed', dreams now started pouring up: punitive authority figures, the KGB, the secret police. He was impotent, tied down by 'them', trapped, amputated, always having to fight back. At first he saw 'them' as his wife. Only by degrees did he realise that she too was a helpless victim. He said, 'Poor kid! Perhaps she's got more in common with me than I've known.' By learning his own map he learned a bit more understanding of her. These dream figures were part of himself; he had to take them back. He promised her he'd 'be a good boy', he would conform. No, he wouldn't have any more affairs (and he had *not* had any more affairs). And his migraines were getting worse and worse. He said to me, 'I hate myself, I just really hate myself!'

Into his dreams came an almost-unseen woman whom he was trying to rescue. She took many forms. Turning her back she would look over her shoulder at him and dive into the water, or vanish laughing into the wood, a beautiful belly-dancer teasing him to sexual frenzy before rushing off and leaving him, always just a second before he could reach her. She was living out for him in dreams the bit of himself that he hadn't known how to handle, as were those 'feeling women' he'd been unconsciously drawn to and afraid of in adolescence.

And now there followed them into his dreams a man who was both fighter and healer. Aggressive against 'them', he was also gentle, quiet and capable. More and more the dreamer saw this figure as an aspect of himself, the strong fighter for causes, tender as well. His father, out of touch with his own masculine side, had given a pattern of masculine weakness. Now he realised it was neither weak nor second-rate for a man to be feminine, as his mother had suggested. The fighter-healer was part of his own style. He had a lot to learn about what it is to be masculine.

In many of his dreams his son appeared, the inarticulate aspect of his own confused child. He began to talk with his son about the child's own real feelings, and by degrees the stutter eased out. The boy had been wondering where his father was. Now, he came to see him as both tender and strong. Finding he had somebody to talk to, he admitted he too didn't like school games. Seen and appreciated, both in his inherited traits and in the differences in him, the boy knew his feelings had been heard.

Where to go next? He began producing amateur dramatics, dance and song. He took up personnel counselling in a management consultancy firm, taking a pay cut and bringing the marriage conflict into the open. His wife was furious. They were very different characters and the marriage was certainly up for question. Among other things, he had to learn to confront her. With the release of his own feminine side, he could choose to relate to her feminine side. He set the pace of understanding; he 'left the nursery'.

He still had a long journey to go, but he began to make friends with the migraines, realising what caused them, recognising he'd been cut off from part of his nature. And the split began to come together.

This was a man whose symptoms were strikingly symbolic. If we had had a contract limited to a very few sessions, we'd have stayed absolutely with the mapping of the migraine. Right at the beginning he'd said, 'I feel I want to crawl up out of it', and I would have taken this and mapped the patterns, asking questions both of the head and of the feelings, bringing it back to the migraine – 'when have such things happened before?' – so that, as the pattern emerged, he would have become much more understanding of it. I might have suggested certain ways of handling it so that he'd be more aware of it.

If the migraine is a symptom and the symptom is a symbol, then the migraine is an outer image of an inner dysfunction. We can take it exactly as far as it needs to go. We do not open up any more than needs to be opened up, according to the contract.

### Bodily symptoms hold out longest

We saw how, when people come in with some psychosomatic issue, almost the last thing to go is their symptom. As the body slowly lets go its charge, its responsibility for what it has been trying to hold, so that the person can go on, the symptom may well open up. They may get much worse physically during the process of counselling than when they started. They are going to say, 'What the hell am I paying you for? To feel like *this*?' We'd be foolish not to mention that this is no joy-ride. When I am starting with somebody with a psychosomatic trouble I say, quite early on, 'Let us work away from the symptom itself, because that will probably be among the last things to go.' Then of course, since people are unique and different, they will have got rid of it by the next session. But generally I think it is helpful. Quite often they'll remember that.

So a simple word can pervade practically every aspect of life in a most remarkable way. The word *hunger*. Ian has an experience of that, a beautiful example of the pervasion of a whole life by a word.

### The hungry man

*Ian Gordon-Brown (IGB)*: I had a client I became very fond of because I saw much of myself and various bits of my history in him. It is fascinating how, when you start to work on something within yourself, a cluster of clients so often appear who seem to reflect the same thing. This was a man whose whole life became a symbolic statement of his original symptom. In his forties, he was doing a professional job that he really enjoyed. He was divorced, with two grown-up children and in a long-standing relationship which should have been very rewarding and satisfactory. However, his presenting problem had to do with this relationship. He was regularly getting into trouble with this woman he had drawn close to.

The actual symptoms – his performance and his behaviour – seemed to suggest a very considerable lack of sensitivity; but exploring it we found that on the contrary he had a highly sensitive feeling nature. It just somehow didn't come out in this close relationship, particularly when there was a difficulty. He had a series of defensive reactions, mostly to do with working things out through his head.

We began to explore the overall patterns of his life. Quite clearly a fair amount of compensatory activity had been going on. There had been little satisfaction in the areas of love or feeling and he was seeking substitute satisfactions, particularly in work. We quickly traced back to the real fact of parental difficulties, fundamentally a problem with his mother. He was the eldest of four children of Catholic parents. The next two were difficult children. The ethos of the family was that he had to be a good little boy and to be quiet. So, by the time he was three, he felt that he was being rejected. He learned how to repress his feelings, having split them from his thinking at a very early age. The undernourished emotions of this strongly feeling child became channelled in other directions.

At this point, I began to feel very companionable with him. Like me, he was of the Truby King era,[9] and Truby King's method was to advise mothers to give babies only limited amounts of anything. *Hunger* later turned out to be a keynote symptom of this man. It followed the lack of satisfaction of those early days. The symptom spread into pretty well every area. You could chart his life by following his satisfaction of hunger. And he really did like his food. He'd always been a good trencherman – he still was. The family had required that he ate everything put before him, whatever was on the plate, whether or not it was too much, which it often was. This parental script was reinforced by his mother's depression, and his own subsequent under-feeding at boarding school. So now, he ate till he was full. And 'full' usually meant not only when everything on his plate had disappeared, but everything in the serving dishes as well (I recognise that pattern.) He would eat every meal as if it were his last, which I suppose had been

---

9    Sir Frederic Truby King (1858–1938) was a New Zealand health reformer and Director of Child Welfare. He wrote *Feeding and Care of Baby*, aiming to teach mothers domestic hygiene, nutrition and childcare. His methods specifically emphasised regularity of feeding, sleeping and bowel movements within a generally strict regimen supposed to build character by avoiding cuddling and other attention.

his initial experience at his mother's breast. He would eat as if his life depended on it.

He developed various ways of dealing with food. He had a habit which others may recognise. While battling to be fair in sharing the goodies, he was fairly certain that he would get the last biscuit or piece of cake if he offered them around, because other people would be too polite to take them. He ate as quickly as he could. Who knows but the breast would be removed if he didn't? Alongside this, he could go for long periods without any food at all, frequently not eating anything until the evening. This came up as a signature in my work with him. He told me that very frequently, after a normal day and a perfectly adequate evening meal, he would sit down at around eleven o'clock, cut great slices of bread, slap cheese on them and pour himself a beer. This was a particularly bothersome pattern. Though already full up to the gunwales, he would have as much food last thing at night as he needed for a whole day. There is a Chinese saying: 'First the man takes a drink – then the drink takes a drink – then the drink takes the man'. What was really happening? On the face of it he had a full and extremely satisfying life. Why should he be doing this quite frenetic and obsessive eating?

He began to look at how hunger was expressing itself in his life. He had just come back from a holiday. He was aware that his driving had been 'hungry'. He had done a fair amount of motoring, 'eating the mileage', feeling he had to be in front of any car ahead of him on the road. He didn't like being overtaken. He had also noticed a hungry attempt to see as much as possible, being very greedy to go to more towns than he could reasonably visit in a day, trying to see too many beautiful places, 'to make the best use of the holiday'. So they would visit half a dozen chateaux in the course of the morning and no sooner had they arrived than they had to move on to the next place. So they never actually saw anything. They had not enjoyed these trips.

This hunger was, he felt, typical of him. At work too he behaved like a hungry man, constantly overestimating what could be done, taking on too much. 'I'm carrying my work-burden like I'm carrying my paunch,' he said. He placated people in authority so that they would feed him with the love, support and approval for which he was searching. He said that whenever he'd been newly in love, he had been extremely greedy and possessive over the woman, so hungry for her that he 'could eat her'. Interested intellectually in new subjects, he experienced a constant, greedy, wide-ranging and superficial pursuit of all knowledge. In his language (not mine) he would 'devour' books and, when really interested, would go at the subject as if it were feeding a long-felt want, a great big gap in his intellect; though very often he didn't do the necessary digesting of it.

He had recently been with a friend to an Indian restaurant. Since he and I were already looking at his hunger, he was alerted. He noted that he had already satisfied himself on the chapatis before the main course had arrived. He was full. He did still stuff himself (because he'd already paid for it; he hadn't quite got to the point where he was prepared not to eat what he had paid for) but – quite a triumph for him – he didn't in fact empty his plate on that occasion. He was beginning to learn how the pattern that had originated with food was affecting him. It was less greed than need. His life was symptomatic of a very hungry person whose initial deprivation of food and emotion spilled out into practically everything. He would eat unaware of what he was doing, just shovelling it in. While, right at the beginning, he had been deprived of food quite literally, in the Truby King style, he began to see that he had also, very early on, felt deprived of affection and support at the emotional level. He came to realise that he hadn't in fact been rejected by his mother (she later said she recognised his early food deprivation). However, he had felt displaced. As the eldest brother, hungry for affection and not getting it, he'd turned to substitute satisfactions. The whole picture was complicated by a strong ego, a very powerful drive to achieve, and also by fairly altruistic impulses. This hungry man appeared to be doing much of all this eating in order to be of help to others.

That brought us back to his late evenings. Why, when he was already full and knew all about it, was he still digging into the larder, cutting himself fresh bread and putting lumps of cheese on it? Why, just as compulsively, would he turn on the television set and simply sit there, watching and eating? As he sensed into it he realised that, whilst he was being well-nourished by his relationship and by his work, there was still no time for himself. The work drive had spilled over. Though constantly eating, he wasn't feeding himself. This is typical. In the evenings, shot of the day and of everything he was required to do, a little bit of him still wanted to be fed, wanted his own feeding of himself. Because he hadn't the wit to do it at other times, and because he was by now so tired, the only way was to get the bread from the larder and cut the cheese.

His hungry seeking (through work, through holiday driving, through his search for knowledge) had been twisted. What he really, personally, wanted to do – that was not being fed. He needed to build in time for himself just to do nothing. He started to do that. However, having experienced the problem myself, I did not feel this was quite enough. The basic pattern of his eating also needed to be changed. It had become physiological, built right in at the body level. It was an addiction. What to do about it?

The aim was, not to *stop* eating but to change its quality at the very root. I said, 'Look, don't eat plain old ordinary cheese. You say at this time you'd be able to afford it, so buy yourself some smoked salmon.' Instead of beer, which he didn't really like, he decided to drink something he would enjoy. He was even finding it possible, as we saw, to leave food on the plate. I insisted he sometimes had breakfast (though, eating so late, he was never hungry until supper next day). Together we were seeking to change the physical pattern, too.

As he gradually began to adjust and give himself some nourishment, so he ceased to be quite so greedy in other areas of his life. He started to say 'no' to extra jobs that he would normally have hungrily taken. He began to nurture his body in other ways, building in time to do things he enjoyed in their own right, listening to what he actually wanted. He spent time in the country, got some new clothes, took out his old flute and played music. He realised that he loved having baths but was always too tired in the evenings. 'Feed your body with more baths.' He decided to have a bath rather than eat bread. He was building in time for himself, creating more beauty around him.

And of course he realised his eating hadn't made him feel satisfied. When he came to see me, the urge to eat seemed to be saying that although he was getting many very satisfactory things, there was no time for himself. During his evening revolt, when he was saying, 'Enough!' and relaxing, an unconscious statement was being made: 'Now is my time; now I'm giving some attention to *me*.' Of course, it can be hard to understand that eating is not going to give you what you want, it is just what you have learnt. Though the habit itself didn't give him anything, he became aware of what it symbolised: that he was doing it in the same compulsive way that he did all his many hungry activities. We were also looking at his inability to face difficult issues. He needed to learn something else to make him feel all right. His switching to a different quality of food, and to having a bath instead of eating bread, were part of that.

Slightly later, he realised he could allow himself to be vulnerable in the feeling area, not only when things were good but even in difficult situations, and still not be rejected. So he went right back and stood at the side of his early, sensitive, loving inner child. Instead of searching constantly for substitute satisfactions for the need for love, of which hunger was the primary symptom, he began to find satisfaction in emotional relationships.

At the end of an analysis or period of psychotherapy, we often return to some very simple things. This man came back to the fundamental symptom that had spilled out into his whole life and been found in nearly everything he did. His hunger and its recognition was critical in shifting from that pattern. Very often the body will then let go of the symbol it has been holding on to, in order that all those aspects be explored. Had the hunger been treated directly, or dosed in some way, it wouldn't have altered the degree to which the whole of his life was making a statement. Then, the symptom would simply have turned round and reflected itself even more strongly in other aspects of this man's life.

### At the end of your tether – exercise and comments

*BS*: This is designed to throw up a lot of material. It is an absolutely invaluable exercise for using with clients when you are working on psychosomatic factors. It involves noting four things about being at the end of your tether; these simple questions have within them two or three years of therapy: [10]

Start by asking them – familiarly – 'Quieten down and go inside yourself; be very much in touch with your body.'

Firstly, now, 'You are pushed to your limits, you are *at the end of your tether*. Get a graphic *image* for this.' We have had, for example, 'falling down a hole in the earth; hitting my head against a brick wall; being smothered by black wings; collapsing; falling over a cliff; being engulfed; disintegrating'. So 'invite the image, if not the actuality, for being pushed to your

---

10    At the end of your tether exercise – Summary:
   1.   Graphic image?
   2.   Body's reactions, medical history, symptoms, if any?
   3.   Memory? What does that sensation remind you of?
   4.   Element?

limits, at the end of your tether. "It is like … " and when you get the graphic image, make a note of it.'

Secondly, take it at the sensation level, reaching to the *body*. Ask, 'Which areas, which organs, are most affected by this? Where does it hit you?' Note how your body reacts. How does it respond to any symptoms there may be? 'Don't think about it, let your body tell you.'

Thirdly, ask, 'What one *memory* comes to you? What does that symptom, that sensation remind you of?'

Fourthly, 'See if you can set the experience in any of the *elements*, air, earth, fire and water.' Placing the graphic image in among the elements is to invite an extra language, another dimension. You can frequently use sympathetic medicine by giving the person the counterpoint of whichever it is they're being, say, drowned in; aiming to give them expression through its opposite. On the other hand, you can help them to have good experiences of the element that they are caught into.

Here are some of my own reactions when I personally did this exercise. When I asked myself, 'You're pushed to the limits, at the end of your tether. What is it like?' up came:

*A graphic image* of myself as a cooked dish on a table; not necessarily a well-cooked dish, just simply grub on a plate with people coming and everyone dipping their spoon in and helping themselves.

*The body's reaction*? It felt as if the blood in my heart was being drained away. And collapse, like overcooked meat falling off the bones, as people dug in. And not being able to breathe properly. Having pneumonia in order to get away from the over-demand to which I couldn't say 'No'. I've had heart trouble, again from that same demand, and hypertension and high blood pressure, headed off because I used the techniques that I have tried to talk about here and was able to get in ahead of it. Obviously I had to do something about the symptoms because I was cannibalising myself. And, with help, I am getting on to that inability to say 'No'.

*What did it remind me of*? Immediately, my father turning his back when I was eleven and walking out of the door as my mother had the second of her three absolutely enormous break-downs. 'I can't handle it,' he said, 'you'll have to get on with it,' which was exactly that feeling of everything falling away. My life-history is beautifully there; every illness and recovery has been the letting-go, by degrees, of the responsibility of that. Including making a profession of it.

As to the *elements*, my feeling of being eaten alive has to do with my body and the Earth – getting food and nourishment to other people. Also with the lack of Air. I felt absolutely locked into matter. An introverted intuitive with much Air and Fire in my astrological chart, what could have been better than to lock me in Earth? I recognise the value of it now; but at eleven I could well have done without it.

So that is one example. The whole of a person's life-experience can show up in this particular exercise.

*IGB*: When I too did *the end of my tether* exercise it tied in with my hunger thing; setting work targets that are impossible of accomplish-ment. Both the image and the body-feeling were of being in mud, lots of mud, and trying to get it out of some container. Marvellously oral and anal! That was Water and Earth, I think. The memories had to do with the pressure of expectation. Too much was expected far too early. Both examples are backgrounds highly characteristic of people in the caring professions, in counselling and therapy.[11]

### Type A and Type B personalities

Consider the circulation of money and the production of goods. Too much effort and too many goods produced may well lead to a harden-ing of the arteries, common in many companies, or to blockages, when the people in charge of development aren't developing. They are producing a lot of cells, but none of them actually works. Think of the migraine headache in the boardroom where, instead of what they should really be doing, they are looking at all the trivial issues. We can see the collective outer form, the phenomenon of the society, as the body with its energies running through it.

---

11   See Appendix 1 for further examples of responses to this exercise.

Associating some of the personality types with some of the more common diseases, people working in the field are trying to link the physical symptoms of certain diseases to psychological states, and also to tie them in with stress factors from marriage to divorce, to having children, to mortgages, to bereavement. A high stress score is likely to lead to some change in health, the particular change being determined to a large extent by the type of personality.

I acknowledge here a debt to the book 'Mind as Healer, Mind as Slayer',[12] looking at the concept of the 'Type A personality'.[13] The correlated illnesses of this type of person have been most studied so far. These people are found to be most subject to heart disease and cardiovascular complaints. Their excessive competitive drive makes them very pushy; they have a time-urgency, always having to meet deadlines. This has been called 'hurry sickness'. In one of the little tests used, they interviewed people to discover their type and instructed the interviewer at a certain point to stutter. The Type A person would invariably finish the sentence for them. They have this terrific drive, urge, ambition to material success. They are impatient, aggressive – and these are all the good things. This is what an executive is supposed to be. They can also easily arouse hostility. Often, of course, there is a very considerable underlying insecurity. They tend to value the views of their superiors more than their peers.

Looking at the Type B people too, the researchers found that if these phlegmatic, non-competitive people did begin to over-compensate, they too could be prone to coronary difficulties, but not to the extent of the aggressive, Type A person.

*BS*: These interesting and useful studies are limited by being based on masculine psychology. Most of the people who have been checked out are involved in business, industry, management, and the findings are going to industry and management. But more and more *women* are getting coronaries and hypertension, whether or not they are in business. The excessive drive, whatever it may be, can fit the feminine principle as well as the masculine. It is not just material success and ambition-drive; it is the over-expectation on herself to stay upright and keep going. She too suffers from the pressure of time, the over-estimation of what can be done and not allowing time for herself. She can generate just as much tension through serving others, with no sense of ambition

---

12  Pelletier, *Mind as Healer, Mind as Slayer: A Holistic Approach to Preventing Stress Disorders*.

13  Type A and Type B Personalities, see Appendix 2.

or drive in the material sense. The whole thing has been narrowed and needs to be broadened out. But it is a fascinating study for its purpose.

*A participant*: Type A personalities are people who have to do more and more in less and less time, and with the greatest difficulty. But it's interesting that we men also collect things. Everything we judge our lives on is in this area? We look upon our lives in terms of 'how many?', 'how much?', 'how long?' We think, 'When I've got this and that, then I'll be all right.' It's a goal-orientated consciousness. I have been very much a product of it. Doesn't this apply to many women, too?

*IGB*: I don't know, I never speak for women. But how do the Type A personalities get like that? What are they running away from, what starts it, what is underneath it? Why do they have to move so fast through life, and also with so little satisfaction, so little pay-off? Often, the job they do is very depressing; they are trying to get somewhere, but the more they try the less likely they are to succeed. Even when they've made their million pounds, or million motor cars, or got their million operations behind them, IT still hasn't happened. 'When I've done this, then I'll be safe' or 'then I'll have made it' or 'then I'll be a different person'. I wonder where that mentality began? What did it replace in our development? Not everybody who is programmed to over-achieve gets into so much overdrive, do they? There has to be some reason. Was it parental approval for achievement at an early age? Is it just weekend panic? But this is how the body gets involved; there's such enormous tension and these people can't seem to close down. It's a transitional object. 'As long as I'm busy and active, I'm alive, I'm living, I'm a person!' That becomes their being.

*BS*: The reasons are multiple, but there is a degree of anxiety at the base of it. The category of people I find caught into this stress and over-drive might well be seen as Personality A types, yet when we talk with them they are not that at all. Often they are highly sensitive but they have become Geiger counters for the collective. Picking up the stress of the world, they don't know how to handle it and so they channel it through their own bodies. They wouldn't in any sense come into Category A, but at the same time they'd be overlooked as Category B types. With their sensitivity and their tendency to introversion they might normally slow down, but their bodies are carrying something for the collective. They need to be helped to steady their pace.

*IGB*: There are people who carry for the collective; but there is also

the introverted, intuitive woman who has a social conscience and therefore does more than her nature is capable of doing. I am talking, am I
not, about nurses, doctors, teachers. Counsellors?

*BS*: But one wouldn't necessarily put these people I am thinking of
into either category. You see, they miss the net. The emphasis in that
study was on material success; but the key is not the success-drive but
rather their over-estimation of what they must do. It could be argued
that that is also a success drive – success by their standards perhaps, but
not necessarily material success.

*IGB*: The heart probably has a particular attachment to feelings.
Heart problems may well have something to do with that.[14] They are
symbolic; the body does it for the person. It happens whether they are
caught in this overdrive pattern and therefore feelings have had no
place in their life, or whether they have just suppressed their feelings.
We saw in a previous book[15] how crisis may follow when we realise we
are not only up the wrong ladder but that the ladder is resting on the
wrong wall. We need to *ask the symptom* and listen to what it says,
heeding the message of the body.[16]

---

[14]  See Appendix 3, Peter Nixon, on the heart.

[15]  Gordon-Brown and Somers, *The Raincloud of Knowable Things*, pp. 200-201.

[16]  See Appendix 4 for further discussion of symptoms.

Lost Memories

# CHAPTER THREE

# Hysteric, Depressive and Schizoid Positions

**Barbara Somers**

*All healthy people must be able to split;*
*it is inherent in our life-experience*

## Splits

Symbolically, and affecting the body, splits are very often part of the reaction to crisis, part of the way the adaptive process occurs within an individual.[17]

Firstly, take the split into the left hand and the right hand. Some people are almost completely out of touch with one side of their body. It is as if they have been split down the middle, right side from left; and their body may be showing every sign of that. The left-hand side of the body (right-hand side of the brain) tends to go with the internal, with heart values, instinct, emotion, intuition, the subjective side, the 'beingness' of life. Very often the other side, of doing and action, is compensated, much to the detriment of this side of the body. Quite frequently, because of this vertical split, *being* people have been pushed over onto the *doing* side, the right side of their body. They always have to placate, buy their way, be seen to be active, be valued for their being in terms of what they do. Alternatively, someone may be too *much* in this being side, the left-hand side, and need to readjust with more doing.

Secondly, there is the classic horizontal split, the heroic stance where people move around as though they were walking above a rising tide, quite stiff, rising above it. You can very often tell an area of split by a person's posture and stance. Part of the counselling is to help them to fall below it occasionally and sense that *it* is not necessarily

---

[17] Some books in this area recommended during the discussion were:
Dychtwald, *Bodymind*, on splits, psyche and soma.
Lowen, *Bioenergetics*.
Reich, *The Function of the Orgasm*.
Keleman, *Your Body Speaks Its Mind*; *Human Ground: Sexuality, Self and Survival*; *Living Your Dying*.

threatening. These people lack grounding and, for that reason, will have neck and shoulder problems and spinal tension. A lot of migraines are about holding energies *up*.

Others walk along as though they didn't have anything below the waist. These people rise above their sexuality and their instinctual nature as though the lower part of themselves was untouchable. They'd been told, 'Ugh! Everything to do with that is dirty, animal, unnecessary, naughty, highly unsocial', and so they try to walk around as though it didn't exist. However, energies within their body will also move

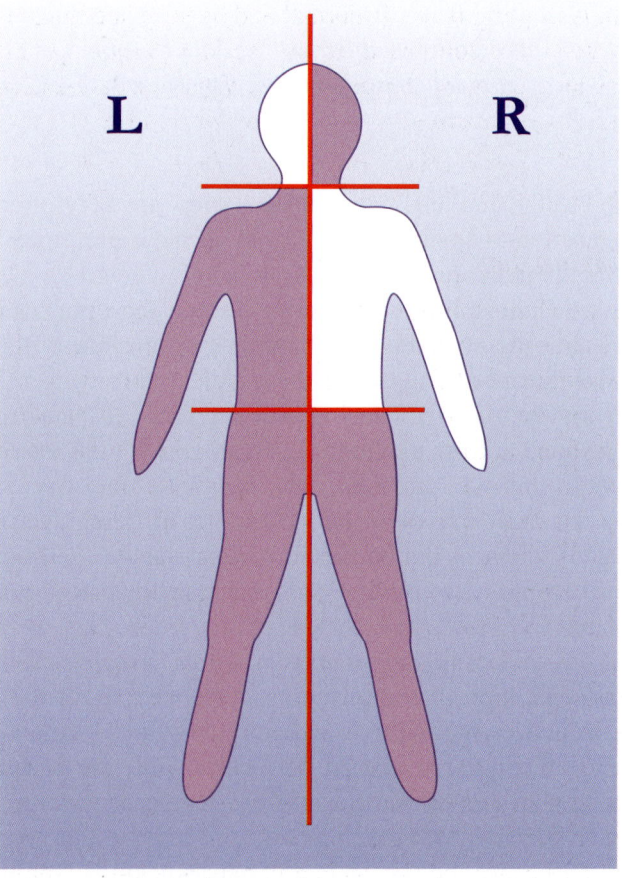

Figure 4. Splits

around continuously, making sure that they do know that it exists, even if it is only to show the degree of deficiency below the belt. Someone observed, 'Not much is happening in my head but my legs are heavy.' Now there is a nice little split, and a rising above it. It's fascinating to look at the body-posture – lovingly hilarious work, this! You can actually see the person's body showing how they have tended to compensate.

To look at the subject of splits at the psychological level, the fact that parents can never be better than good-enough may mean the split goes right back to childhood. We have seen how all healthy people under certain stresses and at certain times show tendencies to splitting behaviour. Accepting that it is normal and healthy and human to react, we only need be concerned when we *too frequently* make that inappropriate reaction to circumstances. What are labelled *hysteric*,[18] *depressive* and *schizoid* reactions are only *clinical* when such inappropriate responses become our *single* mode of handling difficulties. It is very much a layered thing.

### Separation anxiety

These are clinical terminologies for varying degrees and depths of response to the anxiety which a child feels. It depends not only on the separation anxiety that they are given in their early beginnings, but on the seed, the innate, individual nature of the person. We are each likely to respond according to our own particular temperament.

How we move over to an *hysteric*, *depressive* or *schizoid* position depends very much on the denial of our basic needs, primarily as children. It can come out in a later form, but usually it's in childhood, the place where the roots are being put down. If these roots cannot take hold in the parental soil, and very particularly in the internal soil in the first couple of years, then there is bound to be splitting. *Hysteric* is a split; *depressive* is a split; and *schizoid* is a split. Each is from the denial of the underlying needs which every child has in order to ground itself, then root itself and so begin to grow: love, security, acceptance, continuity; and also nourishment of the Self, the personality, its own Self, its own being.

Again, all healthy people have a certain amount of splitting. It is absolutely inherent in all our lives (in our life experience itself and in

---

[18]  See Footnote 4 for use of the word *hysteric*.

the fact that parents cannot be better than good-enough) that we are bound to have splits. We all do. They are unavoidable: we can never, as children, totally have what we would individually require of our background and our parents. But so long as those underlying needs are met, then we can tolerate a considerable amount without splitting off into what would be a *clinical* definition of 'split'.

Jung, Assagioli, Maslow have accepted the great importance of childhood experiences and traumas, but they also bring in another split. It is the split from the original seed, from the original Self, from one's own unique potential. They, and Transpersonal Psychology, would say that behind everything lies that most basic split of all that occurs during childhood.[19] The degree to which the parental background, the environment and later life-experience bend us away from our own original seed – that is the splitting.

### The child left alone

An ordinary, normal, healthy child, feeling abandoned for a period, will manifest every form of anxiety.

> The first movement will be towards hysterics, hysteria. It will protest and cry lustily, loudly and long, which is the nature of the *hysteric* reaction.

> If it is left long enough without that signalling being met, the child will tire. It has gone on protesting long enough. The child comes to expect not to win a response, stops crying and begins to show *depressive* characteristics.

> If it is left for a very prolonged period without response, then it is likely to go over into a split-off state, a *schizoid* state.

That is a normal human being going through levels of response. These are perfectly ordinary human reactions. I remember going myself from hysteric, to depressive, to schizoid when I was researching this subject. Trying to get something coherent, I looked up endless books. I found that the best clinical definitions were certainly among the Freudians, most of all in Freud himself. What he wrote still stands up extremely well. The Jungians drove me up the wall. Here I was, trying to get some description, even a definition, of these clinical states; and, while I do believe that the Jungians have the whole person deeply at

---

[19]   We remember how we are born as a particular seed, each with our own potential. See Somers and Gordon-Brown, *Journey in Depth*, Chapter 1, 'Individual as Seed'.

heart and deal very much with their internal landscapes, there is still a great deal of clarifying to be done.[20] However, in the end it came back to my having to do it myself. So this is one person's guide around this area; but at least it is based on quite a bit of experience over a long time. I find that easy maps are the best way of illustrating these things.

I like my map! I have drawn the parent figure as a two-headed beastie out there, good or bad. It is a conjoined picture; it is anyone's

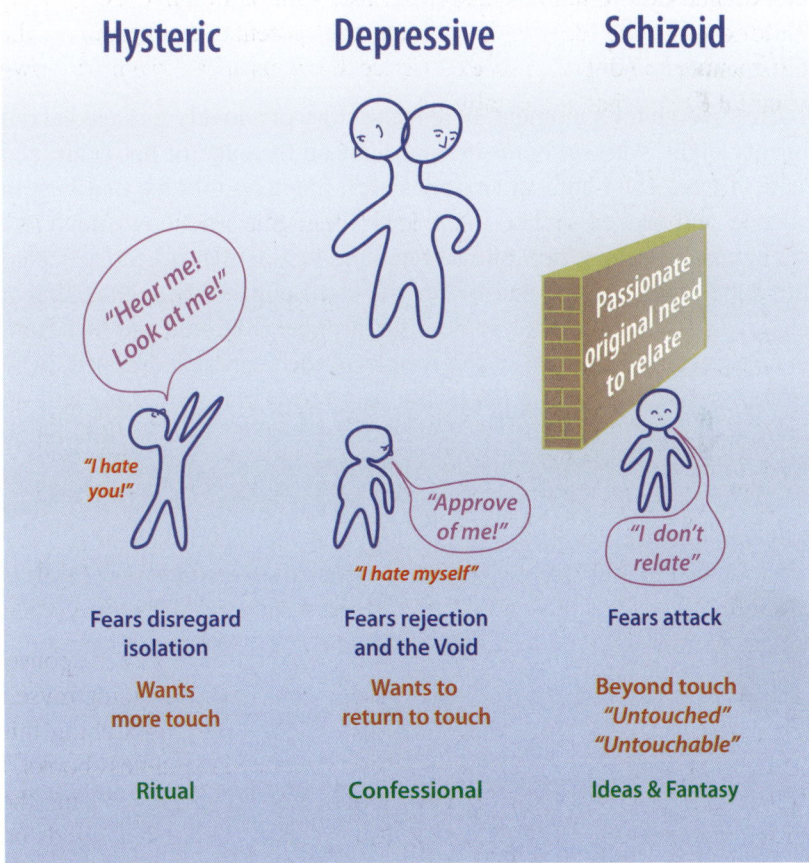

Figure 5. Origins of Depressive, Hysteric and Schizoid personalities

---

[20]  The best book I came across in all my researches was *The Art of Psychotherapy* by Anthony Storr. He avoids definition, gives description and uses clinical examples, and he is very much of the Jungian orientation. BS.

Parent Figure. Visualise three children, not necessarily of the same family but three children with different parents, each child responding in its own particular way to the anxiety of separation from them. Here you have:

the *hysteric* making its demand to the parent figure;
the *depressive*, turned away from the parent figure;
and the *schizoid*, right over there behind his or her wall.

The hysteric reaction is *towards* the figure, extraverting itself by making a noise about it; the depressive is turning *away*, knowing itself unworthy; and the schizoid is *behind that wall*, cut off.

### Clinical labelling

To diverge for a moment: here is the story of a lovely girl aged about twenty-eight, who sat opposite me, right on the edge of her chair, and said, 'I have got a clinical anxiety state'. She later told me that I sat in silence and looked at her for a long time. She said how much my silence had meant to her. She had had the feeling that if I too accepted this label, that was the end of her. At last I apparently said, 'Clinical anxiety state my foot!' or something stronger. She told me that from that moment a great deal of the weight of the years just dropped away from her. She had paid a large sum to go to Harley Street for half an hour, to be told: 'You have a clinical anxiety state'. A nice little label, for all that money. 'Now, go out with it!' So she had done.

How much we love the eccentrics in our midst! The word means 'off one's centre, out of the centre' and it is very helpful. A lady in her eighties said to me fairly recently, 'There used to be so many eccentrics around. Where are they now?' Eccentric behaviour is frequently no longer permissible; it doesn't fit in with the norm. While villages could once cope with a degree of eccentricity, our society (which may in itself be a not-sane society) tends to put people more and more into areas it labels 'clinical'.

This clinical thinking can lead into very negative places. It happens so often: the label inhibits the potential within us all. Another woman came with a short 'psychiatric history' that looked completely black and without hope. It was really shocking for her, because it left out any mention of her potential. I think to have these labels put on them is to make more people ill than has ever helped them. The labels help those physicians who do not know how to deal with this unique person. They don't have the time, and maybe have no sense of the experience being brought in to them. In order to contain the person, they put them into a neat little pigeonhole.

With every ounce of my being I would say I loathe these labels. They are a blasphemy against the human spirit. They diminish the person in a most extraordinary way. I would hope that the thrust of everything that we stand for and believe in is to dispose of such labels, and to put the *person* back in again. I have never met 'an hysteric'. I have met people who under certain stresses make hysteric reactions. I have never met 'a depressive', though I have certainly known people who respond with a depression in certain circumstances. I have never met this strange animal, 'the schizophrenic'; only people who sometimes respond in a schizoid manner (see the story of The man in the dustbin, page 87 below). If they are said to be 'clinical', it is usually just that they're overreacting inappropriately to too many circumstances, as if it were their only mode of action. Over my years of counselling I have seen a lot of people released at least half-way towards health and self-respect and self-centring, simply by *having those labels taken off them*.

## Psychology is new

There are any number of books offering clinical examples of hysteria, depression and schizophrenia. The whole of psychology has had very much to do with this.[21] However, it would be wise to remember that psychology itself in its present form dates back only to about the early eighteen-hundreds. Though its maps of the psyche are equivalent to maps of the world from the fourteen-hundreds, it has become so sophisticated, we have so many fancy words and names and labels that are very useful to the therapist, that it is easy to forget that it is quite a new science and still groping.

It is certainly true that, though many of us very much dislike the overuse of drugs and tranquillisers, at least they are better than some of the treatment that was current in the nineteenth century. Even ECT,[22] which I see as horrifying, is better than lobotomy; and think of being chained to railings, and of Bedlam, and of the terrible animal level at which people were treated not all that long ago. In some parts of the

---

21   The kind of splitting that's happened in early infant life has been handled in great detail by Freud, Klein, Fairbairn on Object Relations, Winnicott and others. I believe all this is well worth reading. BS.

22   ECT = Electroconvulsive Treatment; developed in the 1930s, used widely during the 1950s and 1960s but now confined to a small number of severe mental illnesses. Ed.

world that sort of treatment can still be found.

Again, it is very much a matter of degree. We need to remember that psychology is still searching and nobody *knows*.[23] And there most certainly are people with deeply hysteric, depressive and schizoid personalities who need much care and help and probably the wise use of drugs, in parallel with perceptive, skilled therapy. However, it is not the brief of counsellors to deal with the *clinical* hysteric or the clinical depressive, or the *clinically* schizoid person. Extreme cases are the work of a psychiatrist, or a skilled psychotherapist, possibly of an analyst. But, over and over, the counsellor-cum-therapist will meet people who have a *tendency* to an hysteric personality, or a depressive personality, or a schizoid personality. All these most frequently come into counselling.

### *Origins of depressive, hysteric and schizoid personalities*

So we are considering hysteric, depressive and schizoid *personalities*, from our point of view as counsellors. The early mapping of what happened to the child at the deep root level – Freud, Fairbairn, Winnicott, the whole of Freudian psychoanalysis – has been founded on the idea that everything began in infancy, or at least in childhood; and that nothing would really have happened later had it not been for that beginning in childhood. Frankl, Adler and Fromm varied from that, suggesting that yes, what happened to the child was very important but that later experiences must also be taken into account; for they too could have caused splitting reactions along hysteric, depressive and schizoid lines. Examples are found in war, in prison camps, in bereavement, loss, rejection, job redundancies and the rest. Alfred Adler particularly said these later traumas counted. His work showed that the *will to succeed* was the basis of it all, while Erich Fromm held that it was the *will to freedom*, and Viktor Frankl that it was the *will to meaning*.[24]

So someone's natural reactions perhaps had little to do with their parents, who may well have been 'good-enough'. Perhaps the person was a slow starter; or maybe innate characteristics of their own true temperament made them unable to take the pressure at some earlier time. Perhaps during adolescence they couldn't grasp their own self-image or build in any sense of identity or personality. And the perils

---

23   This was the late 1970s and early 1980s. Obviously, very much progress has been made since then in the development of successful treatments. Ed.

and difficulties they encountered at school may have had an unimaginable effect, confirming or counteracting the influence of their parents and arguably as strong. Setting aside these factors, and whether the reactions started early or built up much later, by degrees a habit formed. That response was established as a pattern and they began to act in an hysteric way, or a depressive way or a schizoid way. Then, particularly if they met someone who *labelled* them like that, they really began to take on the characteristics of the labels. Thus it is that their reactions were pulled out, attenuated to the state where these categories started to be used inappropriately.

## *Crisis, stress and anxiety*

So we see that, while anxiety may be converted into *bodily* symptoms and postures, it may also be converted into *psychological states*. Although usually treated clinically as a specific area, I believe that anxiety can take the level of the hysteric state, or of the depressive state, or of the schizoid state. In fact, these are all anxiety states. (It can also, as we shall see, lead to panic attacks and phobic reactions, to obsessive or compulsive ways and to difficulties with sexual relationships.)

Under certain present crisis, it is a natural, human, healthy reaction to go back into the past, to regress, to recoil. Particular stresses may cause any one of us to act in any one of these three main ways. I know for example that if I am overtired I tend to talk a great deal, a typical reaction to anxiety; and if I am pushed too far, this can go over into an hysteric state. It doesn't usually because, in my case, it tends to convert itself into a compulsive/obsessive state and I find myself wandering around in small circles picking up bits of paper from one pile and putting them on to another. However, push me too far and I will split off and go into a schizoid-type withdrawal. I believe, hope and trust that these are my ways of trying to deal with over-stress; but they do give me some experience of what it must be like to live in those states in a fairly permanent form.

The great danger is, of course, that very many people are being *treated* for what is perhaps only a light degree of each of these states as if it were the full clinical measure. They are being given drugs, or ECT, or the heavier kinds of therapies, for what are after all mostly healthy human reactions.

---

24   Frankl, *Man's Search for Meaning*. According to Frankl's 'Logotherapy', the striving to find a meaning in one's life is the primary motivational force in man: it is a will to meaning in contrast to the will to pleasure on which Freudian psychoanalysis is centered; and also in contrast to the will to power stressed by Adlerian psychology, and the will to freedom of Fromm. See also Fromm, *Escape from Freedom*; and *The Art of Loving*.

## *A healthy response*

To sum up: we respond in an hysteric way, or a depressive way, or a schizoid way and, under certain stresses, it is *appropriate* to respond in these ways. Just as every normal, healthy human person splits, so we all tend to our own temperamental reaction in a current crisis. The splits of early infancy will have caused us to respond quite characteristically to the stresses of our later life-experience. We make conversions of psychic energy or over-stress into somatic form. We can all get various forms of psychosomatic illness or dis-ease at certain times. It is a way of adjusting the body, bringing the *psyche* and *soma* together, trying to adjust towards a better way of living. This is why, fundamentally, we consider symptom to be symbol.

## *Counselling with a Transpersonal orientation*

Counsellors need always to have in mind that we are dealing with a whole person who is perhaps responding inappropriately and partially to anxiety. Once again, we deal with the degree, trying to establish just how far their responses are inappropriate. We all have a toleration level which varies with the individual; but under certain pressures and at certain times we pass over into some degree of these reactions. It is very wise, when we are being counsellors to other people who have these tendencies (perhaps in greater, perhaps in lesser degree than ourselves), to remember that we are dealing with something which is a natural human phenomenon.

We need only be concerned if clients begin *too frequently* to make inappropriate reactions to circumstances. We notice if a lot of stress drives them too far over into one or other, so that they too often behave with an hysteric reaction, or too frequently react to life's pressures and demands by becoming depressed, or split and withdraw and isolate themselves too frequently from normal pressures in the schizoid way. If they are not doing that, then it is not a matter of concern. It only becomes clinical when such inappropriate reaction becomes their only mode of handling life and circumstances.

Using the map in Figure 5 (page 37), we shall look at each of these states in turn, considering the types of illness or psychosomatic function that tend to go with each. We haven't moved away from *soma*, but we are beginning the movement of *psyche* and *soma* coming together. We shall be looking at people who have *tendencies* towards the hysterical personality, the depressive personality and the schizoid personality, all of whom are quite likely to come into counselling. As we have seen, anyone *extremely* 'hysteric', 'depressive' or 'schizoid', who has often been given a clinical label, usually needs therapeutic, analytic and very experienced handling.

Mother, Child and Dancer

# CHAPTER FOUR

# The Hysteric Personality

## Barbara Somers

*These people are writ large … in their company we rise up through our colour dimensions into the spectrum of our own feelings*

So the trio of personality types most likely to come into counselling are the hysteric type,[25] the depressive type and the schizoid type.

## The hysteric child

Every single one of us has had to a degree the experience of *being* the hysterical child. The hysteric is the one who, in childhood, met the two-headed parent of Figure 5, – mother or father, or the combination of both – and the parent did not hear. Or didn't seem to; maybe the parent was in fact responding, but for that particular child it wasn't enough.

This is the forceful child with a fair amount of fire in its nature, demanding to be heard, trying to reach across the barrier between the self and the parental figure: 'For God's sake listen to me!' A great deal of the 'Hear me! Accept me! Love me!' of the hysteric may come down to this. The child felt disregarded at a deep level, un-met as a person: 'My basic needs are ignored – I'm neglected – no one understands!' Though it might have been a later experience that caused such children to slip over, or be flipped, into the hysteric response, usually it started early on. Practically everything they do reflects that 'Let me be heard!' This reaction towards getting attention, attracting attention, buying attention comes from the innate human need for stability.

It also comes from their search for *identity*. This kind of splitting, this larger-than-life stance, will have begun as a demand for the recognition of who they were. It often manifests through being histrionic, overstated.

---

[25] See Footnote 4 for use of the word *hysteric*.

Needing people, these hysteric personalities dread being alone. They have had to establish their identity through demanding, attention-seeking, seduction, trying to discover an identity through role-playing, play-acting. The adult will argue with us and exaggerate, which was exactly their way of trying to elicit from the parent figure (and later in life from the world around) some playback to their sense of *being*, their sense of identity.

Maybe there was some real lack in the early parenting. Maybe the child did have a reason to feel that she didn't exist in her own right, must always shriek her unmet need. So, characteristically, the adult continues to go on shrieking. This fiery one is demanding, 'Pay attention to *me*! Listen to me! Love me!' In a clinically hysteric client, this demand, this requirement, this calling out to us to fill that gap, is almost insatiable.

### What is the hysteric personality?

I went to 'The Harvard Guide to Modern Psychiatry' and looked it up:

*The hysterical personality* (as if it were a thing, not a person) *' … is dominated by the urgent need to please others in order to master the fear of being unable to do so. This results in restless activity, dramatisation and exaggeration, seductiveness either socially or sexually overt in manner, often creating disappoint-ment in the other person, and [an] immature and unrealistic dependence upon others'.*

Which describes a very, very small part of this extremely colourful personality who also has hysteric tendencies. This is an active, vocal, dynamic, 'do something about it' person, fiery and gristly and gritty and extremely energetic temperamentally. Nearly always they are feeling people with a very powerful colour spectrum and affective range. Someone with another temperament – gentle, internalised, passive – will respond differently. Few quiet, intellectual, receptive people react in this hysteric way.

Over and over we find that their toleration of aloneness is very low indeed. It is a polarity: they dread being alone but they also want to be free. Feeling that they did not exist in their own right, they need to be among people and have a profound need to relate. Like children, by demanding, attention-seeking, dramatically exaggerating their needs, they gain enough emphasis to leap the gap and get themselves from the periphery into the centre. Often they will subtly manipulate in order to gain their own ends. Oozing charm and seduction, they insinuate themselves so as no longer to feel disregarded and unmet as a person. And the shouting, the screaming, the threatening: 'I will run away, I will do away with myself – unless you do what I want!' It is no good pretending that people who talk about overdoses aren't likely to take them, because it simply is not so. They very frequently do. It is difficult to know whether it is the genuine distress-signal of someone who really wants to die, is too tired to handle it, has been pushed beyond the end of their tether and genuinely wants to end it; or whether it is an early-warning signal, a cry for help. Or is it an act of revenge on the people around? The hysterical-type personality might take any one of those routes. I know quite a few counsellors who have lost clients that way.

Since feelings and body are closely related, the hysteric, who is a very feeling-type person, goes naturally over to the body. Illnesses which draw attention to the person, and actually to their real needs, are the indirect approach. For instance, under the anxiety and stress of war, soldiers may take a 'hysteric conversion' (an evasive action serving a useful purpose), going into trench blindness or partial paralysis. Remove them from the front line and from immediate danger, and by degrees the symptom releases itself. An over-stressed surgeon may become paralysed in the right hand; a teacher may be too tired and their voice gives out. Note that the blindness or paralysis or loss of the voice may well point to some deeper thing too.

## We are all hysteric

It seems that hysterical symptoms serve three major purposes: [26]

*Evasion and manipulation.* Firstly they enable us to evade distasteful, frightening or potentially threatening situations: the diplomatic headache which comes at just the right moment; feeling dizzy or sick. It is natural for children to shout their demands to make them heard. We have all done it. In childhood, did we not avoid alarming or boring situations by feeling just exactly such things? We have all worked up symptoms in order

---

[26] See Storr, *The Art of Psychotherapy*. I like this book because he talks of there being if not a creative then at least a purposive factor behind the symptoms. BS

to get out of things. And we have all seduced or tried to seduce in order to draw attention to ourselves. We have subtly manipulated our environment as best we could. How very quickly the child under five is able to pick up the exact point at which to split the parents down the middle. These are natural ways of surviving within the environment. But if one goes on doing the same thing into adulthood to avoid something which is likely to be too threatening (feeling the migraine starting, having the energy run out), then it is an inappropriate reaction and we are in danger of being labelled 'hysterical'.

*Retribution*. Secondly, these hysterical symptoms can be revenge against people whom we resent or are angry with. A lot of frigidity and impotence, a withholding of oneself from a partner, reveals itself as a punishment. 'If you won't give it to me, then I won't give it to you!' This may be carried over into later life and begin to dictate the pattern of all relationships. The man may behave like Don Juan but, as a form of revenge and punishment, never follow through. And the woman may dress to the nines and look very seductive, acting like a siren but again never following through. When that behaviour becomes a way of relating, we may be looking at an hysteric personality. Work back through the symptom, see it as a symbol. Invite pictures of it. Ask, 'What does that remind you of?' We often reach back to a withholding – to something felt to have been withheld at a much earlier stage.

*Splits against ourselves*. Thirdly, the symptom may be there to attract sympathy, attention and focus. Frightened of making direct demands on people for fear of rejection, hysteric-tending personalities draw attention to their own needs and distress by behaviour symptoms which require other people to notice. They are divided against themselves (more so in the schizoid position, but it is also true of the hysteric): there is a discrepancy between what the symptom has made clear they need, and what they *say* they want and feel.

Try pushing in through these levels using a cushion to represent each. While they respond one way at one level, they have a completely different response at another. 'I would love to have gone to the party with you, but my headache/backache/earache stopped me.' So their outward behaviour is distancing, but it is because their inward need is so great. Or: 'I really love my wife/husband, but I can't bear her/him to touch me', which is both a come-on and a put-down, a distinct polarity, and also discrepant to their own real need. It is sad when it goes on too long. Like the depressive personality, the hysteric is very much concerned with other people; but many a sad person with this tendency pushes away the very thing he wants.

There are no 'them-and-us'. We really do all have the capacity to become hysterical under the right pressure. This helps to keep it in focus. We have to watch the degree to which we, too, try to insinuate ourselves, get our way through this hysterical approach. We all do it, seducing, going round behind the scenes; we all press on other people's boundaries and make demands. We are not just dealing with some other person, a client. We are dealing with somebody who is an extension of that which is within ourselves.

## Acting and play-acting

Hysteric personalities play games with others, or themselves, or with us. Their tendency to over-exaggerate emotions – gratitude, love, distress, anger – makes it all seem a lot bigger than it need be, and that can get very tiring. The overstated, histrionic quality around the longed-for relationship strikes a false note. 'Surely this person is different underneath?' we feel. 'Isn't this all on the surface? Is it real – which is chicken, which is egg?' A key question, this. Bear it in mind and it will be easier to keep these clients in the right perspective. I would say that everyone is a unique, individual seed with a certain temperament which belongs to it and, under pressure, some will go one way and some another.

With great actors, that wonderful energy is channelled and turned outward. Many of the finest actors come within this description and they can be most marvellous on stage. The acting profession would be much impoverished without its hysteric-tending personalities, larger-than-life and highly creative. To encourage other such clients to extravert their creative energy in some tactile form can be one of the best ways of dealing with it, even if it is just shouting out and then turning the shout into a sound, the sound into a note. But first the boundary must be clearly established for them or they will go rushing out over-emphatically, losing heart equally quickly.

## Hysterical depression

If someone with an hysteric personality were to go into a depression, it might just possibly be a way of drawing attention. However, it would be an hysteric type of depression and would not have anything like the same feeling-tone as the depressive type's own. A depressive person would sink into it. The hysteric's movement into depression is far more colourful – there is a totally different feeling about it. It is definitely the hysteric's style to extravert out to everybody, signalling around. Where someone with depressive traits might move into themselves for quite a long time, perhaps eventually contacting one person, the hysteric would retire to bed and telephone everyone.

There are those who think about cancer as the end product of untreated hysteric symptoms. That is a fascinating subject. The hysterical-tending personality – extravert, communicating, wanting to get out and perhaps not being able to get there – might well develop a rapid, overtaking form of cancer, while the depressive type might tend towards the slow-burning, quiet, eroding form; there are gentle cancers too. We need to look at the typology of 'cancer', a cover-all umbrella word for a much wider thing. Get a sense of the person's energy and we may well have the whole syndrome. The out-going hysteric will tend towards the outgoing, fast-moving, taking-over, no-inhibitions-about-boundaries type of cancer, whereas, with the depressive, there is a subtle half-tone to it. This is why it is so important to have the whole picture of the whole person. Then we can begin to look at the details within the ambience of it.

## The value of the hysterical-tending personality

When I catch myself thinking, 'Oh no, not another one!' – when someone is gazing into my eyes one minute and throwing cushions at me, if not worse, the next – then I remember the value of this hysteric personality. Without it, we would lose a whole dimension. The very demand from life of the hysterical-tending person demands life from others. As a counsellor, we cannot sit back on our laurels (supposing we have any) with one of these personalities. They certainly demand a reaction – and by God they get it! If it is handled well they can be the life-enhancers who, frequently highly creative, demand much from life but also evoke life in others. Things aren't dull when they're around; their colourfulness creates colour. They are so full-canvas in their approach that they draw out the full range within anybody they deal with, helping other people break out of their rigidities and extend their own boundaries. We need to recognise their aliveness, their vividness, their ability to enhance life. They are writ large, a bit too big for the containers they're put in. We cannot sit with an hysterical-tending personality and not rise up through our colour-dimensions into the spectrum of our own feelings.

One person who came to me was very able. She sometimes acted on radio and eventually became a Gestalt therapist. In our exploratory session she fought me every inch of the way. She answered questions when put to her but if I pushed a little too far into the emotional area she would say something like, 'Do you always wear that colour? Because I think it looks terrible'. I'd respond by saying, 'Oh, what a pity, I'm rather fond of this colour myself and I wear it quite often.' And then a bit later, 'Do I have to sit with this cushion beside me? I can't stick this cushion.' So I'd say, 'Well that's fine, just chuck it overboard if you want to.'

This happened over and over. I countered it each time. She'd say she was coming and then wouldn't turn up, or she'd come late, or early. When that had happened three times, I said, 'Are you trying to tell me something?' So we faced it: 'What are you doing?' I guessed (I didn't at that point say it to her though we talked about it later) that she was really asking me to prove that I loved her, that she was acceptable whatever she did. The playing back of that is important. Once the trust has been built in, such people often test the parameters of our tolerance and love by non-payments, missed appointments, 'bad behaviour'. And, after their over-exaggerated admiration and gratitude and seduction, we'll suddenly get something like, 'I want you to be my friend but I know you are only doing this for the money'. In comes the boot! It goes straight to the guilt areas we have about fees and it is very difficult not to respond in kind. Or they say, 'You looked at your watch, you don't really want me to be here, do you?' And so they put our integrity to the test.

She might not have liked me, but I genuinely liked her, her forthrightness, her coming straight at me. She had fine bone structure, lovely expressive hands, beautifully-shaped feet with high insteps like a dancer. Her hair looked as though it had been done in a wind-tunnel (a mass of strong hair, lots of energy) and her face was very energetic. She wore a gorgeous combination of greys and browns, and she needed all the colours. I was able to respond with love. It was rather like riding a bucking bronco, but I would say that in the very uproarious sessions that we had together she came much more to herself, to a sense of her own being.

## Counselling the hysteric personality

While the clinically hysteric person is, as we have seen, best dealt with by an extremely skilled analyst or psychiatrist, the *hysteric type of personality* can respond extremely well to a counsellor who is there for them and provides a continuum. However, we need to know our limits.[27] We must be able to avoid stepping in and responding to the roles being played, or taking projections back into ourselves, so that what is said will actually stay with the client. It is difficult. We too will receive the histrionic range of over-exaggerated emotions. These people certainly do not lack colour. Oh, the overwhelming degree of gratitude and love they feel for you. Haloed one week, perfect, all-giving, wonderful, be pretty sure you'll have a forked tail and horns and a slap in the face the next. There are devils and there are angels and there is nothing in between.

While we can feel very sympathetic towards the depressive and deeply understanding of the schizoid type of personality, it's easy to get tetchy with the hysteric. The doubt somehow remains: they do not ring true. We can find ourselves being very unfair to a client of this nature, missing the moment when they are speaking the truth simply because it is too strongly stated. This over-dramatisation makes it very difficult to be patient, to stay with it, to hold it and to respond. There is also that subtle sense of being manipulated, which alienates the very friend or employer or lover they so much need. The only way is to keep in our vision the *child* who's with us in that adult. This is their survival method.

The hysteric personality type is not just playing games. This is the only way that such a person can relate to the world, which is a very different matter. They are actually playing through their own survival, their way of staying here on Earth at all. But it is not always easy to hold on to this. We will have our love put to the test. The degree of

---

[27] Someone commented that Frank Lake is said to have remarked, in the early 1950s, that the difference between the brilliant psychiatrist and the merely good one is that the former spots the hysteric first and passes them on to the latter for treatment! BS

attention these people require is exhausting and we may well feel spent. And if we consistently do not like someone, we need to stick to our right to terminate the series. After all, if they are role-playing and we also start role-playing, there are two people doing it. And that's not counselling, it's play-acting.

Is it possible to work adequately with an hysteric person if we do not feel that we genuinely like them? Well, it is certainly more difficult without that liking of them behind us. But, be with someone over a period, get to know them, and love is drawn out of us. It is extra-ordinary how we can learn to like, sympathise with and eventually to love people when we never thought we could.

The feeling tone of the relationship between us will be very important to such a client. The hysteric personality is rarely particularly intellectual. Because they feel so strongly, and express themselves so vividly through the colour, the vibrancy, the immediacy, the histrionic quality and the writ-large side of their emotions, it is little use working at rational understanding or helping them to come to 'insights'. Any insight from counselling is less important to them than the feeling that at last they have found somebody who meets them at the feeling level and appreciates and understands the quality of their being.

Although we may sense we are being put to the test, even that the whole thing rings false, from the Transpersonal orientation it is terribly important to be true to the relationship and to ourselves. We can push this person back into a regressive state if we are not. It may involve being very firm, perhaps being more directive; but most of all we have got to be true. This kind of client can bring out some of the depths of counselling, testing the ability to stand by our own integrity.

## Space and boundaries

So, saying one thing one minute and doing something completely different the next, they are stepping out of their own boundaries and trying to force a breach through the boundaries around other people. But on a deep level they are trying to balance the relationship, to gain parity, a sense of equality. We can go with that, but also realise that it can be a con. They can be quite seductive at getting from us extra care and attention which they feel is normal because they don't have many boundaries themselves. Keeping well inside our own limits, we give them the sense that, by degrees, we can help them to be contained within theirs. If we are not careful at laying down our own with them at the beginning, we may give too much. We then find ourselves on an elastic string where we withdraw what we have been over-giving and they end up feeling rejection and separation anxiety.

And we know about 'roots and splits' and how it is the original acceptance and affirmation that gives a person a sense of rootedness. The child who has not been rooted will not have the parameters; therefore they will always test all boundaries to see if we will let them in or if we're going to reject them. It is is a continuous trial but, if we can work with them, very rewarding too. A colleague told me of a client with this sort of tendency, whom she needed to hold with great firmness:

> *This person was always trying to control the situation. She wore an enormous watch on her wrist so that I could always see the time very clearly, far better than I could from my own clock, which is too far away for my weak eyesight. She asked if she could move my clock out because the ticking annoyed her – and I let her do it! This gave her a sense of power. She used every ploy in the book, including the telephone call in the middle of the night, and 'I'm going to commit suicide' and (though she paid very little), 'You're only in it for the money'.*

> *At last one day I felt she'd tipped me upside down. I don't think I showed it on the surface but I decided to take quite a different stand with her. I stopped trying to play the usual counselling games and began to come from my own personality, my own centre. I became directive with her, answered her questions straight. She plugged in to my new state and it made a lot of difference: she offered to pay more, and I went out and bought a clock that didn't tick. She never again tried to move it. She probably taught me more in counselling than anyone before or since. She became an artist, which she was by nature, and was in a pretty good space.*

If we are aware of our own space and boundaries, recognising and respecting them, then our example helps the person discover respect for their own. Full stop. We help create that middle ground. Whatever else we do or don't get right, that has to be right, and it takes a lot of preparation and a lot of centring.

Less often (except among those great actors referred to) do I come across an hysteric type of *man*, though sometimes men with a strong feminine *principle* are of the hysteric type. A man with a lot of feeling within him may go into the hysteric reaction, but it generally goes more with the feminine principle than the masculine. However, I do have a male client who used to flash sexually through his car window, which was his form of hysterical reaction. He would park near places where children were playing, or in woodlands, and do it from the safety of his car. Whereas before that he was in trouble and there was a small court case coming up, now he shouts instead, and even sings, behind the wheel of his car.[28]

A double-handed movement is needed towards such clients. Since they are so relationship-oriented, anything which mobilises the feminine principle (non-rational types of expression appealing to the instinctual, emotional, intuitive nature) might well give them a new language and help them to set up a dialogue with life which later they can take into relationships. We need somehow to hold on to the positive value of this hysteric tendency within people we meet, as well as within ourselves, and recognise how it might be led into other, more extraverted, more socially acceptable channels. Though in a way even that is a pity: in another century (as we saw when looking at clinical labelling) such eccentricity would have been dealt with very lovingly.

---

[28]   See Note 68, p. 197, on paedophilia. And see Chapter 11, p. 195, on exhibitionism.

Enigma

# CHAPTER FIVE

# The Depressive Personality

## Barbara Somers and Ian Gordon-Brown

*Here are the most exquisitely sensitive of people*

So, to the *depressive* type of personality and the feeling of the counterpoint with the hysteric. Not always, but very often, this too has its roots in childhood. The person is not necessarily depressed all the time, but depression is the line of least resistance. If someone spends most of their time in depression, or in several degrees of it, then they are liable to have a clinical label stuck on them: 'a depressive'. But this is a *person*.

From a Transpersonal point of view, I believe that the human being is fundamentally healthy, not sick. Referring again to Figure 5 (page 37), I suggest that all three types, hysteric, depressive and schizoid, will have started out unique, strong and healthy. But depending on the energy, the strength of the soul, perhaps the typology of the Self within, they react to pressure in different ways. So two small children may have very different reactions to what seem equal challenges from the parents. Perhaps, for instance, they receive a lot of attention but absolutely no understanding. One, the hysteric type, will try to win that understanding by shouting, 'Hear me! For God's sake, hear me!' battering away, always turned towards the parent. Whereas the other child, given the same parent but having a different temperament, might turn away and become a depressive adult.

### The too loose and the too tight hold [29]

This is to do with roots and grounding. Both hysteric and depressive people may have been too loosely held by the parent. The *too loose hold* would give the child tending to the depressive stance a sense that

---

[29] See also Somers and Gordon-Brown, *Journey in Depth*, p. 75.

it was abandoned early and therefore must be rejectable. It will feel that for some reason it was found wanting, that it did not meet up with some unknown specification and has no hope of doing so. A child tending to the hysteric, on the other hand, will have felt disregarded, un-heard, having to keep insisting, 'Notice me! I'm here! Don't ignore me!'

But the depressive person could equally well have come from *too tight a hold*. Constantly hearing, 'Now come on, this is what I really want of you', the *hysteric's* reaction would be to feel too tightly held and to shout back: 'Hear what *I'm* saying, you're not listening to *me*'. But a child going over to the *depressive* side, given a heavy expectation from parents thus over-concentrated upon it, would have felt that it simply could not hope to come up to some unseen specification and has already been noted as never likely to do so. Thus the child picks up a sense of guilt.

*Relationship* is extremely important both to the depressive and the hysteric type of personality. If hysteric people didn't care deeply from the beginning about relating, they would not respond to separation by reaching out. Depressives also care very deeply about relationship; if they didn't they would not respond by longing for approval. (The schizoid person, as we shall see, may not care so much about relationships at all, perhaps being naturally isolated.) But each of these is deeply concerned with relationships. Where hysterics feel disregarded, depressive people usually feel not only disregarded, but *judged* and found wanting and inadequate. They have been tested against some invisible measure whose nature they cannot know. It may actually be inside them, but they sense it came from key figures in their life, very often the parents. Always falling short of this invisible, maybe fluctuating, measure, they have to keep doing something about it but, whatever they do, they are hopeless and helpless in the face of it. Thrown back on to themselves, they have no sense of inner worth, no way back to being valued. They feel full of generalised, non-specific, free-floating guilt about *being*. It is not around anything specific. It is as though they have no right to exist at all.

The depressive is the most usual type of person to come into counselling and also, perhaps, the most likely to be helped. It can be extraordinarily enriching, as indeed it can for the hysteric-type personality.

## *We all know depression*

All healthy people experience depression at times. It is really a matter of degree. As pain can run along a scale of intensity from mild to excruciating, so depression can run from the gently sad to the totally annihilating and catatonic. Words and labels in plenty have been added on to these things (psychotic versus neurotic depression; major versus minor depression; endogenous versus reactive depression). We need to bear in mind that, though we can categorise depression, take these descriptions and make them into useful raw classifications, yet there are subtle fringes and very wide ranges of variation and interplay between them.

Talking with people, we often find their depression was triggered by some apparent external cause such as we have all experienced: bereavement, divorce, loss, failure, job-redundancy, the after-effects of glandular fever or 'flu (and we do need to allow for the depressing action of some of those infectious illnesses. It often takes six weeks at the very least to clear such a depressive reaction). And then there is the sadness that can come as winter draws in. And what about post-natal depression? Miscarriage? 'Shall I be sterilised?' What for one person might mean a very important release from the burden of possible pregnancy, for another could mean a total end. Abortion – 'Should I go for this option?' Infertility – 'Shall I choose IVF treatment?' It often has to do with self-identity, potency, the power to initiate, or end, a birth of something.

Again, I never give a view. At a rational level, taken as a logical decision, any of those things might be well justified, but at the deeply emotional level the depressed person is not ready to take that extreme step. These things mean something quite different to each person. We ask the question, 'What does it mean to *you*?' The symptom is the symbol.

When, on the other hand, there did not appear to be an outer cause for it, depression was often labelled *endogenous*, 'born from within', a nice fancy Greek name to describe something that nobody knows anything much about. This seems to originate from the client's own inner attitudes and personality, without any apparent reference to external causes or triggering mechanism.

So: all healthy people experience depression at times. From a Transpersonal point of view, I suggest we look out for the *interlude*.[30]

---

[30] For more information on the *interlude*, see Gordon-Brown and Somers, *The Raincloud of Knowable Things*, pp. 148-149.

This is a low, flat state associated with change. A lot of people go into a hiatus when something is gestating within the psyche. The energy that would normally be out in consciousness is drawn back into the unconscious to encapsulate and en-womb something in process of development. It is not true depression, but it can certainly feel like it.

### Labile depression

Then there is the personality whose depression fluctuates. It runs from high to low rather like labile blood pressure, which goes up and down between extremes. Not much is known about the causes. It could be that there is an imbalance in the body system, a deficiency or over-use of some brain chemical. It may be the 'manic defence' pointed out by Melanie Klein: the ability to deny the reality of our inner world. It is said to defend against our depressive guilt, the fear of harming the other by our own aggression. We can adopt this defence as a depressive, hysteric or schizoid type of person. Just possibly there is some consciousness-changing mechanism going on (and that may be true of all psychological states; we have to bear it in mind).

This 'manic-depressive' or 'bipolar' personality can fly very, very far, like somebody 'high' on a drug. They certainly need great care. A lot of people walking around are like this, oscillating between mania and depression. Usually quite biddable when their mood is low, when clinically high they can be extremely dangerous to themselves and others, completely losing their sense of groundedness. Right off the earth, they are quite liable to step out of a window – and take somebody with them too, thinking they can walk on a cloud. It is a totally unrealistic view of what they can do: a God-like omnipotence. Someone I knew described it as 'going out as though you owned the town, feeling everybody is going to come to you and you could walk through walls. "Whoopee, the world is fine! Yes of course I can get between those two posts" – and CRUNCH!' Or they believe they are Mahatma Gandhi. It is extraordinarily difficult. They run the range: up in the heights one minute and a little while later, right down in the depths.

Generally speaking, these people do not come into counselling. They may have to be put into hospital and held in various ways - it's to be hoped by loving arms, but generally by sedation – even tied in. Their low, depressed side is perhaps less exaggerated than with true depression; just because of its lability, this bi-polar condition often gives way more quickly. True depressives lack this defence, lack the externalising energy to be able to be manic. Less labile, they do not have these 'high' phases, though they can have times which are less grey. Their depression has a slightly different nuance. Compare the over-work, the dedication and sacrifice of the truly depressive type of personality – the drudge on the endless wheel. So the one that comes into counselling is probably not the more labile kind, though we will need to check that out.

## Clinical depression

When people become clinically depressed (which is distinct from having a depressive *personality*), there is a sense of being 'totally wiped out, without redemption – damned'. Those are words I hear from people who have been, or are moving towards becoming, extreme cases; and I only began to work with people like this when I had had some experience, not in my early years. There is no centre that will hold. They are terrified of going into their own inner world in case they find nothing there. 'Nothingness,' they say, 'void, condemned, annihilated.' Here are Dante's levels of hell. 'Absolutely worthless, evil – annihilation would be a relief.' They are just not here. And it is very understandable, if we keep in mind the picture in Figure 5 (page 37). Having been assessed, weighed and found wanting, they were rejected.

In this state of serious, chronic depression, the person certainly needs skilled help. There is always the danger of suicide when somebody is coming out of or going into a depression. And the most deeply depressed people cannot hear. In their abyss, they have dropped below life-level. No amount of talking, or holding verbally, is going to get through to them. Those who have been in a profound depression know. It is like being behind a great thick curtain or veil, where other people on the surface are talking and saying things which are absolutely meaningless.

How to deal with that?

## Drugs

Well, we do not deal with it as counsellors. We may think we can bale in there and help, but it actually needs somebody who knows what is possible. *This is not a counsellor's job.* It may be that wisely prescribed drugs administered by a qualified doctor or psychiatrist, running hand-in-hand with skilled psychotherapy, are the only methods we have of helping to handle this extreme situation. It is necessary to help the person reach a point where they can actually begin to hear what is being said. So, pass it over to an analyst or a psychiatrist. It needs most skilful handling. The clinical states of depression belong with a very experienced person, because that client may need to go into care, and suicide is very high up on the list of what might occur.

*IGB*: I worked with somebody who did need drugs. At one stage he was determined, with great guts, to get off them (and if a person is *not* determined to get off the drugs eventually, there is not much a counsellor can do). This man gradually learned how to manage the symptoms that he experienced when in an undrugged state. He found that by going with them rather than against them, they were not quite so bad. Then he learned that he could discharge some of his tension *through* the symptoms he was experiencing. It was all right for him to shake and shudder and wobble and scream on the floor for half an hour. He did succeed in coming off them, but kept them in case of a crisis. However, I don't know what would have happened if he hadn't had this determination for himself.

*BS*: I think this is always a touchy area in counselling. We cannot underline enough that we must stay in close contact with our clients and know what sort of drugs they are on. It is not really a counsellor's job unless they are very experienced. We also need to make it extremely clear that we will keep in very close contact with the psychiatrist.[31]

On the other side of the story is a client of mine who has been very badly depressed over the years. He is a writer, so fortunately already has a creative area of his own to work to. He was on lithium when I first met him, and kept trying to come off it. However, I told him I wouldn't work with him unless he stayed *on* his lithium. I kept saying to him, 'You've taken yourself off it, haven't you? What are you doing with it?' 'Oh well,' he'd say, 'I just left it off.' I said I felt that the lithium was being helpful, that in his case it was actually holding at bay symptoms that he wasn't yet ready to handle. By degrees we managed to modify it and bring the dosage down. He would bite the full five-gram in half and take two-point-five. However, I don't think I could have helped him to handle it without the lithium. We have been able to

---

[31]  The authors were always emphatic that counsellors and psychotherapists should work closely alongside the medical profession when appropriate. Ed.

run it in parallel and ride the two horses. We have done a considerable modulation, and now he's taken over the monitoring and modulating of it himself, which is the major thing. It is not for me to do it. But any time he comes in again, I say, 'Well, increase the dosage a bit.' The only time I ever got really strong with him was: 'I will not work with you if you are not taking these drugs'. Then one can hope for that kind of modification.

After all, God also made chemists. There are times when drugs are immensely valuable, as long as the counselling runs in parallel with them. Think of some of the alternatives: lobotomy, ECT, chained to walls in bedrooms. Some may be crude, but at least they are better than some of what went ahead of them.

However, our brief as counsellors is with the depressive *personality* and, as we shall see, many of those do come in to counselling.

### The depressive personality

So we have seen how a *clinically* depressed person talks about more than emptiness; they talk about annihilation and 'total wipe-out'. But someone who speaks of being empty may have this depressive characteristic without being clinically ill. 'Deep down, I fear there'll be nothing there.' The depressed personality dreads that there's nothing inside to come out: 'At my centre there is – nothing'. Because they felt (rightly or wrongly, but this is how the child experienced it) that they were judged worthless, they feel worthless. Their low self-esteem is one of the most marked things about them, and a general sense and fear of failure.

Typically they expend a great deal of their life-energy in trying to gain approval and esteem from others. They desperately need a response from those outside to feed back into that sense of emptiness, fill it out in some way. Where hysterics would demand it, shout to get it, depressives will actually turn away, but as if they are in search of some way of *buying* themselves into that place of acceptance. 'Anything but confrontation.' To speak up for their need is to court the rejection which they are sure is coming. They tend to hit backwards over their shoulder, relate backwards, developing antennae for others' feelings, but in order to adapt to them and so avoid direct confrontation and rejection. They are, in fact, building a wall which continues the cut-off which they felt they had in the beginning. This is the child put out of Paradise.

These are the most exquisitely sensitive of people. Depressive personalities have a disproportionate response to anything which is even by simple nuance a criticism. What another person would take as just the ordinary knock-about of ordinary daily living and conversation, they see as denoting failure on their part. Each reversal or slight can have a devastating and cumulative effect. (I begin to feel a bit depressed contemplating it.) It is as if they lack a protective skin. They have learnt to handle their world by extreme sensitivity to hurt. Again, the strong people around them may be drained, going to the wall trying not to step on their feet. For it is terribly easy to fall over some hidden trip-wire, and we sense them going all spiky, mortally offended, rejected. It is very difficult to see where we are because they don't have parameters, so we're over the edge before we know it. With this hypersensitive person, we're so busy trying not to crunch on them that we begin to lose our own ground. We can end up feeling like great big brutes, while they feel wounded.

Depressive people often overvalue others to their own detriment. They can sit in a room full of people and believe that everybody else has it hung together, or is doing better, or knows all the answers; it is only they who don't. 'Oh, you're so wonderful, everything you do is marvellous. But little me out here, I could never achieve anything.' We hear these comparisons over and over. Other people, particularly any people they are attracted to, have a magic formula which they themselves lack, some potion that grants achievement or affirmation. Things come easily to the other person, but never to them. Uriah Heep in Dickens, a scraping, unlovable person, was a marvellous example of this hand-wringing placating of others; probably a highly depressed personality there.

In fact, this low expectation ('How could *I* ever hope to be like that?') is a very selfish viewpoint, because they have become the centre and judge of their universe. Quite a number of depressed people, as they begin after a while to move out of it, can be shown, very gently, the degree to which theirs has been an egocentric view. They have been using themselves as a measure of perfection; or continually measuring the world out there against their own worthlessness, which comes to the same thing.[32]

---

[32]   See Rowe, *Depression: the Way Out of Your Prison.*

However, crack that shell, bring these potential fledglings out of the egg and when they really start flying – they fly.

Depressive people are much less overtly, outwardly demanding than the hysteric personality, whose demands cannot be mistaken. But nonetheless they have a near-bottomless pit of need for pats, strokes and affirmation from other people to help bolster their own lack of self-esteem and fill their sense of having an empty hole inside. They will very often hide behind a sacrificial stance, giving and giving and giving. There are no boundaries to their giving. Or they fall into a pattern where they must be either saving everyone else in order to redeem their own sense of identity, or else being victim to all these dominating people. The effect is to get people to notice them, pay attention to them and give of themselves.

These people can seem highly cynical. It is their safeguard against rejection. They want to reject before being rejected. Start pushing into it, though, and we rarely find a true cynicism. More truly, these depressed cynics are deeply wounded romantics looking for the happy fairy-story ending. It is because they care so deeply about relationships. If they pretended they didn't, they'd be going against their own nature. This is why the Transpersonal approach, looking with the talisman for a point of centredness from which we can work, can very much help this romantic person. We are not giving them an elixir, but we are giving them a rabbit's foot on the road to the elixir.

Our biggest workers, those who hold up industries and organisations and professions, often use continuous over-activity to mask and defend against depression and to hold back the experience of their sense of emptiness. Workaholics may actually be holding depression at bay. 'If I stop doing, I will have to *be*. If I'm no-one, then how can I be? What can I be? Even if I could just be, would it be acceptable?'

### How depressive people seem to themselves

From their own viewpoint, they can be so over-concerned with others' opinions that they have few of their own, not even knowing what they think and feel. Ask them, and they can honestly reply, 'I don't know'. They're so busy taking their colouration from everyone around them that it has never occurred to them to ask that question of themselves.

'Do you like green, or do you prefer pink?'
'I've never thought about it.'
'Shall we go to the park?'
'I don't mind, what would *you* like to do?'
'Would you like tea, or coffee?'
'Oh, I'll leave it entirely to you.'

And the answer, one of the keys into understanding this nature, is that they actually *don't* know. One comment from someone who put herself into the 'depressive' category:

> *I went shopping but I couldn't choose anything, I had no idea what I wanted. People said, 'Well, are you coming out or are you staying in?' and I was just stuck in the doorway, because I didn't know whether I was going out or staying in. I couldn't make any decision.*

This is why they respond very well to therapy. The therapist or counsellor can throw back to them, 'Well, perhaps you'd like to begin to consider what your own needs and feelings are in all this?' To the depressive personality, to choose seems monstrous at the time, so self-indulgent and greedy. They say, 'If I like this and somebody else doesn't like it, then I'm offending them.' Or, 'I'm committing a sin by expressing my own feeling (and I may well be rejected.)' They're already split off.

This can, of course, lead to a very symbiotic way of living. Their chameleon-like natures are so ready to identify and take on the colouration of other people that they find it difficult to have any colour or identity of their own. They tend to seek out someone with strong opinions and views, lose their own nature and feel even more annihilated. They always have something of the masochist about them. Inevitably they draw to themselves those who are going to hurt them, crunch them down; strong, possibly quite ruthless, people, who will respond with, 'How could you possibly like green – or pink! How horrid!' Thus the sadist is befriended by the masochist.

I speculate as to whether a cyclic depression may not, in its odd way, sometimes be providing a safe continuum? Is there ever a *comfort* in depression? Some people are depressed only in autumn, or only in winter, or only in summer. There's no anniversary, no major break, trauma or bereavement. They are not still unconsciously grieving. It is a cycle more to do with the seasons, as though their nature were tuned to a particular rhythm. Could there be a creative mood within such a cycle, the return of the known? Even depression can be familiar; there can be a certain comfort in it. And also it avoids complication and demand.

## Aggression and anger

I am positive that each person starts out as a good healthy seed. Jung, and many another in this area, held that every healthy person who makes an attack on life, who takes a grip and faces up to their experience, needs a certain amount of aggression and assertiveness. We need the ability to be angry and express that anger, then to learn through our life-experience to channel it. It is not healthy if, over a long period, we do not do so.

However, the depressive personality has so early had to turn any 'negative' response inward that their aggression, anger and hostility (which can of course be positive if properly channelled) are redirected back upon themselves. One of the major definitions of depression has been 'aggression turned inwards'. It is very true in some ways. Instead of attacking life, or coming back at the other person, they turn their energy into attacking themselves. They don't really see the other person; they relate to people out there by projection. Everything is turned back, bent towards the self, taken inwards into the solar plexus area, which is where the depressive always catches it. However, 'aggression turned inwards' is not the only definition. From a Transpersonal point of view, when we go behind the depression and discover the anger, we can practically always go behind *that* and find the need to assert the self – or the Self.

If they can be assertive at all they may do it suicidally. Or absolutely violently. Feeling 'if there is no way but into depression, I might as well go the whole way', they may try to blot life out completely with drugs and alcohol. But, give them a holiday, a drink, a change, and with that one trigger they can suddenly assert themselves. These sensitive, sympathetic people can blast away extraordinarily and absolutely terrify themselves, completely flummoxing the other person with their anger and hostility. I knew a woman who really loved the friend with whom she often went on holiday. However, there was always an explosion, particularly if there was a bit of alcohol flowing. She would say the most terrible things to this friend of hers. She did deeply love her, but because she trusted her and was away from everybody else, and the drink helped, she would express all, saying the most desperate things to this friend. But this aggression was really directed at people to whom she had never said it, as far back as she could remember. Since she was also a very lovable person, the friend tolerated it for a long time, but in the end refused to go again.

Or they may assert themselves by 'yapping like a little dog', as one man put it. His wife was usually quiet and gentle and kind ('droopy', he called her – certainly a depressive type of personality). 'But get her away from home and, even with me there, she'll become like one of those terriers, nipping at your ankle, snapping at everybody.' Apparently she would frighten the wits out of herself until, back in her own environment, she was soon down into the droop again. Very often, depressive-type personalities have no experience of bringing out straight statements, so they do come out inappropriately, with biting little ways like small dogs, and then they hop back in and hide. It can take us by surprise if we are counselling them. We don't expect it, we're looking across at them, and suddenly we're nipped in the ankle.

## Self-assertion

Real self-assertion is the claiming of the light around us and the ground under our feet, from which we need neither to attack nor defend ourselves. The hope is that these people learn to assert themselves positively. Again, we help them by slow degrees to face, accept and learn to re-channel their own ability to express anger and aggression. They *need* to take a grip on life, attack life. After all, that is only self-assertion. When treated positively, it is just a statement of themselves.

I heard of one very depressed young woman who had slashed herself since the age of ten and later attempted suicide several times. A court case was to decide whether she would lose all parental rights to her children. 'I asked her what she would do if this occurred,' said my colleague, 'and she said, "Well, a year ago, I would have gone out and tried to kill myself. But now, it's them – I'm going to shoot them all, all the lawyers, all the social workers!"' The aggression was coming out. Now, she would kill the lot of us, but it was turned out and no longer turned in on herself. I saw that as healthy.' That is a very good example of the layers of depression. Work behind them and we find the rage and the anger, the expression of the person. And get in behind that bombardment, help it to be contained and taken back and very often, behind the lost unhappiness, we will find once more the creativity of the essential Self.

The more aggressive among depressive type people are seen less often. Usually men, they will go over the top in anger and rage and then sulk when opposed, manipulating by silence. Churchill is a good example of somebody who was at his best and most positive when admired, affirmed and in action. Strangely enough, he was not of the hysteric mode, although with his very strong, extraverted type of energy one might have expected him to be. His body was probably strong enough, although he frequently became ill before or after major stress. He simply did not know how to modulate his self-assertion. I met someone who had known him very well indeed and said that, underneath that, there was very real depression. He simply could not tolerate being alone. Although more aggressive than repressive, when he stopped working he spoke of there being a great emptiness.

Yet Churchill could go into a different depressive mode, manipulating the environment by silence. And, as we read in his biographies and autobiography, when he was left alone – and silent – he managed to stay out of the terrible depression of not being in office by painting, building walls; the creative transmutation processes of the depression. Or going to sleep. But oh, the sulk of the depressive personality! It has to be experienced to be believed. It is punitive. By not saying anything, not doing anything, not making a response, it manipulates all. It can come in various textures and layers, from the wounded, 'How could you hurt poor little me, I never did anything to hurt you?' to a deep, quiet, long-suffering silence. (The hysteric will also go into a sulk, but it will not be long-suffering.) The depressive's sulk, though! You can hear the electric charge running through it, its enduring, masochistic, sacrificial silence. It is the most difficult of all to get through; and of course all our own guilts and depressions come out in response.

### The value of the depressive-tending personality

Demanding, draining as they are, I love working in these areas, for these people are also pulling out the sensitivity of those around them, deepening the caring nature of others at the most positive level. They are at their best and most positive when admired and affirmed in action and in work. This is very useful to the world. Because of their ability to identify needs, developing subtle antennae and putting others above themselves, they can be the most helpful, most genuinely lovable people we could ever meet. Just as the acting profession would be weakened by having fewer hysteric personalities, so most businesses and organisations, and all the so-called 'helping professions', would be very much impoverished without the depressive personality and its ability to love, care and put others' needs before its own.

And so they are in action in the world, sacrificing themselves, caring for others. Nursing and the social services are full of them. Here are those therapists who inappropriately put their clients above themselves all the time until they nearly kill themselves, and pretty nearly kill the clients as well. They often have this fear of being found wanting, this fear of *being*. So, although they are the most sincerely concerned people in the world, their danger is that those they help will themselves be drained in reaction. There is all the difference in the world between giving out naturally in service, a spontaneous outflow, and *buying* our place. All counsellors have to watch their motivation, not to be a part of that.

Those with this depressive characteristic are by nature highly creative people. Moving like willows to the downbeat, the minor chords of life, they tend to be extraordinarily sensitive. Their musical ear is tuned to the minor key. Others are major chord people, but there is a poetic quality about these that goes for the heartbreak in the heart of things. Writers, artists, musicians – maybe only those who have known the abyss can best imagine the heights. Conversely, those who know the heights can also know the depths. The *sad clown* is almost a cliché. There are many very good examples among our greatest comics, their clowning and fooling about masking a depth of sadness. Depressive people are nearly always *introverted*, whether thinking- or feeling-types. That's not an absolute rule of thumb; you can have extroverted depressive people. But take a singer's voice away, a guitarist's guitar from him, pinch a flautist's flute and very often you will discover that they have very little sense of identity and may even go into quite profound, near-suicidal depressions.

While it can give them joy to create, many creative artists feel that creating is a terrible agony, that their creation has been brought about by fire, by friction, that they are being driven by something greater than they are. Sitting outside, not actually caught by that daimon, we would imagine it to give creative joy. But for them it is not like that at all. It is like having a great beast on your back, and when it's not there the lack of it can be as agonising.

Every creative artist when completing a task will suffer from a post-birth reaction, just as any normal healthy person, after putting out a lot of effort, needs the counterpoint of relaxation. Muscle tone has to come down to quiescence in order to regenerate itself. So creation seems to have in counterpoint a tendency to feel empty. Creative artists have this sense of being hollowed out. As we have seen, if they are feeling deeply depressed they will use the word 'empty' (while, if they are going over towards clinical depression, they will say 'totally void, totally wiped out, annihilated'). However, after a time, back they come again. For nine years I worked with writers, artists, playwrights, poets and so on at the Society of Authors, addressing with them some of their problems. I remember once at a meeting saying, to a roar of laughter and affirmation:

*When in the birth pangs of the idea, writers show generalised anxiety.*
*While actually writing, they demonstrate schizoid delusional states as their characters take on lives of their own and become more real than external people.*
*This is followed by post-natal depression.*
*While looking for a publisher, they're distinctly paranoid.*
*During publication, they show every sign of bipolar disorder, and after publication, of omnipotence.*
*When the critics get at the publication, it's persecution mania.*
*In the space between books, they're depressive, often suicidal, convinced that they'll never be able to write again.*
*And then, when they do pick up pen and paper once more, they're obsessive and compulsive.*

All people are creative, depressives as well as hysterics, but they do it in a different way. Both are artists in *being*. That is what we need to hold on to: to be creative, we don't have simply to *do* things; the depressive has a great skill in *being*, a quality of being. Since, we hope, they have so far survived the struggle, they will use every mode of manipulation and request in order to *be*. The hysteric on the other hand is still demanding the right to be.

It has been said that the outflowing, positive *hysteric* person has the ability to enter into somebody else's experience and can make the best kind of counsellor for that reason. I am not sure I agree. Such people are likely to superimpose their own desire for identity on the client's identity. I don't say they can't make very good counsellors; they can, and perhaps even better consultants. But, if they are true to their hysteric type, they would probably be better identifying with an acting role. They are very well able to do dynamic drama therapy or Gestalt. But the ability to sit there for ever, helping other people sort out their gold – panning for gold – it is very often the *depressive* who can do that. The depressive has a very particular quality of entering in and often makes the very finest counsellor.

### Counselling the depressive personality

As we have seen, the truly, profoundly depressed person may well need to be taken into care, and certainly needs skilled therapy. They simply cannot hear other people's affirmation; that is part of their non-hearing. Yet the depressive *personality*, somebody who hasn't gone into that deepest level, is going to turn up fairly frequently in counselling. They are very responsive to therapy. If a continuing quality of trust is built in for them (over time, obviously), these less extreme cases can be helped to hear, and not only to hear but to learn to trust. I think the reason why depressive people are much easier to help than hysteric people is that, over a period and with the right degree of holding and loving, they can be encouraged to begin to validate themselves; and so their own lack of self-esteem is bolstered. Eventually, often in a surprisingly short time, they come to have a very much greater sense of personal worth and self-valuation, because, in fact, they *long* to hear. And, in a similar way, the hysteric also longs to hear (while, again, the schizoid person is a different matter).

Part of what we do is meet the depressive person's need of loving affirmation over what may be a long period. We help them to feel that someone cares, that their achievements and potential are supported. This outside reinforcement is terribly important, because there is nothing inside that can give them any such reinforcement. The majority of them can survive a great deal if there is *one person*. One person to be there as a continuum can often in itself do the work; they don't necessarily need a whole company. After a while, they don't even have to see that one person too often. Just the knowledge that someone is there to believe in them can enable the client, by degrees, to introject that confidence and build inside themselves what the therapist has been trying to help them hold.

### Beware the power of the weak

The difficulty with the depressive type personality is that the backlash of their lack of self-esteem is a forked tail. They will, if they can, manipulate the whole situation by their sacrifices and their hyper-sensitivity, sacrificing themselves to the hilt for us and then resenting us bitterly for it. 'Now look what you've made me do to myself!' Unlike the hysteric-type personality, this person is not usually going to mess us about over such things as money, being late, mentioning the important thing just as they go out of the door. They will be early or exactly on time, pay on target, get everything right.

And quite a lot of depressive-type personalities will bale us out (if we're lucky) by showing us their own humanity in order to save us. They will be exquisitely sensitive to us: 'How are you? Did you enjoy your holiday? You're very pale today, are you tired?' Because they love us they will then come to our assistance, which gives them a sense that, since that is something they can do, they have a role. It leaves us wondering, '*Now* what do I do? Now I'm as depressed as you are.' And then, when we have got through all that, they say, 'By the way my brother died yesterday', or, 'I'm really ill, but I didn't want to tell you'.

So from the area of their guilt, if we are not careful, we are pulled out to meet their needs, drawn right off our ground; and now that's two of us out there. Whereas the hysteric comes in over our boundaries and makes us back off and hide, the depressive person moves away, luring us out from our own space. It is almost as if they are saying, 'I'm so lonely out here. Please come and join me! Come and coax me back, tell me you do want me.' The therapist must be able to sit back and parley with them, getting them to turn around and address their own boundaries. The boundaries are there but the client feels there is no way across, since they have been set up to keep them *out* from life. So a lot of coaxing is in fact needed.

It sounds funny. It's very tragic, it's very painful, it's lovely. It takes a tremendous amount of patience. We sit in and help them to create the pearl out of the grit in their own system. That takes time. It can't be rushed. We are very often in for quite a long sit: first, to build in the trust; secondly, to help them to get that sense of boundaries; and thirdly, for them to dare to express it in the outside world. The danger is, they may prefer to feel that the therapy room is the only place they can find the pearl and want to recreate themselves only there.

### *Eye-level*

*If you look up to the other, then you are going down; if you look down on them, then you are going up.* We need to practice keeping our own eyes level; it is tremendously important to maintain that straight look *across*. This helps them in turn to keep their eye-level as equal as they possibly can. Outwardly, the depressive person is nearly always looking *up*, so that the other person seems much taller than they are. They are sometimes very judgemental; as we saw, judging themselves but quite often judging others as well. After all, it is a judgement to feel that everybody's taller than you are, isn't it?

However, we very often discover that in their unconscious is the reverse: inwardly, they may be looking not up, but *down* at other people. Deep in their psyche is the sense, 'I am special', an unrecognised prince or princess. There is sometimes – not always, but quite often – a powerful unconscious figure in the psyche of a depressive person which has to be taken into account. It is an over-idealisation within themselves, coming from a fear of under-idealisation. Small people can still be Napoleons, can they not? Looking at it in a Transpersonal way, this sense of 'I am of the blue blood' may have something to do with the nature of the Self. They may have been forced to turn to the image and the archetype of the Self because something was unavailable from the parent figure. Crossing over to it, they have discovered within themselves a real centre, but they don't know what to do with it. It takes a long time to get at that bit inside themselves. Helping them adjust their eye-level helps that internal figure – if it's there – to be less high, over-idealised and judgemental.

## *The effect on the counsellor*

Depression is very exhausting to have, and also very exhausting, even draining, to work with. We feel that at last something is beginning to happen, something's cracking. And the person comes in next time as resentful as they were before. We sit there patiently. Sometimes we are dealing with a bottomless pit of demand that leaks out, runs out like a siphon. I do not like using words like 'seduction' because it sounds too conscious; but there is a kind of seduction when we are working with these clients.

I remember one depressive client, an absolutely enchanting young woman, delightful to look at, like a mermaid, as though she weren't quite there and would vaporise. She had a very small, tiny voice. She whispered more and more quietly, till one session I suddenly woke up and found myself trying to hear what she was saying. She had her eyes closed. I pulled myself upright and saw what was happening: I was like a snake following a snake-charmer. She wasn't doing it consciously (or was she?): the dropped voice, the slightly averted eyes, having to fix my eyes on her all the time, trying to coax back her gaze. I was lying practically horizontally across the floor. It was useful, having seen that. It brought me back. Trying to hear can be incredibly draining. We need to watch for it. It is good to sit upright and say, 'Could you say that again in a voice we can both hear?'

This is why it is wise to look at our caseload and spread any depressive type personalities out across the week if we can. Avoid having them all on one day. And though maybe it is a little disturbing for them, it is quite a good idea not always to see such a client at the same time of day but to vary that a bit, in case of this diurnal swing. Somebody we see at, say, nine o'clock each morning may be a very different character at four-thirty in the afternoon.

Counselling of this caring, exquisitely sensitive human being requires, as always, respect for the individual and recognition of the value of what they are capable of at the subjective level. Again, it's space and boundaries and a coming-together as equals on that true meeting-ground, which is in the middle of the counselling room. We meet them at the interface between the two of us, where the boundary is. It is terribly important to be most real with somebody like this. If we are simply pretending to believe in them but are actually a bit tetchy or edgy, we come over with the most ringing inauthenticity. These people are testing our worth, our mettle, as well as trying to discover their own worth and their own mettle. If they push us up onto some pedestal, we may need to hold it for a while until, because they've got an example which they feel is worth following, they hear their own gold ring true. So, we keep the humanity and the equality but know how very easy it is to fall into the trap and find ourselves taking the posture that we are pushed into. This may do nothing but increase their sense of worthlessness. We can only respect their boundaries and their worth very genuinely from inside if we respect our own.

### Doing and being

The depressive person certainly needs to be helped not to be overactive. However, to find themselves out of action too soon, too quickly, is an excessive counterpoint to over-action and can put them into that sense of emptiness again. They do need to keep in action. We help them to say 'both this *and* that' so that work and relaxation are in counterpoint, and even in the relaxation they know that they can come back into work again. If we can keep them on their feet and interacting with life as far as they are capable, that's the way to do it. It takes time. It is a matter of breaking the either/or position so that they understand the nature of 'work *and* play, do *and* be. It is alright to pause and breathe'. For people who have been frightened of *being*, it needs a tremendous amount of trust to take that risk. After all, they have worked very hard since early childhood to protect themselves, and are not quickly going to let that safeguard go.

We help them to realise that you do not have to save the world in order to buy your place in it, although saviours do have qualities of caring. And by degrees, because they are affirmed by someone outside, they have the strength to take back into themselves the power which they have invested in the outside world. So, with all depressive people, our aim is to give them a sense that someone cares and will provide a continuum. Be around, honour the times set up for them. If we make a promise, keep it. This applies with every client of course, but very particularly with the depressive.

> *We hope to help them to stay in action but not to be over-active; to balance being and doing; to gain a greater sense of perspective about people (they probably over-idealise their parents, and thus their friends, the authorities and everyone else). Help them face, first the possibility of their own anger, resentment and hostility. Then, by very gentle degrees (not frightening them too much, because, after all, their anger, resentment and hostility have been going inward for many years) we help them to see that it can be expressed without loss of love. Very often it has to be expressed in our counselling room and they find that we still continue to love them. They can curl up in a foetal ball and weep, and talk about their emptiness, and we still love them.*
> *And we hope to help free them from their own guilt of being.*

It really comes back to *space* and *boundaries*. We help them to build in more boundaries and put down more roots; and we aim to provide the affirmation of their being which they felt, almost certainly rightly, that they lacked as children.

### Both hysteric and depressive personality types

Though these general tendencies are fascinating, I certainly do not think it's possible to put people into clear-cut categories. However, we can roughly summarise by saying that hysterics have a prime need for *attention* and depressives for *approval*. Obviously these fringe over into each other, but the hysteric's need for attention is because of an original sense of *disregard*, and the depressive's need for approval is because they felt that, though they were seen, they were *found wanting* and rejected.

We saw how both hysteric and depressive (though not schizoid) people, are still deeply concerned with *relationship*. Both depend on feedback from others, both fear abandonment by those who can 'save' them. Therefore they concentrate most on the issues, difficulties and problems of relating. In counselling, the major discussion point is not only relatedness to people but relatedness to life. So we need to concentrate primarily on helping them to relate to themselves and then to others.

Both have problems with aggression and assertion. The hysteric tends to be critical and angry, and project out on to *others* when they have stopped over-admiring them or when they don't live up to imagined ideals. When depressives can't live up to their own imagined ideals or the ideals they imagine that other people have of them, they turn criticism and anger in on *themselves*. The one is extraverting to get others to live up to the ideal; the other is introverting in the belief they can't live up to their *own* inward ideals. Both are quite angry underneath.

With the *hysteric* the therapist has mainly to honour and respect the boundaries, saying, 'I hear you, I see you, but you needn't make such a noise about it, because that is how you alienate people from you'. As therapists, we help them tolerate their own fear of not being seen, of isolation, of not being acknowledged as being there. That is done by respecting their dignity. This clarity of guideline is terribly important. It is rare for an hysteric personality to meet somebody who can hold them, contain their excesses, even contain their lacks. It is because they feel they cannot contain *themselves*, cannot hold themselves, that they need that help. One person able to do that can give them enormous confidence. Patience and forbearance are needed, yes, but also the firm line. It is all about respect, about lovingness; but rugged lovingness, not sentimental slop. Otherwise these people may say, 'You're not holding me enough, you don't love me enough to have a good argument with me – enough to give me a good hiding.' Well, we don't need to have an argument with them that will 'give them a good hiding', but we do give them this clarity and firmness of line. It is terribly important.

The *hysteric* personality listens, waiting only for the moment to dive in themselves; we may be lucky to get a word in edgeways. *Depressive* personalities, on the other hand, are good listeners and often loath to talk about themselves. They're not used to communicating anything from deep within, not daring to confront the inside of themselves in case it's void, empty – in case what they felt in the beginning is so. We aim to set up a reciprocal relationship where the person is encouraged to talk back and express their sensitivity: 'How do you feel about what has just been said?' (If we say, 'What do you mean by that?' they will seize up.) 'Would you mind saying that again? I sense that there was something more subtle there that I've missed.' And very often they can be persuaded to tell us what they *might* have said.

Just to be there is helping. And so they find love and dignity and respect, and are also coaxed back to their own boundaries. If they are taking their colour from other people, we get them to turn round and observe their own colour, not just where it filters over into other people's, but where they are drawing other people over to filter into them. They are often defined most by being needed. They are most deeply concerned, loving, exquisitely caring people. Since they have an artistic, aesthetic, creative side to them, which very often brings itself out in the form of poetry and music, the non-verbal modes, we find very often that working with dreams and artwork is the best way through.

## Hysteric and depressive 'conversion'

I remember the man who trained me saying, 'If you're trying to take away, or help somebody remove, a symptom – trying to cure a "nervous breakdown" – do be very careful to have something to help the person replace it with'. Working in Transpersonal Psychology, we are fortunate to have the possibility of a replacement at a higher level. We are listening to the language, asking, 'What is this illness saying to you? Is there an alternative way of handling the energy? Can it be *converted* into a different form?' We're certainly *not* saying, 'I don't believe in this, it is only in your head, it's just your imagination.' But very often a psychosomatic illness or symptom will throw this up into question. Could the energy which is being taken down regressively into tension be converted again in a totally different way?

To amplify it out: if someone with an *hysteric* tendency gets anorexia or cancer, might it be that they have gone into a *hysteric* conversion of energy into illness? It might be, 'Now look what you've made me do to myself!' Is it perhaps an active signal to someone in their life at a self-dramatising level – a way of communicating? Rather than making an attempt to destroy themselves, are they taking revenge, avenging themselves on the person they feel caused them to do this? Will some of them be getting the attention that they have been screaming for? With the hysteric person, the illness may actually be a play for life. Their demand to be heard may have caused them to relate backwards and respond inappropriately, regressively, hysterically to outer stimuli.

The counsellor can say, 'Well, that's one way of using the energy, and it may be the best way for you at the moment.' But, working with them from the interface, they may come to recognise that the energy that has gone down has within it the possibility of being 'converted' back again. Might it not rather express their colour range, their sense of drama? Be with the Transpersonal polarity, the other side of the person; sense their intensity of living and of feeling, and help them seek expression through extraverted activity. Then, instead of their going back inwardly to that parent body with, 'Why won't you listen to me?' they may begin to put the energy out into movement, song, dance, sound, colour, acting. The 'conversion' is now taken up from the lower to the higher. So though for a time somebody runs with their symptom, we are not trying to take it away. We are working alongside the symptom to see how the energy may be also converted back.

Again, take somebody who gets ill and has a tendency to a *depressive* conversion of energy. Might they not unconsciously be trying to obliterate themselves, to vanish off the scene by putting an eraser over themselves? Is their depressive bit regressing in order to be held, to have that touch, that intimacy? We are looking at the *depressive* person as having been weighed, measured and found wanting. They have tended to relate to life inappropriately, always placating, trying to buy their way back in, or even to obliterate themselves off the scene. 'Well, this way of using your energy may have been helpful once,' we say, 'but there are other ways of converting it.' So, again we are standing with them at the interface, helping them by degrees to recognise that there are ways of claiming their ground, their centre. Then they may use the ability to pour themselves out, to buy themselves back, in service to other people.

The depressive conversion is a very self-centred stance: *Self*-centred. It is centred on the Self. They are trying to find a centre. This centring on the Self can be enlarged beyond the range of the small self and amplified out into wider contexts. I have seen many a depressive person – absolutely churning, seeing no way through life – beginning to move out to others through the exploration of dreams, story, myth, legend, astrology, counselling. They recognise that out there is a great big world. They do not have to spend the whole of their energy trying to buy themselves back into the original nursery. That again is a conversion of energy back and up: it allows them to have their depression, but also to recognise what happens when the mist begins to clear. In the process, they have gained a great deal of sensitivity as to what makes people tick.

So for both hysteric and depressive personalities, counselling is about *relating*. Next, we shall be looking at the schizoid and later the obsessive/compulsive type of person. In the beginning they too were concerned about relationships, but their experience of life has driven them right away from that and now they care much less.

The Edge

# CHAPTER SIX

# The Schizoid Personality

## Barbara Somers

*I have made it a rule myself*
*to consider every case as an entirely new proposition*
*about which I do not even know the ABC.* [33]

Everybody splits off at some point. It is our survival factor. If we can't take ourselves physically out of an intolerable situation, we *need* to be able to cut off, to put the lid on, to detach and take ourselves to an objective position. It is quite natural and normal in the human being as a mode of survival under unbearable stress.

And we usually return; we come back again to be where we were before. But if it becomes a way of life, a way of handling every situation, then we are beginning to talk of the truly *schizoid* position. It's when we go out over the wall and *live* on the other side of the split, so that the split acts as an abyss, a schism preventing any kind of relating. When a person spends a large part of their lives on the other side of the split or schism, they are liable to be called 'schizoid'; and if they stay there all the time, they'll be clinically labelled 'schizophrenic'.

Think again of the *hysteric*, the *depressive* and the *schizoid*. Which is which? It is like making a difference between a dragon, a unicorn and a phoenix. We all have a tendency to move between these three positions. The hysteric and the depressive are still seeking relationship, intent on it, their life energy turned in towards it. Their anxiety is the anxiety of separation and their life energy is given towards coming back into relationship again. As we saw, anger and resentment are closer to the surface than with the schizoid type of personality. The truly schizoid position is different. Someone here can quite often hold an objective working relationship together but, if they are fringing over towards the non-splitting type of schizophrenia (see pages 88-89), then

---

[33] Jung, *Man and his Symbols*, p. 82.

when another person wants to get close to them and become subjective, panic breaks out.

## The schizoid-tending person

It is as if some trauma has happened to place them beyond a much wider barrier. It is not that, like the hysteric, they feel that they have not been seen clearly enough, nor that, like the depressive, they have been measured and found wanting. It's just that relationship is for them not a reality. Words we hear are 'futility, apathy'. Their despair is infinitely more integral. It is not depression; it's below depression. It is not the void; it's below the void. It is profoundly part of them. It is as though they have never known relationship, never hoped for meaning, and are totally locked out. Alienated, they have alienated themselves.

If as a child I was handled and held, then a sense of myself as a subject will have been set up. Therefore I will sense 'out there' as the objective world. This gives most of us our sense of where reality and fantasy are defined.[34] Both the hysteric and the depressive have had the feeling of somebody else holding them, tracing the outline of their body, giving them their first sense of reality. The child who emerged from that original symbiotic rapport with the mother, for whom that touch was profoundly and truly there in earliest bonding, will have experience of relationship. Even if it has later been a bad one, even if we have been put out of touch, we will continually demand the re-establishment of relationship so that we can be put back in touch. Being handled and held, we can sense that at least there is one person who feels for us, to whom we can relate.

By contrast, the truly schizoid person has never been put in touch. For someone deeply marked by this, the original emergence from the symbiotic relationship with the mother will have been affected. Nothing and no-one has ever drawn them over the borderline into the realm of relationship with the outside world and the person out there. They were never bonded enough in the beginning to have the sense of relating to anyone, and at a very deep level they don't expect it. They may have been institutionalised, or repeatedly fostered. The necessity of a mothering figure to hold, outline, define the emerging child or emerging personality, to give it a sense of being a subject, not an object, was not met. There was nobody there for this abandoned infant over too

---

[34] This was discussed in connection with the Child in the Adult, and also with Space and Boundaries. See Somers and Gordon-Brown, *Journey in Depth*, Chapters 3 and 8.

long a period. There has never been a relationship against which to protest, or of which to demand. Lacking in the first years the *hold* that is so vital, they have been put out of touch – or they have never been put in touch. Sometimes they have been alienated totally beyond touch. And all this means that they have not less but *more* need for relationship. The schizoid personality has a *passionate original need* to relate.

So, we can say that the hysteric is expressing the need for *more touch*; while the depressive is out of touch and seeking to *get in touch*. But the clinically schizoid position is where the whole person is *beyond touch*, set apart and outcast.

### Subject – or object?

Thus the deeply schizoid person has never bonded, never been helped to be a subject. Or it may have been some later trauma that placed them outside the touch of human relatedness. A truly schizoid situation is where somebody feels that, since they were treated like an object, they *are* an object. They don't think of themselves as a subject. They see and experience the world as a place where they are *used*. They have come from the womb simply to become a thing. There is no sense of 'I-ness', of becoming 'a little "I" in my own right' and then learning to objectify that, since there has been no subjective relationship, no gentle movement from the primary, holding parent. Treated like an object, not feeling themselves a subject, they have a very small sense of what's inside and what's outside. They are more like a parcel than a person. Their own name means nothing; there is no 'Paulness'. Paul is just a label on the parcel. There is no sense of a boundary to be defined. There is no one on the other side to help create any tension of relationship. They are simply put out into the world as a thing, to find their own way. Hence there's no sense of clarity between the subject and the object of reality.

Feeling themselves to be a thing not a person very often leads someone truly schizoid into alienation from their own body, their physical being, their own instinctual nature and that of others. They look upon their own needs, instincts and urges as animal, as something which has nothing to do with them. It is as though they were in another place. They have no relationship to what is happening to their body outside; simply none, a total disconnection. The body, if thought of at all, is carried around as if it were some appendage, a long, long way away.

So, treating themselves as things to be used but not related to, they tend also to treat other people as things, more or less useful. That is how they relate to the world because that is their experience of the world. The truly schizoid person is deeply frightened by emotional intimacy. It is such an unknown that it's an enormous threat. Their defence is to withdraw as far as possible from the chance of any kind of intimate touch.

## Solitude, fantasy and paranoia

You will sometimes get schizoid-type personalities who 'go away': lighthouse keepers, long-distance runners – solitary pursuits. They are most real when they are alone, dealing with life by taking themselves to another place; but that place may for them be very rich. Their vocation, if it's chosen, is often in line with it. Shepherds or mountaineers are often schizoid-type personalities making their own adjustment. They can tolerate the aloneness and isolation that depressive and hysteric types are all the time trying to hold at bay.

Of course, a lot of people do this. Relating to life in our own way, we can tolerate so much externalisation, but then we have to split off. Most creative, sensitive people have the experience of *sometimes* feeling most real when they are alone. We are talking here of people who feel it all the time. I can see how that happens. I would have to put my hand up as being more in the schizoid personality line (I don't think the 'schizophrenic' because I'm too *related*), but certainly a point comes when I cannot take any more and I quietly pull out and withdraw myself. Then after a while I am back again. Certain loving friends through the years have said, 'One minute you're there, and the next minute you've gone.' I'm here physically, but I have actually gone away. I know when I am doing it, I can feel it. 'Where are you, where have you gone?' they say. 'Away, away!' I couldn't survive without it. Ask yourself, have you too had that experience?

But there is a certain marked coldness about the very schizoid person. From a warm, living human being's point of view, they live in a cool, Icelandic realm. It may not feel like that to them, but certainly the feeling of that coldness, that chill.... Hence their capacity to live in a completely fantastic realm. For these people, reality and fantasy have no definition. Since there has been no patterning, no experience of what is in and what is out, they dwell on a borderline between the two. Their tendency is to exalt the mind and to exalt fantasy. They may never leave its realm but hide in it, touchy and suspicious, always in danger of attack from 'out there', from outer space. From where they are, all is out there. They are often paranoid: seeing a tape recorder, for instance, a deeply schizoid person may go into 'one of their episodes'. They can think that the walls are bugged, everything is spying on them, there's an all-hearing ear, an all-seeing eye everywhere. Paranoia is very close to the schizophrenic type of reaction. I will look at the more extreme cases first and move later into the less extreme.

### The man in the dustbin

I knew one person who managed usually to hold that schizoid split remarkably well. A very inventive man, eccentric to a degree, he was an exceedingly fine musician. Typically, he lived at night, playing very fine jazz piano in Soho clubs, and in the daytime he lived his other life as a teacher of classical music. Teaching all day and playing all night, he managed to hold the split together through his music, which was for him as near an enormous love as he could feel.

He hadn't quite gone over the edge – hadn't split totally – when, trying to replace his own mother, he met a woman who it appeared might help him. Old enough to be his mother, she moved in with him. She was an absolute cow, and he was just open enough to relationship to stay with her. From an outside point of view it was terrifying to see what she could do. Through this man, she punished just about every other man she'd met. They were together for about a week, and when she had finished with him he fell over the edge and into the split that was waiting for him. I had a telephone call from Victoria Station one night. Could I please come? Gerald was in a dustbin at the end of the platform.

They called me because I was one of the only names in a notebook he had with him, with my telephone number and a note: 'Barbara, help!' So they called me. I arrived at about one o'clock in the morning. I remember the terrified station master standing at the barrier in a peaked cap with gold stuff round it, and a very, very frightened policeman who must have been all of eighteen. As soon as they saw me coming, they pulled me through the barrier and rushed me down the platform to this large dustbin. I knocked on the lid and it opened up and these terrified, panic-stricken eyes looked out at me. I was the only one Gerald allowed near him, since he knew and, as far as he was able, trusted me. He held the lid up and I talked with him for about an hour and a half through the gap. He was speaking of 'the Martians out there'. The little touch he had begun to make with the outside world had been so invaded that he'd just gone off into space (in imaging, you get a lot of this invasion from outer space). It took a long time to coax him out.

It struck me as a wonderful image: this lovely, lovely person in the dustbin, isolated, acting out exactly the true schizoid split. Fortunately, it was 'an episode'. He was helped by others with more skill than I and, in his case, drugs were used to bring him out. He might have been thinking of throwing himself under a train but he had seen the dustbin, got in, sat in it and pulled the lid down on top of him. 'I was attacked from out there. I didn't know what to do. The only safe place was in here, in my fantasy world, sitting in the dustbin, pulling the lid on me.' It had flipped him over but he was able to come back at least roughly to where he had been before it started. That is another difference from the deeply schizophrenic place (see below): the ability to flip over the barrier and perhaps come back again.

These people nearly always fear attack from outer space. Even if the voices come from inside, they are ringing with a quality of space: the voice from on high. Most people can go to films about triffids and aliens and invaders from far away in the universe. They are great fun if we have a grip on outer reality. We sit in the cinema and have this wonderful frisson of fear, and then we get up and walk out into the street and come to a world that is outside. And most of us can do that, or turn off the box, and have our relationships with each other. But just imagine people in that space all the time, with no way out. What would it be like to go out of the cinema and find the same world outside us as inside? It gives us some idea of the inscapes of the schizoid.

## Clinical schizophrenia

Where the whole being is split off, it becomes extreme clinical schizophrenia, obviously not the work of a counsellor. It is a dedicated calling. None of us, neither psychiatrists nor therapists nor anyone else at the moment, *know*; we put it together as best we can.[35] And it is privileged work. In someone seriously damaged in this way, where there is no expectation of any reality in a relationship, there is rarely any hope or belief that therapy will be any use. And maybe they are right. That's why they anyway don't turn up in our therapy rooms, and only if we are working in an institution or organisation are we liable to come across such a person, or if we find ourselves married to or working or living with one. Generally, they just won't be there.

We recall Jung, whose every case was a new proposition 'about which I do not even know the ABC'.[36] So, right at the beginning of his work, in talking about psychiatric activities at the Berghölzli Hospital, he was pointing out the danger of labelling people from a place of ignorance of their story. His approach was to discover the meaningful reality behind the so-called 'fantasy' world of *dementia praecox*, looking at the symptom as symbol, listening to the language.

## The shoemaker's fiancée

He had started his career by watching an elderly lady. Year in, year out, all the time, she made the same movements. Jung sat day after day, night after night, watching her, feeling there was a meaning in that movement, yet not being able to understand it. She couldn't speak and took only fluid nourishment, eating with her fingers and letting the fluid drip into her mouth. It sometimes took her almost two hours to consume a cup of milk. When not eating she was going through strange motions, making curious rhythmic movements with hands and arms. What was she was acting out? Concerned over what this meant, he had found no clue, only that she'd been there for many decades, though no one remembered how or why she had come in.

But because he thought there was a meaning in it, he looked up her very old case-notes. People had just presumed she was barmy; that was it. At clinical lectures, she was presented as 'schizophrenic'. 'That meant nothing to me, for these words did not contribute in the slightest to an understanding of the significance and origin of those curious gestures.' He pondered and watched. 'One evening, I saw her making her mysterious movements.... Why must this be?' Fascinated by the idea of symptom as symbol, Jung asked the old head nurse whether the

---

[35] See Note 23, about the subsequent development of successful treatments.
[36] See Note 1.

patient had always been that way. 'Yes, but my predecessor told me she used to make shoes.'

Then she died, and Jung asked her brother who turned up at the funeral what had happened. He learned that she had been in love with a shoemaker who had rejected her, and she had gone mad. She had been admitted after the loss of this fiancé. Jung then saw it: the old-fashioned shoemaker working at the last – putting nails in his mouth, hammering them in, taking them from his mouth – and she, going through the movements just as the cobbler did. Through the years, nobody had recognised the movement as the village cobbler's. She had been telling people all along what it was and nobody had taken any notice. But the shoemaker movements showed an identification with her sweetheart lasting all those many years.

'Henceforth,' said Jung, 'I devoted all my attention to the meaningful connections in a psychosis and came to understand the language of what had hitherto been regarded as meaningless.' Others would have called such a patient a very unattractive old lady, asking how he could bear to work with such people. He couldn't take that in. It was not what he had seen. It was the attempt to enter therapeutically into the story of the patient that led him into his work from then on. (This is in 'Memories, Dreams, Reflections' and is well worth reading.[37])

### Control

Again, the majority of us have experienced love to some degree, though we may have had pain and trauma along the way. But, not having experienced love, very schizoid people may substitute *power*, which is the energy they are accustomed to. And as they have been done to, so they do to others. Because they have been *used*, turned into an object, because others have had power over them, they've got to win. It is in order to survive. Ronald Laing, in his book 'The Divided Self', mentions a patient arguing with other people in a therapeutic group. 'I can't go on!' said the man. 'At best you win an argument, at worst you lose an argument. *I am arguing in order to preserve my existence!*'[38] Win, or be annihilated.

Or control can involve an almost total withdrawal from outer reality. The person retreats into isolation so as not to be affected by other people; they go into a world of fantasy where they can play the superior role,

---

37  Jung, *Memories, Dreams, Reflections*, Chapter IV, 'Psychiatric Activities', pp. 145-147.

38  Laing, *The Divided Self*, p. 43.

be in total command. It can be a sort of omnipotence. The splitting that can occur may lead to sexual fantasies, often very strong and largely tending to the sado-masochistic, with the person as the powerful component. It is domination in order not to have to submit. They split people up into parts. This is where fetishes can quite often come in, say for genitals, or a single eye, or one ear or whatever.[39] It's almost as though they are broken up into sub-personality people,[40] and with the multiple splitting that some disturbed people go into, the parts do not meet each other.

### Jekyll and Hyde

Some people do a simple two-way split. One part functions in the external world, but another part has 'gone away' and is actually maintaining their 'real' world. They have a sense of walking around as a cover-up. Robert Louis Stevenson's classic story is a marvellous example of this splitting. One side is quite unrelated to the other. There is the conformist, 'good works' Doctor Jekyll, and the Mr. Hyde who, to begin with, was only mischievous – getting drunk, misbehaving, putting a brick through a window. Hyde was revealing a much more baleful side of his nature *because* the Jekyll side was splitting away, saying, 'This is not me, it is nothing to do with me, I distance myself from it.' Though they may tend to go the same way, people with a schizoid personality are not quite the same. The schizoid split is a very real place, but do not presume immediately that this is a 'schizophrenic' person.

### Severe trauma

Trauma can come early, but it can also come later. There are a number of things one has to watch out for: perhaps an accident occurred when they were adult; perhaps something dreadful happened for them and traumatised their life; perhaps they were involved in war, taken hostage, shocked, imprisoned. And they have dealt with it by developing this kind of personality; more likely if it was an already natural tendency, and more likely still if it was also accentuated in childhood. So painful traumas can cause a partial split-off in the schizoid personality. Over the years, I have known two prisoners of war who were forced by their experience to split off and then, to some

---

[39] Fetishes, see below, pp. 188-89.

[40] See the Sub-personality Exercise, Gordon-Brown and Somers, *The Raincloud of Knowable Things*, Workshop I, pp. 20-31.

degree, stayed that way. They were not really schizoid-tending people but conditions in the camps had been intolerable and that was their survival factor.

I particularly acknowledge Viktor Frankl here. Working from his own experience, his idea for Logo Therapy grew out of Auschwitz and Ravensbrück and Dachau.[41] The spirit of what he said is that those whose values were extroverted, whose valuation was in the outside world, tended to crumple more than those whose valuation was in the inside world. If they couldn't survive outwardly and yet did live on, one of their major modes of survival would have been to go within. Though this would have forced some into a schizoid split, others would have been lucky enough already to have a touchstone, an inner richness from which to draw. This is why I think it so important that we, with our clients and with ourselves, work on building an inner space. We never know when the bottom will fall out of our external world, and we need always to keep in contact with that inner touchstone.

So people probably only go the way of the schizoid split if some earlier history has predisposed them in that direction. Lots of schizoid people have very well-adapted lives, where they split off and the two sides live side by side in totally separate compartments. If someone has the rich privilege and problem of being the partner of a person like that, they will have the fairly fortunate insight, short of having to go into a profound split themselves, into what it's like to be living in those two compartments.

### Fear of relationship

As we have seen, the schizoid personality has a passionate original need to relate. Yet 'I don't need relationship' is their first major safeguard. 'Relationship is sentiment, relationship is an animal instinct. I am above this, beyond this, this is not me. I can manage very well, thank you.' There is a whole range between this schizoid-type personality and the true schizoid split. This person is not necessarily split up into multiple parts; they may just be being themselves but they are on the other side of the split. If they do go into relationship, they remain emotionally uninvolved, retreating from anything remotely emotional, vanishing off the scene in a crisis. I remember a client saying of her husband, 'He made babies as if from another planet' – and they had six of them.

---

[41]    Frankl, *Man's Search for Meaning*. And see Frankl, *Man's Search for Ultimate Meaning*.

Secondly, there may be a fear that 'any relationship risked won't last, so don't get involved'. That need have nothing whatever to do with early bonding. It may be that what has happened around a person has pushed them into not daring to risk involvement just *because* it will inevitably end. For some, that has happened with a whole series of relationships. They may have known a whole lot of people who have gone away, or died. One client came in and said, 'I've had three therapists die on me.' And then I couldn't be ill, or have a cold, or not get to the door at the speed of light, without her immediately thinking, 'That's another one. I've put the evil eye on her!'

Thirdly, the person may be in a schizoid split out of a fear of being dominated or engulfed by the other. Because they once *were* dominated and engulfed by others. Or they may fear losing their hard-won, isolated identity. They have such a poor hold on it that they are not going to risk its loss and can often retain autonomy only by withdrawal. Isaac Newton probably came into that category. Abandoned by his mother at three, he never made close relationships with men or with women. He was extremely suspicious of his colleagues, was reluctant to publish his findings and accused others of stealing his discoveries.

And fourthly, they very often fear they will destroy or harm the person to whom they become attached. This usually results from the early loss of a parent, perhaps followed by later losses. Or there can be the sense of having drained or emptied a parent so that no love was left for them. They may well have been told, 'You were a very difficult child'. Or perhaps the mother went into hospital when they were young, and then, if she is later angry with them, they feel they drained her life-force away, even killed her, and they go through such guilt that they won't risk any involvement or relationship.

### Life in compartments

I knew someone, highly creative and talented, who had this kind of split. One of the manifestations was that he could be talking in the morning with his family, then the moment they'd gone out, he would lock the door and go into his inner fantasy world. Once his wife forgot her handbag. Going back for it, keyless, she had practically to beat the door down to get him to open it. He had two clear-cut compartments. 'They've gone.' He'd cut them out and was into another, a fantasy world.

That was a mildish form of it, but quite usual. Outwardly he led a very well-adapted life. Such people are liable to follow isolated, sometimes intellectual pursuits. It may be as well not to look too closely at those who are drawn into scientific research, philosophical work, pure academia – the 'back-room boffin'. And yet they are highly creative there. They make an adjustment of the psyche which allows them to be in relation to life in a creative way, while yet staying within their split-off positions. They will often have an air of superiority, the ivory tower, the keeping at a distance. They appear to be indifferent, giving the impression of being untouched by lesser mortals. You may have to scratch them a bit before you get to that. If you see it with a client, watch it. They perceive relationships as being about superiority and inferiority. They just don't know about equality.

It is when they are *forced* to be spontaneous that their avoidance of spontaneity shows. This is because they *can't* respond, not because they don't want to, or don't choose to, or are frightened of doing so. It is simply that they are unable to. We get the sense that they are weighing everything and apportioning words, replies, reactions – putting it through a filter with a gauge on it.

The slightly hysteric-tending personality may well make a relationship with the opposite kind, someone slightly schizoid, very quiet and indrawn, who does not easily express their feelings. One person said, 'I've experienced a *switch*, both in people I work with and in myself. If I am in an untouchable, schizoid space, I can bet that the person I'm with will go into an hysterical state and come after me all the time. But when a crisis happens, *I* go into the hysterical state, and then the other person will turn around and withdraw into the schizoid space.… ' She went on, 'If I am trapped and tired and over-stressed, I will come off my centre and run around like a scalded pigeon.' This is a marvellous example of space and boundaries: the middle ground and the boundaries are under attack. The hope is that we can at least to a degree choose which we go into, hysteric or schizoid.

### The value of the schizoid-tending personality

Many of us are caught, trapped into this schizoid place by the stresses of life. We use a phenomenal amount of energy just to hold the external world at bay. Hence that movement away to refresh and go deep into our own imaginal, quiet world. And then we come out again. That is one thing (though, as we have seen, to go there and stay there as an almost permanent way of life is quite another).

The person with the schizoid tendency does seem to have an extraordinary gift for turning up in odd places. You may not have seen them for four or five months and then ... you are standing next to them in the tube. A week later, you'll be on a train and there they are in the buffet. Whatever magical process this may be – and the word 'synchronicity' still doesn't explain this coming-together at one moment in time – they seem to be part of that internal landscape. They dwell there, wherever the law of synchronicity dwells.

They also know what you dream before you dream it. They have skills for counselling that leave most counsellors gasping. They simply cannot contain what they know. Or they objectify it into the external world. Because they are an object in the subjective world, they feel they have total control of it, and sometimes you believe them. That's why, very wisely, there is a high turnover among people working with those seriously disturbed in this way. After two or three years, you may really be questioning who is sane and who is not.

### The lady who danced around the tree

I do not deal with people in psychosis; it is out of my area and it is not my brief. Other people are better at it than I could ever be. However, I have over the years come across the true clinical level of this schizoid state, and we do sometimes hear some very surprising things. The mind boggles, but the imagination plays with these things. There was a little Welsh lady in a green emerald felt hat, and her little skirt pulled down over her knees, sitting with her ankles crossed, talking to me for at least three-quarters of our hour together about all sorts of things. She had been to a place in the country where there is a tree which has people dancing round it in the moonlight. 'This is a marvellous tree,' they say, and start dancing round it – literally lunatic. If ever there were an unpeaceful tree, it must be that poor tree up there. 'Sitting by that tree, I had an experience of Pan,' she said. I took that in my stride. 'Oh, tell me about it?' She did. 'You see, I *am* Pan,' she explained. This lady in her green hat! I was able, because I was standing at the interface, to listen to her. All through her time there, in the small hours of the morning which she said was her reality, she'd got up to some extraordinary things – as Pan.

Well, they may have been true, I don't know. That was one of those cases where you open things up, have a quick look, close them again and sew them up tight. I could see the degree to which her imaging, which might well have originated around the age of ten and the approach to adolescence, had simply transferred itself over. She was following spiritual gurus and that whole energy just built up for her at night. A sad little woman she was, because she couldn't relate to people. I suppose you couldn't relate to people if you thought you were Pan, because Pan, being very close to panic, causes panic in others.

## Working with the deeply schizoid person

It is because the schizoid person has never had a continuum or a connection with anyone (or has had so little of it that the dialogue of relationship has become two objects speaking to each other in alien space) that the most delicate, most loving, creative, artistic work in therapy often lies along the line with them. The extreme schizoid goes into delusional voices, is inundated from the unconscious. A lot of them, as we saw, are fighting for their lives. Voices speak to them and may befriend them, and the voices have to be honoured.

Referring again to Figure 2, the Inner, the Outer and the Interface, we see that there is nothing to stop most less schizoid people from moving back and forth through the overlapping interface between these two separate realities. However, because schizoid people have very often had no one, nothing, to help them define the difference between inner and outer, they hold them far apart. For them, there is almost no overlap, no interface. They have gone right over and far away into the inner, an 'inner' of their own making. They live in their own 'no-place' within. If you work with them, which I have done a good deal, it is very important to treat their no-place as something you can work with. The more we can take a posture with our client *between* their inner and their outer reality, the more we can stand at that interface, the more we can begin to listen to their quite extraordinary language. We are listening to the interplay of the symptom, whatever it may be, and the symbol which lies behind that symptom. Though they are usually highly articulate in their own way, they rarely talk about it; they have to have a great deal of trust to do so. We accept their language, we listen to its poetry, the way it speaks. It is the most incredible, wonderful dialogue.

## Counselling the schizoid personality

As we have seen, working with someone in the *schizophrenic* position is certainly not the job of a counsellor. They would rarely come to us as a therapist anyway. Since they do not expect help, they don't normally come seeking it. But they are nearly always put into care by others, simply for their behaviour, and often have counselling thrust at them.

However, a schizoid *personality* may well come into our therapy room. If they do, we have to know how far to push their relating to anything, without it becoming a threat. They are interesting. I find them delightful and fascinating. I get in the split with them and try to imagine it from within. They can use language in the most incredibly descriptive way. They write about life, observe it. It is the profundity of abstract thought. As Descartes wrote, 'I think, therefore I am' – a very schizoid statement, but also an extraordinary formulation towards a viewpoint. They have got to cope, to defend themselves, or they will be wiped out. That is a very real statement of what it is like to be in that schizoid split. It is a matter of existence, of 'beingness', at a level and of an order totally other. Here are some key points in working with them:

> Firstly, have great respect for their inner landscapes and their personal boundaries. See their view, their reality, as being valid, however wild it may appear. I believe a great number of our truly pioneer, 'map-making' people are labelled 'schizophrenic' and are in hospitals for just this speaking of a different language, this hearing of a distant, different drum. One always has to have a tremendous respect.

> Secondly, it is enormously vital to provide a continuum. Do not, under any circumstances, violate their space, and assure them that they do not violate yours. Somehow, give them the sense that you are still there for them as a hand-hold in the outer world. And so, incredibly, in an atmosphere of increasing trust, they may begin to unfold the richness of their inner life.

*Thirdly, I need to trust myself as counsellor. And trust the client.*
*They are probably not going to trust; but at least, over a period,*
*they can act as if they trusted.*

We are dealing with the artist here. I am constantly amazed by the
enormous artistry with which people go along a particular line to
accommodate, to adapt to life. I often use painting, sculpting, poetry
when I am working with people in this schizoid split and very often
they have a consummate ability to express themselves creatively.

Avoid deliberately evoking imagery. People come in seeking the
nature of their identity and of their journey. Since behind appearances
in the outer world lie all the levels available to an individual, the deeper
we penetrate the more we move from the objective outer into the
subjective inner world. This is why, when dealing with the truly
schizoid person, it is simply not appropriate that we help to evoke
imagery. These people are full of images already. Perhaps they are
more closely in touch with the inner because they are so cut off from
the outer. In any case, it is much more important that we take the
imagery that they have already and help modify it, anchor it back.

### The falcon

I often compare working with a schizoid kind of person with
falconry. They fly and come back to the wrist, which is the interface.
They fly very easily into the fantasy world, with which they are
altogether *au fait*, so if we encourage them to fantasise we'll just send
them further and further out. The job is to try to bring that fantasy back
and anchor it. We help them see how it links them, through the
subjectivity of the personal relationship with the therapist, to the
objectivity of the external world. So, as with the falcon, we familiarise
them with the wrist, let them know there is a place to come back to, and
let them fly. We help them come back on to the interface – then fly –
then bring them back again – a continuous flying and grounding,
flying and grounding. We are being falconers. More and more we are
helping them to give form to the image.

Most schizoid people, once they do begin to hear, once they come
to live at the interface themselves, do have the most wonderful voices
going on. These are the people who teach us to fly. That is their great
gift. Among many of these deeply schizoid people we are looking at the

flying artists of the future, speaking a language, exploring an imagery, that has not yet been itself anchored.

Though, as we have seen, I try as far as possible to avoid too much imaging since they have so much already, I do try to handle what they give. It is very difficult. Their inside reality out-distances me every inch of the way. When working with this kind of person, we have to have double ears, treble ears, and an inscape and an outscape. They increase our own sensitivity because they are ten steps ahead of us the whole time. There is nothing that we know about the internal landscapes that they are not already infinitely more familiar with. However, as I said, if they image too much and we are not very careful, the falcon will go off into inner space again, and we will have a job anchoring it back. We have to get it to return to the wrist, usually by relating outwardly, by the tactile arts and by outside reality.

### The talisman

If we suggest anything to the schizoid person, well, firstly they certainly won't come back and, secondly, they will know better anyway. But if they do appear, they can sometimes relate remarkably well to the talisman, so long as it is of their own choosing.[42] Giving them this anchoring principle for their very rich fantasy life will help. The talisman is nearly always a wonderful delineation of their own omnipotence and their own sense of the void. Make quite sure that you are working with where the power lies; then their talisman can become their greatest help – and yours, too. A colleague told me of somebody split by incredible damage: 'We can go into the abyss; but how far do we go *up*?' she asked. 'He was dragging me up after him. After some time he was able to respect that I was there *with* him, and we agreed I wasn't the object. Then we began to work with the talisman. He chose a boat with which to come down, bridge the gulf, sail some of the gaps. And he externalised this by getting a small, real, sailing boat.' Just as you can sometimes feel, 'Move over, there's another one on the way up', so the gods must be pleased that here's another human being on the way down.

So we generally bring down the stream of their energies, not by helping them to image even more but by listening and getting them to express the inner world in a tactile way, with things. They are liable to respond to music, to non-verbal arts, to gardening, perhaps to working

---

42   The *talisman*, imaged as an inner mediator of wisdom and compassion. The understanding and knowledge of the non-judgmental talisman exceed those of the ego. Once it is invoked, acceptance is given to any image from the unconscious. The talisman stands in for the Self and can at any point be turned to for advice and support. See Gordon-Brown and Somers, *The Raincloud of Knowable Things*, Chapter 6, pp. 198-199.

with animals, if they can be coaxed out to do it. However, as we know, they can get deeply frightened and threatened if anyone tries to force a relationship on them. Tell them that they ought to relate and they are absolutely terrified. *People* create huge demands for them. I suppose it's like parleying with monsters. They may move completely into a fantasy realm, holing-up from any attempts to draw them out, 'out there'. One psychiatric social worker said to me:

> *I frequently see the orthodox approach towards those in schizoid splits, which is continuously to try to get them to relate, perhaps to animals, more likely to people. This, to me, feels awfully wrong; it's making too much of a demand. If they feel like being apart, surely they should be apart? But that is not happening; there's this endless insistence on their joining the club, the discussion. So obviously they put up barriers.*

Generally speaking, they do much better with *things*. They can very often relate to some job, such as making sure that the garden shed is tidy. They often like working on the land, maybe with animals, or with objects at the tactile level, which can give them a greater sense of being a subject. Even so, working with living things, even animals, can make them feel like an object again. It is mobilising the energy which has caused them to split inner and outer. We are using that energy, that degree of creativity, that clear delineation between inner and outer, using the very strength with which they are holding that split apart. Using what they have, helping to explore their inner imaging and giving it an outer form, so we help them bring inner and outer together in a new way.

This is why some of these people do respond to crafts. In therapeutic processes within hospitals, the use of tactile materials – clay, finger-paints – has of course been enlisted, encouraging the idea that it's all right to dabble with paint and giving the person a tactile anchorage. However, the majority of them do not like that kind of thing: dirty, messy, it reminds them of their body. And as we have seen, body and instinct and feeling are but appendages, animal, not acknowledged, 'Not mine, nothing to do with me'.

## *'Resistance'*

This is one of those cover-words which is highly variable with the individual. A student described 'resistance to getting better' in a client who had said, 'I'm afraid of going up, I don't want to go up'. The student questioned whether this might have to do with 'the fact that they are going to have to lose their omnipotence.' But there is a moment at which the psyche of the client knows when they have climbed far enough. They will begin to resist, and one needn't necessarily presume that the psyche, in this area, is not wiser than we are. They know it is not the right moment for it. I would say, *never know first and never know better*.[43]

So I always listen closely when someone 'resists', to hear what type of resistance it is. We can ask, 'Does that seem to you the right thing to do? Or would you prefer not to reply to that question?' This gives them the responsibility. It helps them to see the difference between themselves deciding whether they speak and relate or not, or go into the omnipotence which is really a withdrawal from relating.

## *The counselling contract*

With a new client, I listen to the level they are coming from and do an initial mapping. We make a contract together, setting up an initially limited number of sessions rather than leaving it open-ended. We arrange times and costs. Whether inexperienced or quite well-practised, we may well encounter somebody whose deeps turn out to be a bit deeper than we can handle. This contract is a safeguard in both directions. It gives us the opportunity to see whether someone who may have an hysteric or depressive, or schizoid tendency really needs more help than we can offer.

How might we tell if a seriously schizoid-tending person walked in for the first time tomorrow? Student counsellors sometimes worry about this a lot, asking, as I have myself, 'How will I recognise someone who's beyond me, if they come?' Well, it is a very common sense, human thing. We forget that we are ordinary human beings; our bodies are excellent Geiger counters. When we are sitting in the park reading the paper and someone comes and sits on the other end of the bench, we sometimes – not always – feel like getting up and walking away. An energy field emerges and we pick it up.

---

[43] 'Long experience has taught me not to know anything in advance and not to know better, but to let the unconscious take precedence'. Attributed to Jung and said to be in *Archetypes of the Collective Unconscious*, CW Vol. 9 i. The reference proves elusive. Ed.

Exactly the same thing exists here. Keep your sensing equipment attuned. Don't presume you are going to hit trouble. However, if you have any doubts at all about this person, keep the sessions going and penetrate a bit further, but do not go out of your depth, because it doesn't help them. This is why it is extremely important to know your limitations as well as your extensions.

And I try to know as much as I can about the back-up in my environment. It is important not to feel as though we are letting ourselves down by referring someone on, otherwise we too are in danger of playing God. With the safeguarding of the contracted sessions, we can be free. People respect that if I've made it clear to start with. It is quite valid to say, 'I feel the intensity of your experience, what you've had to go through. However, you bring something that perhaps I'm not the right person to understand as well as I should, and my suggestion is that you could speak to someone else.' People accept that. It both respects the individual and gives them an opportunity. Also, by saying, 'I genuinely feel that this is not my brief – I am not as well-equipped here as quite a lot of other people', we are taking the onus onto ourselves. It is better to say it in the beginning than to get deeper and deeper into the water and end up with a rejection from the person, or becoming frightened of them, which is no gift to them.

## *Which am I – hysteric, depressive or schizoid?*

Or all three? I know we have all got the lot. I hope we have anyhow, or we are missing a perspective. I would invite the reader now: go into yourself, confront yourself and sense which of these three positions you are most likely to go into under stress. Ask yourself, would you happily recognise your own tendencies to each? It is very important to accept them all within ourselves. Note how the outer character can very often indicate the inner. Also, decide that, if you know about it and can keep it up in consciousness, you can probably handle it. Then, make friends with that position.

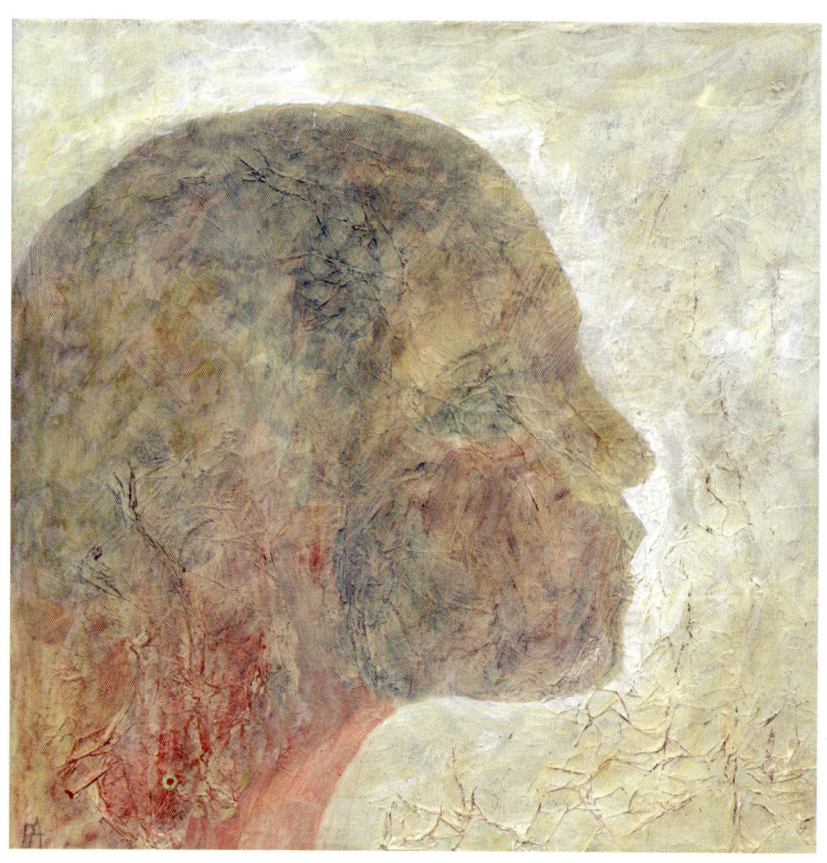

Emergence

# CHAPTER SEVEN

# The Obsessive/Compulsive Personality

## Barbara Somers

*If they can be regarded as having a speaking symptom, a symbol,*
*then areas of creativity that they wouldn't have*
*believed possible may be opened up*

S
o, as we look towards the *obsessive* or *compulsive* person, and the way the *phobic* personality can grow out of this, I remind the reader of what I have said throughout: although these words – schizoid, compulsive, obsessive and so on – are clinically used, they are not definitions of people. They are *labels*, descriptions of personality types. And the degree to which they are treated as definitions, the degree to which people have these labels stuck onto them, is the degree to which a lot of work in this field is non-therapeutic. The more we recognise that this is a *person* with a personality trend, and that the symptoms are speaking very loud and clear about the solution as well as about the problem, the more we are opening up the therapeutic possibilities of these words.

I will start, as I have before, by referring to the 'Harvard Guide to Modern Psychiatry' for a definition of 'the Obsessive/Compulsive':

*The patient experiences persistent thought-patterns which he tries to prevent* [that's the obsessive half of it] *and repetitive tendencies to behave in a way which he does not wish to* [that's the compulsive side].

I would add that the obsessive half of the definition is the internal side, and the compulsive half is the external. I think we are looking at the tension between the inner and the outer worlds.

### The child

Figure 6 shows the child contained originally within the mother. There aren't many maps around on this. This one, derived from Edward Edinger, is based on experience and is very speculative.[44] It is meant to evoke these things out of our own experience. It has an enormous value in encouraging us to ask, 'What is my role and function now, within this therapeutic process?' With this Emergence map behind us, we are

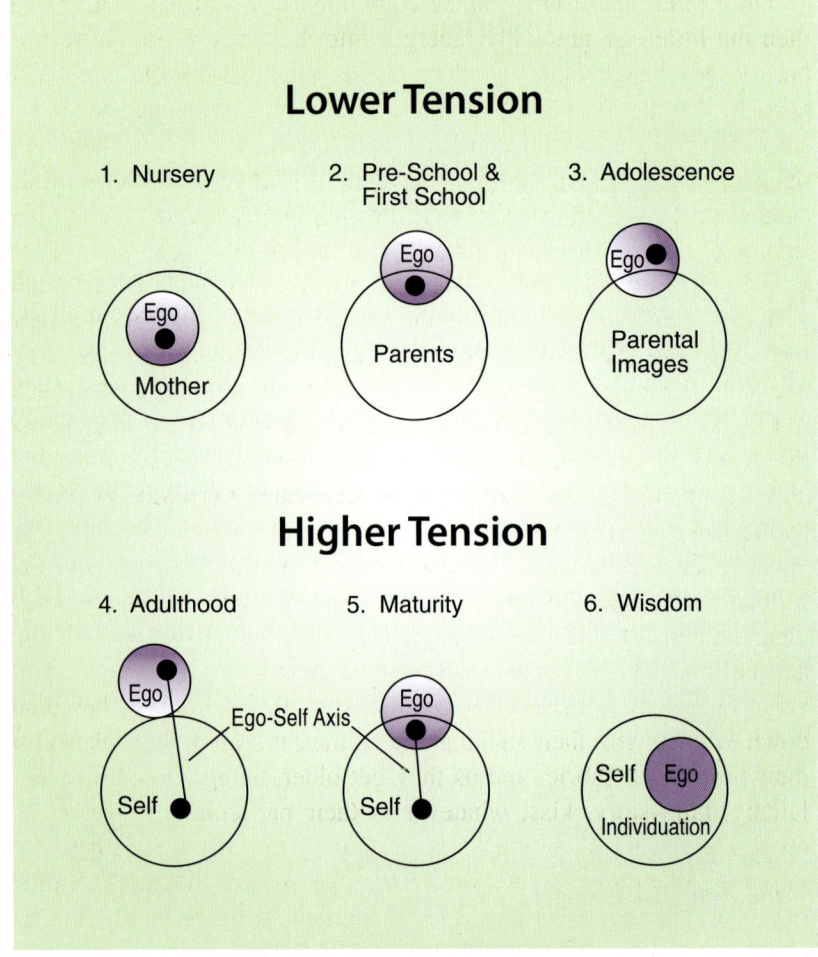

Figure 6. Stages of Emergence

---

[44]  See Somers and Gordon-Brown, *Journey in Depth*, Figure 3 'Stages of Emergence'. Also, see Edinger, *Ego and Archetype*, p. 5. Edinger gave only the first four of these diagrams and did not refer to Mother, Parents or Parental Images.

reminded, in our hearts if not on our note-pads, of where we are at any given moment in the therapeutic process. I have added the words 'lower tension' and 'higher tension' to the original map and put the lower as a tension in the instinctual root-life, the 'negative' side. This can push somebody over into being obsessive or compulsive in their behaviour. The higher is a creative tension. We look at what can grow out of that kind of tension and out of the experience of the individual on the interface.

Until three, there is complete containment within the mother, and then the little ego gradually emerges into the outer world. In fact, at both stages 1 and 6 the boundary of the ego is permeable, since it is absorbed in the surrounding matrix. Turn this map around and it suggests the Interface map of Figure 2 (page 9) again, with the father or father figure leading across the bridge from inner to outer, from the subjective to the objective world, from the over-emphasis on the feminine towards the world of the masculine. Note how, in the first five years, development is a movement from that symbiotic relationship with the mother's psyche. The child makes little forays across the inter-face. The interface is like a bridge and it is father who holds the bridge and leads the way across it. Thus the child is moved from the total hold of the subjective and begins to build a sense of an outer world. Note too the degree to which good bonding and 'good-enough' parents help the child to stand at the point of interface, to explore both inner and outer and to feel that they are not in a place of threat.

Let's have a look at the development of the 'normal', natural, fortunate child with the good-enough parents. A continuum is absolutely vital to them. At a very early stage, they set up rituals of continuation and need which, if met, can ensure their peace. We find it even with very young babies: the need for regular feeding and holding, being put down to sleep with their sucking object, their thumb or their blanket or their little bit of fabric, and as they get older, being tucked in with a lullaby, fairy-story, kiss, whatever is their particular routine. If it's missed, we hear, 'You didn't kiss me', or 'I want my story'. It is very important that things are not only repetitive but that they are repetitive in the same order. 'You didn't say the bit about the wolf.... ' For the child, this is absolutely essential. It is part of their sense of identity, of having a continuum in life.

Around the age of two or three, children markedly show the ritual nature of play. Again, the order in which things are done, the repetitive words they use, the pecking order, playmates, the repetition of actions – these things matter. And so they begin to set up rituals which allow them eventually to emerge and explore the unknown. Toys play a huge role as part- and transitional objects. They belong to the internalised, subjective, fantasy life of the child, but can also be taken out and carried into the external world, helping to make a bridge across the interface between the inner and the outer, the subjective and the objective worlds.[45]

And then, at around five or six, dreams come to them from the subjective world. As the child has more and more to deal with the tension of both inner and outer experience, nightmares emerge: 'Mummy, there's a crocodile under the bed!' 'There's a man in the wardrobe on the stairs, Daddy, will you come with me past that?' Calling out at night, wanting a night-light, having that sense that someone is around who can come in and help hold outer and inner together for them. 'Please, I want a cup of water' very often has to do with. 'Are you still there? You haven't gone away, have you?' The child is beginning to safeguard itself, consciously having to experiment to find whether inner and outer are still there. That is typical behaviour for a child and very appropriate.

It is not so appropriate when you get adults using the same kind of safeguarding. This is what we see when we look at obsessional or compulsive behaviour.

## We are all obsessive and compulsive

Any normal, healthy human being can show certain obsessive or compulsive reactions under particular stresses. On going on a journey, for instance, a lot of people have anxieties about separation, or about meeting up with the unknown. We displace this anxiety on to *things*: 'Do I really have the tickets?' We unpack the case and have a search. 'Have I turned off the gas? Did I put out the lights?' Some of us will go back and make sure. 'Did I really lock the door properly?' We all do this, as I have said in connection with all the previous examples.

But others will actually go back and have a look nine or ten times, and miss the train or plane – miss the journey. This is the difference of degree between normal anxiety ('Did I put the letter in the right envelope?') and

---

45    See Somers and Gordon-Brown, *Journey in Depth*, 'The Child in the Adult', especially pp. 38-39.

a tendency towards the obsessive or compulsive. Again, I hope I can put myself in the 'normal' category here, but I have certainly noted that if I am over-tired or over-anxious, I will walk around moving piles of paper from one place to another. It can give me quite a sense of containment. We all have these small ways of displacing our anxiety by doing something. Speakers giving talks may pick up the glass of water and put it down again without drinking. I know I do that; it is a way of centring myself. Abnormality is when such inappropriate behaviour becomes essential to a person's living. That's the difference. The truly obsessive/compulsive person feels that they absolutely have to go on using this displacement behaviour in order to survive.[46]

## Obsessive-Compulsive Disorder, OCD

However, for clinically-inclined people, both the external and the internal worlds are places of threat. They are preparing for some unspecified disaster. Their symbolic rituals help to keep that threat at bay. We see it in children too, the tendency to hit each sixth railing, or step on every third paving stone,[47] to kick a stone, to carry something around, to touch wood, to keep whistling to keep danger at bay. Typical of the obsessive/compulsive person is behaviour such as washing hands excessively, over-concern about lavatory seats, fear of contamination by doors and sofas and chairs, having to straighten pictures, tidy desks and drawers, get everything squared up in line and, if one is interrupted, go back and do it all over again. One client I knew couldn't leave home on the thirteenth until he'd seen a Number Thirteen bus through the window. It was to 'avert the evil eye'.

## Anxiety

We need to recognise that this kind of ritual action is only the symptom of the person's internal fear and insecurity. It is all about anxiety. Remember Figure 5, the two-headed beastie as mother-and-father? We saw the *hysteric* personality[48] as having the tendency, even in adult life, to stand on the interface and turn in toward the parent figure, shouting with a tremendous concentration, 'Hear me! Don't put me out there!' We saw how *depressive* personalities on the interface turn rather to the outside, yet are looking back over their shoulder: 'Don't leave me out here.' This is the child, or the adult, who feels they have been put out

---

46  See Rapoport, *The Boy Who Couldn't Stop Washing: The Experience & Treatment of Obsessive-Compulsive Disorder*, Collins, London. An excellent book on this subject.

47  See Milne, *When We Were Very Young*, 'Lines and Squares', p. 12.

48  See Footnote 4 for use of the word *hysteric*.

from that warmth, been measured, judged, found wanting, rejected in their feeling. And the *schizoid* personality has gone to another place entirely, saying 'I am safe *here*. Everything and everybody is out there.' This person has turned to an inner place all their own. Obviously this is a crude way of saying it, but shows how each of those three types is responding to their stance on the interface, looking inward or outward.

So how does the person who moves later into *obsessional* and *compulsive* behaviour deal with being put on to the interface? They may be attempting to displace the build-up of anxiety that results by this imaginative acting-out. It may be the anxiety of guilt, of loss, of abandonment, of separation. It is an active defence against being disregarded in the way that the hysteric type fears, against the despair of the depressive type, and against the splitting of the schizoid type. Some people (at a totally unconscious level, of course) go over into the obsessive and compulsive to avoid going into any of those areas. By their displacement behaviour, they get a sense of being able to master themselves and their outside world. They are trying in some way to control the environment. A lot of their obsessional acting-out is aimed at easing the internal tension of having to stand on the interface between inner and outer and be caught in the pressure of those two pulls, those two tensions, which are bearing in on them and pulling them apart. They are like the baby Heracles struggling with the snakes.[49]

In the same way, the approach of primitive peoples was aimed at averting threatening situations. Going out beyond the containment of the campfire, the huts, the kraals, the teepees, they would take a fetish, carry an amulet, a transitional object as a reminder of the God; and so they could step over from the subjective containment of the extended family into the world out there. They would invest a great deal of libido in that totem, that talismanic fetish object, to the degree that, if it was removed, quite frequently they would die.

## *Origins of the obsessive/compulsive personality*

Working with clients with a tendency towards the obsessional or compulsive and checking back with them, we find that (insofar as it stems from the environment) it seems to come from two areas. Firstly, a strict, rigid, formalised, severely structured upbringing with a lot of

---

49  Heracles was born in a normal manner, from a human woman. His immortality sprang from the Queen of the gods, Hera, whose milk he drank at birth. Hera didn't know whose child she suckled, just that its mother had abandoned this baby. But when the newborn sucked too hard, Hera threw him from her breast with a cosmic spurt of milk that created the starry Milky Way. Thus from nurturer she became enemy and later, learning his identity, sent snakes to strangle the infant Heracles and his hapless brother, Iphicles. But Heracles only chortled as he in turn strangled the snakes in his chubby baby fists. Ed.

guilt and Jehovah stuff – 'Thou shalt not', shibboleths. They have learnt that one must be good, never caught off one's guard. There is often talk of an eye looking at them: 'They are watching me. She is watching me. He is watching me'. This eye brings the sense of being always in somebody's critical regard. Frequently, too, these people have been over-protected by that strict, fearful parent. For them, 'out there' becomes a very threatening place, and so does 'in here'. It can often result in their shrinking up very tightly on that interface, unable to go either out or in for fear of 'them'.

Secondly the opposite, which has the same effect: the unpredictable, shifting, chaotic environment, giving the sense that impending chaos is always only just held at bay, that there is no order, that people will never do the same thing twice. They attempt to control their mounting internal anxiety by following repetitive, familiarising outer action. This will make a safe guideline to hold chaos at bay.

### The young woman who picked at the wallpaper

I worked with a client who had nine siblings and a highly hysterical mother. 'What's going to happen?' It was a constant worry; she never knew from one moment to the other. Meals didn't appear at the same time; moods were always changing. One moment it was all hugs and joy, the next and everything had fallen apart. Finally, when she was about eighteen, this young person took to her bed, turned her face to the wall, pulled the covers over her and began to pick at the wallpaper. When she was taken to hospital, she picked endlessly at bits of the wall. After a while, she went into an asylum and picked at the doctor's jacket. The only thing that seemed to give her any sense of order was to handle tiny little bits. She could feel that *this* was the tip of her finger, and she could handle that bit. She used this action to hold at bay the threatening chaos, the imminent disaster which was always pressing her boundaries. 'To avert the catastrophe, somehow I must impose order on this mess.'

### Sexuality and aggression

So extreme rigidity and extreme fluidity can both push the individual over into compulsive/obsessive behaviour. And very frequently, in adults, it has to do with the instinctual drives held down by that very rigid early environment; or, conversely, by the person's need to be formalised and to set up their own guidelines in order to avoid chaos. In each case, people who are compulsive or obsessive are usually unable to express either sexuality or aggression very well. These very powerful libidinous instincts are threatening. The person will go in like a lion tamer with a whip and chair to keep them at bay, to beat back the beasts, to create a reassuring ritual that will hold them. Very often, of course, they are holding at bay the richest part of their own nature. One of the works of counselling is to help them to discover what is the value of the ritual that they have set up, at its highest level as well as its most profoundly regressive. Why is it there? What is it saying to them? Very often it will release something more of their aggression and their sexuality in the process.

### Domination and submission

Again, because of their experience, the obsessional personality tends to relate in terms of superiority and inferiority. For a child to be in a conflict of love and hate is usually very healthy. With a 'good-enough' parent, the child is permitted to love and hate the same person and is not put out of parental containment for it. However, the person who is unsure of this, of what's going to happen to them, somehow has to keep the love/hate polarities of their nature under control. Therefore, in their later relationships they go over into domination-or-submission, superiority-or-inferiority. To disarm others, they themselves tend to be either authoritarian or submissive. We are conquered – or we conquer by submitting. Two animals will come up to each other baring their teeth, testing each other's strength, but if the situation can't be handled they will go over into the surrender posture, grinning up at the victor. However, by doing just that they have become in fact the conqueror of the situation.

### Relationship and feeling

This kind of personality has no expectation of equal or reciprocal relationships. They are always caught in the tension of the opposites, trying to keep instincts and emotions at bay as unacceptable, threatening, guilt-causing. For fear of letting go, of being caught unaware, of something coming in while their back is turned, they very often go over into strong intellectualism. They tend to use words compulsively, obsessively, to distance rather than to express, repeating phrases in a very pernickety, exact form of speech. These are people trying to hold a lot of feeling at bay.

## Perfectionism

And, dangerous in the neo-Transpersonal area, are the image of and the impulse to perfection. The need for perfection is the need to support some insecurity. Therefore perfection becomes a destructive ritual. One client, who at his woodwork class had made 'the perfect table', spending whole days at it, said, 'And I heard my bastard manager say, "Well, that's not good enough, is it?"'

## The value of the obsessive- or compulsive-tending personality

They tend to live in the future. Much of their present energy is channelled ahead, taking precautions now against some unspecified event to come. They may be isolated, cut off in relationships, stereo-typed, un-spontaneous, miserly – the tight grip. As we saw, the virtues of it are in areas where meticulous exactness, order and predictability are required, where experiments need to be repeated over and over and recorded very clearly. Businesses, offices in accountancy and research benefit enormously from people like this. In counselling it is very helpful to point out the values and virtues of this mode of life, standing at the interface with our client and exploring why they have felt the need to barricade themselves off, to set up these parameters and containments for themselves. What it is they are holding at bay inwardly and outwardly? And we are there with them.

## Getting alongside

I once spent a long time with somebody like this. I had been talking across to him, feeling I had to shout across the space. He was shouting back. I stopped, got up, walked round and sat down beside him. 'Look, it's two of us in here.' I listened alongside him to what he was saying, and after a little while he put his hand out to me, held on very tight, broke down and cried. A lot of material came out simply because I remembered what I was doing. I'd been the 'outer', shouting to his 'inner'. He'd been on the interface, frightened of what I was going to raise out of him, that he was afraid of saying to me, unable to hear what I was shouting at him. But the moment I went into the interface with him, he felt that he had a little more strength to look at these monsters. By degrees, having faced it, we brought it down to size and looked for the values in his way of containing things. Thus we could go from a rigid to a more flexible kind of containment.

## Dr. Johnson

Although this is a fairly flat-footed example, yet even as he was manifesting the 'lower tension', Dr. Samuel Johnson was creating his dictionary. Here is Boswell writing about him:

> *The doctor had another particularity, of which none of his friends ever ventured to ask an explanation. It appeared to me some superstitious habit, which he had contracted early, and from which he had never called upon his reason to disentangle him. This was his anxious care to go out or in at a door or passage by a certain number of steps from a certain point, or at least so as that either his right or his left foot (I am not certain which) should constantly make the first actual movement when he came close to the door or passage. Thus I conjecture; for I have, upon innumerable occasions, observed him suddenly stop, and then seem to count his steps with a deep earnestness, and when he had neglected or gone wrong in this sort of magical movement, I have seen him go back again, put himself in a proper posture to begin the ceremony, and, having gone through it, break from his abstraction, walk briskly on, and join his companion.*[50]

Boswell's keenly observed, pre-psychological language defines very well the meticulous accuracy that Johnson showed here. It is fascinating to consider that he was also working on the dictionary, which required the same degree of meticulous accuracy. We often get very detailed behaviour being turned to analysis and dissection and exploration, breaking things up into small pieces and putting them together as a mosaic.

---

[50]  Boswell, *Selections from the Works of Samuel Johnson*, ed. C. G. Osgood.

Johnson's is an excellent example of the way this behaviour can come out as a distinct symptom which nowadays might be seen as 'tending towards the clinical'. And yet we always have to bear in mind that these symptoms have a positive as well as a negative aspect in the life of the individual. Nowadays, too, could not the creative tension being held by some people be transformed into a different external-isation? A great number of those who have this ability for accuracy in detail might well be able to transform their tendency towards the obsessive or the compulsive and transmute it into research, analysis, anything that requires that meticulous approach. If a lot of people labelled as obsessive and compulsive can be regarded as having a speaking symptom, a symbol, then areas of creativity that they would not have believed possible may be opened up.

### *Obsession and the transcendent function*

I think imaging can be exceedingly helpful in all this. Very often, after a little while, we can replace the fetish, the object, the compulsion, with a talisman, and begin to look towards other values. Maybe ritual, which at its negative end is displacement activity, is at its positive end transmutation, a transformative element which takes energies up and gives us the transcendent function.[51] Can something be both obsession and transcendent function? I think it very frequently can; indeed, they may go hand in hand.

---

[51] See Chapter 12 below, which draws on Somers and Gordon-Brown, *Journey in Depth*, Chapter 10, 'Polarities and the Transcendent Function', specially pp. 175-176. The transcendent function is the transforming symbol which unites the pairs of psychic opposites in a synthesis which transcends them both; it includes the personal but also transcends it.

Journey into Spirit

# CHAPTER EIGHT

# The Phobic Personality

### Barbara Somers and Ian Gordon-Brown

*The need is to get to the root of the fear rather than
to the nature of the symptom*

The question of the 'phobic' personality grows out of the obsessive and compulsive area, talking to us through the displacement onto objects which is shown in phobias. It is another way of managing; it is an extension of the obsessional impulses and recurrent thought-patterns which can certainly make for some very difficult paths through life. Phobias are apparently slightly different, yet I think they grow from very much the same roots. They are a way of handling anxiety through action. I would like to talk about a case which I think could have led to a phobia, because it seems to me to throw up what I believe can be the genesis of various phobias.

## Katherine's story

This was a woman of thirty-three with a husband of thirty-seven. They had two children under ten, they both came of 'good-enough' parents, they had a very 'good' relationship and did a lot of talking with each other. Then he contracted cancer. It wasn't discovered until a very late stage, and the hospital said that he had anything from six weeks to live, eighteen months at the most, but more likely six weeks to six months. They said to her, 'Don't tell him that.'

At that point she came to see me. He had been sent back home by the hospital. I talked with her about the relationship and what she was going to have to handle. She decided, and agreed with me, that actually they did need to talk on the basis of their good relationship. It was going to be an intolerable thing for her to bear alone, and it was no service to him, because previously they had always talked with each other. I got in touch with the consultant at the hospital and said this was my view. We discussed it and he said, 'If you're going to help her, fine, go ahead.'

My brief was to stay in touch with Katherine over the period of her husband's illness and to his death. We had been working together for some months when one evening she telephoned me. She didn't often do this. Her voice was very tight and I knew something tremendous had happened: 'Can I come and see you?' I told her she could come that evening, as soon as possible. 'I've got one or two things to clear up and then I'll come,' she said. She turned up at about nine, rang the bell and told me what had happened.

Her small son had had his birthday that day and she'd organised a party for him and his sister, and about five other children. They were due to have the party at five pm, so she tucked her husband in after his lunch at about half past two, and made sure at intervals for the rest of the afternoon that all was well with him. And the party began as planned. An hour later, she went upstairs to make sure that he was all right. He was not in the bedroom, so she went into the bathroom, which wasn't locked. He was dead in the bath, in a pool of blood. He'd cut both his wrists.

She described to me how she went in through the bathroom door – this is the way that women in particular handle things, I think – and leaned against the inside of it. And then she swore at him. She cursed at him in an absolute rage. How could he do this? How could he do it when she wasn't there? How could he do it this way? How, most of all, could he do it with those children downstairs, any one of whom might have come up and gone into the bathroom? She went on and on and on about it. Then she managed to steady herself, went downstairs, gave the visiting children back to the parents coming in, sorted things out with her own children, telephoned the doctor (Katherine had a very good GP), went back up, dealt with everything, telephoned me. Then she staggered into my room.

She was absolutely horrified. I could see it was essential that we went through that experience, because most of all she was displacing her shock onto the dreadful guilt of standing there and saying these terrible things to this man she loved so greatly and had been caring for so much. She stood with her back to my door and she went through it again and again and again. She went through it right up to midnight, re-living the whole thing over and over. And each time she described it and went through it, she mentioned the butterflies on the wallpaper in the bathroom.

She came in very early the next morning and went on going through it, playing it over until finally the energy that was locked in it could begin to release. And of course it did, letting itself go in tears. She was reacting as a normal human being does in the face of death, which is always a blasphemy in life, however it occurs. We go first to rage, and then to grief, and then by degrees begin to come to terms with it; but the rage is required. I think, knowing Katherine, she would not have raged, she would have risen above it. She would have gathered everything together, handled the situation and probably, for the sake of the children, not have grieved very much except in private.

However, this butterfly motif kept coming up through the months that followed, and I suspected that in five or ten years' time she could well have become phobic to butterflies. That's what happens in a crisis: suddenly, something gets fixed in time and some detail is etched into us as if with acid. It becomes the carrier of that experience, that trauma. I am not saying she would necessarily have reacted in this way, but I suspect that this is how these phobic things are built up. Katherine is a good example, because she hadn't had a traumatic childhood; she'd had good bonding and not till she was thirty-three did this crisis occur. But the degree to which the butterfly motif kept coming up was interesting.

After a few days of the de-conditioning we did together, she was able to handle a further shock. She was standing at the sink on the third morning doing the washing-up and her little son came beside her. He had brought the tomato ketchup from the table and he poured some into the washing-up water and said, 'Is that what it was like with Daddy, Mummy?' And she was able to steady, to hold, to get down to his eye-level and say, 'Why do you ask that?' And he said, 'I heard you ring the doctor.' She was able to help him work it through. We didn't know what effect it might have had on him. (In fact, he might have become phobic to tomato ketchup later on, without being conscious of any personal connection to it.)

So the shock doesn't always come from a long way back. Work in through the fear of birds, cat fur, flying or whatever the phobia is, and we usually find that it is a displacement for fears and traumas lying deeper. They have been distanced and put onto something else in order to hold and contain them. At base it is a very healthy reaction, a way of stopping the person flipping or going mad. They can't handle it inside, they can't handle it at the interface. The inner tension is too big for them at the time, so they put it onto some object in the outside world. If they didn't do that, they would internalise it, keep it in the inner world as a subjective thing; then, of course, only later would they begin to show phobic fears.

### Various phobias

Phobias include unnatural, exaggerated and compulsive fears of many things, for instance of animals, illnesses, heights, water, storms, open spaces, enclosed places. The dread of these things is easier to handle than the original dread. The loathsome object stands for some other fear, perhaps sex, or the devouring mother; or for some desire, some hunger in disguise which the condemning self makes loathsome. I think most human beings have a tendency to be phobic about something. We are going back to our monkey ancestors. A lot of people dislike and feel at least slightly phobic about spiders and snakes and rats. It's as if the mind is saying, 'I don't want to think about that', and the phobia is a symbol. After all, our theme, our title, invites us to look at the symptom as a symbol – at our phobias as symbolic language. Address the language, set up the possibility of a dialogue, and of course things will begin to open up.

> *Claustrophobia*. This fear of closed, confined spaces often comes up as a sense of one's own self-identity not being given air and space. Check the phobia with the person and over and over again we find that it is suffocation of the Self. That is an obvious one. It may be that they lost the good object, the good person, and they dread that that will lead to loss of all separate existence. They have no life of their own, and thus flee to the safety of the open space, feeling swallowed up inside. It is also dread of their own dependency; they want to be born in a hurry. But through imaging work, through dialogue with it, we reach the fear of being engulfed, suffocated, trapped. And we often reach a trauma, whether of childhood or later.

*Agoraphobia.* Fear of open space, the market place, the *agora.* These people stay at home. The market place can stand for either the outside world 'out there', or for the forbidden inner one. The orthodox view is that it is flight back to the womb, giving up the battle of life – the fear that, away from home, the person will be swallowed up by the bad mother, possessed, devoured, suffocated, robbed of freedom and independence. But if someone is suddenly hit by agoraphobia, it is likely that they were in a chaotic outside world from an early age; or again, it may take them to a more recent trauma.

*Acrophobia.* Fear of heights; here, it is a good idea to check out somebody's expectation level and ambition drive (their own or someone else's). Heights give vertigo to these often highly successful people. Working with them, we may ask them to stand on a chair, and hold their hand.

*Monophobia.* Fear of being alone. These are people who, on a beach, will come and sit right by you, having parked their car immediately alongside yours in the empty car park. How far is the person simply feeling unable any longer to hold at bay the threats on the interface, whatever these threats may be? They dread that they cannot themselves parry the threat, and desperately need the presence of another person to give them a sense that they do not have to handle it alone.

*Pathophobia.* Fear of disease and contamination. Could this come from fear of guilt and sin? 'Jehovah's eye is watching you!'

*Pyrophobia.* This fear of fire is the dread of emotional eruption and the heat from the fire of their own instinctual nature. It is worth noting here that pyromaniacs are usually very controlled people from rigid backgrounds. Setting fire to things is at the interface of inner and outer, aiming to objectify the irruption.

*Necrophobia* is well-known as fear of death. However, what about the fear of loss of identity?

*Phobia about anaesthetics.* Fear of the chaos of unconsciousness.

*Fear of going home.* Again, maybe conversely, some people dread going out of hospital. They felt babied there and dare not leave; and, if they are kicked out, they may be quite without defences.

*Fear of Flying.*[52] This may indicate lack of roots, fearing the insecurity of space and air. Also perhaps a particular trauma? Or is the person unable to control their lives and so fears to let go?

## The language of phobias

These are perfectly obvious things – and yet they are not all that obvious. Least of all are they obvious in their treatment. And yet if we talk with the phobia, with the symbol, it nearly always throws up what it was about. Get into the feeling of it; ask, 'What does it remind you of?' To try to talk it away, to dissuade the person, to de-condition them or use aversion therapy, can all be very helpful but I fear it may just move the symptom around to some other area. Whereas treating the symptom with the respect that is due to it as a symbol, dialoguing with the symptom, recognising that it has a negative but also a positive element in it, seeing it as an adjustment towards health, rather than a non-acceptable aberration away from it, can very often bring the person off that interface and give them the courage to explore what it is about. The need is to get to the root of the anxiety rather than to the nature of the symptom and, as we saw with obsession and compulsion, to recognise that this kind of phobic reaction is only the symptom of internal anxiety and fear. Again, imaging can be extremely helpful.

Words that come up when working with people with phobias may include 'continuum, toys, play, playmates, father, nightmares, dreams, symptoms'. Or again, 'faith, religion, belief, talisman, guru, teacher'. These may suggest helpful figures to help the person past the interface. Also we may encounter huge experiences, revelations. Whatever we are exploring, and however clinical it may sound, there is always the possibility that it has in it the roots of something infinitely bigger. Stay with the client at the interface, and the small self that is frightened is enabled to use imagination in this unconscious way to project their inner fear onto an outer object. Then they can use the same quality of imagination to begin to get in touch with the bigger, wider aspect, the same thing seen from a different level.

## Nightmares and big dreams

Some big dreams can be related directly to this phobic characteristic. One woman who came to me in her fifties was phobic about any smell

---

[52] Fear of flying has several names, aviatophobia, aerophobia and pteromerhanophobia among them. Ed.

that suggested corruption. For her, the smell of a violet did that. She could smell what other people couldn't, and the phobia was already there. She was in danger of being looked on as a very odd-ball character and had lost a number of jobs because of her violent aversion to smells. So we worked at de-conditioning, helping her to image, and finally she told me this repetitive and frightening nightmare of a rotting corpse. She told me she had been dreaming it since she was twenty-two.[53]

Of Jewish extraction, she had been a child in Europe under the Nazis. Before she was three, all the people in her young scene had vanished into the gas chambers one by one. The entire family had been wiped out except for one aunt, who was only fifteen or sixteen, little more than a child herself, and had managed to get this little girl out across the sea and into England. So by the time she was four, the dreamer had arrived in an alien country with an alien language, cut off from almost all her roots. Her later childhood and adolescence was spent in one room with this young aunt, a single tap on the landing and a shared lavatory, and night after night she would wake from sleep to hear her aunt weep and weep and weep – waking to this endless weeping.

She had pulled herself up by the bootstraps and managed to get herself very well-placed in the Civil Service. But such a large part of her was locked back into the pain of the past that she was really a shell of a person. Although she had managed excellently and showed a very commendable front to the world, she told me that the moment she had come into a relationship, her own sense of poverty and inner emptiness had risen up because of all the disappearances from her life. Because most of her energy was still locked back with that endless weeping, she had felt there was no hope for her.

Then when she was twenty-two, up had come this recurring nightmare. She dreamt not of a nice clean skeleton but of a decaying, rotting corpse coming out of the grave with the grave-clothes hanging from it. It stood at the end of her bed. She would wake up sweating all over, sometimes screaming, horrified at this awful thing. Recently it had not just stayed at the end of the bed but had begun to come close, grinning and leering and leaning over her. Now it had begun to appear in the daytime, emerging in her imaging as a sub-personality. 'Am I going mad?' she asked me.

---

53  This woman's story is also told in Somers and Gordon-Brown, *Journey in Depth* pp. 26-27, in connection with unlived life. Here, the same story is used to illustrate how a phobia can develop and be transformed through imaging.

### The robin and the eggs

We stayed with that one motif. Getting her to relate to it, and by degrees visualise it – well, it was so horrible dealing with that corpse, she was so absolutely averse to recognising it, that she had to work from the feet towards the centre of it. And eventually she was able to confront it, even approach it. I won't say 'befriend' it, but at least she set up some sort of dialogue with it, if only by looking at it. And finally she was able to visualise herself putting her hand out and touching it. And what was her horror when it collapsed and she could see inside it. And suddenly there was something inside....

It was a robin sitting on a nest of eggs. It said to her, 'Why did you keep me waiting all this time? I couldn't have kept these eggs warm much longer if you hadn't come to me now, at last.' By degrees her robin – and it was *her* robin – told her what was in the eggs and why they were there: 'Whatever happened to your music? You once thought you'd like to play an instrument'. She certainly loved music, but it was ages since she'd so much as listened to any. 'What happened to your love of art? Just to look at paintings once gave you a sense of fullness. when you felt so empty inside, but you never do that now. Why don't you occasionally go to the country, as you used to? Once, you thought you might like to make friendships, but you don't do it.' The robin talked to her about the degree to which she was keeping her terrible early traumas alive: the gas-chamber and her family vanishing one by one. It was a great moment when I said, 'Whatever happened to the corpse?' and she said, 'Oh that! it blew away in the wind, but you see there's this *robin....* '

It was her scene, her robin, her eggs. She had been jeopardising her whole future and missing out on the essential nature of herself and her various talents, which this robin had kept alive for her. That was a big dream, a nightmare, repetitive, always telling the same story; and it scooped into the phobic side, which began also to give *her* a story. Gradually the strange smells troubled her less and less.

A normal human approach has a great deal to commend it inworking with people with phobias, given that we are aware of ourselves and our own unconscious hassle (for instance, we may be anxious for the person to get well, or to be successful). Our ability without fear to hold the tension of light and dark, good and evil is terribly important, infinitely more important than anything we may say. It is our ability to face whatever may come. That horrible, hideous corpse eventually showed the robin. When she was describing it to me I really had to centre myself to stop the horror that she felt, which was practically in the room. I could smell that corrupting flesh, I could see that corpse as she described it to me; the damn thing was standing between the two of us! But later she said that the quality I had of 'not looking disturbed by it' was very important to her. Our acceptance of such things is very often the first threshold. Cross it, and we're working equally with the person and the image.

Listen to nightmares. They come riding on horses, mares, but they are still dreams. We walk on the edge, in these borderlands between inner and outer where we meet with dreams, with symptoms, with symbols. The counsellor somehow has to walk that border in order to have a foot in both these realities. Borders and interfaces are terribly important; we need to explore them still, in our own consciousness.

## Roberta's story

To show how a healthy individual can nonetheless sometimes react in ways which, if led to their logical conclusion, could pass over into the clinical, here is an example. What had come up for Roberta when she and I did the 'End of your tether' exercise together [54] was so absolutely bang on target that I later invited her to talk briefly about it. It shows the splits that a reasonably normal, healthy person can have - those who are pretty well hung together - although Roberta confirmed that she had *not* had a very good childhood background. Her replies certainly fed into the area of 'symptom as symbol'. What she gave us is absolutely the pattern of the thing. This is our conversation about it:

*BS*: So, Roberta, you visualised yourself being at the end of your tether?

*Roberta*: I felt restricted, bound very tightly.

*BS*: We noticed you pressed your arms in and closed your thorax, which I drew your attention to. And then I asked you to get a graphic image for it.

*Roberta*: Immediately I felt there was a strap around my body, and a table, like in that series where the heroine is going to meet her fate. My fate was a buzz-saw at the end of the table. I was being pulled along

---

[54]  See Chapter 1 above. I had asked her to get a graphic image for being at the end of her tether; then to get the body feeling; and then any symptoms coming out of it; and finally, one memory which it triggered. BS

to it, and I had a most vivid feeling that I could not leave my house.

*BS*: And then the body feeling?

*Roberta*: I think at first I felt tight, crunched in round the skull – like that – to protect it, because I anticipated being split open by this saw.

*BS*: And then I asked you if you could get one memory?

*Roberta*: Immediately I saw a dead puppy. I saw myself as a very young child, about four. I cannot imagine how I had this image. I felt absolutely rigid. I remembered that a puppy had died and had been buried in the garden, and the next day I'd dug it up, because I had never had any experience with a dead animal before. Now, I was looking at it, and that triggered the other image. I looked at the dead puppy when I'd dug it up again and I felt numb and frozen. Again, I couldn't imagine, but then I suddenly remembered what had gone before. A bitch we owned had given birth to a litter of puppies, and I used to visit her. She was off in the cottage and I was in the big house. I loved the puppies. They were kind and lovable, and I was going in every day and holding them. After I'd been doing this for about four days my grand-mother – not the grandmother I loved, but the other one – told me that I mustn't do that, I mustn't disturb the puppies …

But I did, because they were irresistible. I can still remember picking them up, lifting them off the bitch and holding them, dear little things. When my grandmother realised I had continued to go to see them, she told me that if any of the puppies died it would be my fault, totally my fault. So I must not touch them. One would probably die and I would be responsible. So that night I prayed and prayed that nothing would happen to the puppies. The next day when I went and looked at them they were all fine. I was longing to hold them, but I didn't. I couldn't reach out to them.

Then, one of the puppies did die. I thought it was because I had done this. And that's when I felt 'strapped'. I'd prayed and prayed, and the puppy had still died.

*BS*: First, Roberta, we talked about symptoms and, going from an immediate contraction down the thorax, I asked you about lung and chest troubles?

*Roberta*: Yes, and I felt tight all over, restricted and frozen.

*BS*: Your arms straight away had given the layout of where most of your problems over the years have come. And *frozen* was the major word: when we went on to talk about it, it was the emotions which you couldn't express, frozen to ice. There were a number of mentions of ice.

*Roberta*: Which I've had in very many images. But immediately from the past I could see that I was still split off. I realised that over the years I had kept myself from reaching out – very much aloof, even though I know that really my impulse is to reach in.

*BS*: And we talked about how, when remembering the puppy, your impulse had been to pick it up and nestle it like that, hadn't it? And as soon as your grandmother put that taboo on you, 'Don't touch!' your hands wanted to go forward but were drawn back and clamped tight, and the feeling of warmth was frozen. So that triggered off a whole lot of other material that has come in.

Talk about splits! Without Roberta's knowing what the whole thing was about, we had gone straight into the exercise. And she was being split in two, left hand from right hand, thinking and doing (outside) being cut off from being and feeling (inside). All of which is very much in the nature of the split. We asked together where her own nourishment had come from. It certainly was not from her parents; that was where the crunching in the head had come straight in. She said it was that other grandmother whom she had loved and who had cherished her. We went on to talk about her relationships and the tendency to cut off and reject before she could be rejected.

Roberta and I agreed that, had she not had the ego-strength she did, and obviously the integrity of the individual seed, which seemed given her to survive her very traumatic childhood, she could easily have set up various phobias. For example, she might have developed a fear of anything furry. The degree of her health is that, instead, anything furry sends her absolutely cuckoo with love. But without knowing, without being able to remember something like the death of that puppy, another person could very easily have had bodily pains, or broken out in a rash, the moment they saw anything furry. Without realising or recognising it, they would be going back to that original scene, not remembering, having blacked it out. So it is a taboo: 'If you touch that (lovingly, warmly) it will die! And we will know that it has died.'

*Roberta*: You asked me how I felt when I approached the anticipation of the split, and I'd said, 'To one side'. The moment I'd said it I realised that I'd tried very much to go to one side, leaving out the left side, of emotion.

*BS*: Looking back, we realised that many of the trees and plants you had drawn were leaning over to the right, growing on the right, and the left side were left un-green.

*Roberta*: What we talked about was an unrealistic, wishful perfection, a perfect world, a perfect healthy puppy. I didn't want to do anything to destroy that perfection. And I thought I had destroyed it.

*BS*: Another person could have taken it too far over and become obsessive or compulsive, putting everything in neat lines, touching every third railing. You, Roberta, could well have been placed in that position beneath the all-seeing eye, with the voice saying, 'Touch that and you will destroy it!' Thank you very much, Roberta.

In order to touch it at all, the obsessive person's got to have it absolutely perfect, be always on guard, always right. However, the integrity of the individual and the strength of their ego-structure can hold, does hold, and frequently can be helped greatly to hold, despite the most ghastly traumas in life.

### Ritual

Note again the degree to which, for the healthy child, it is natural to set up rituals to hold the borderland at a tolerable level in a 'normal', healthy way. The parents play their part in holding the devils or the gods at bay for them, and giving them a place where they can grow and develop. Take the example above of Katherine, the wife of the man with cancer. She had had a good home life, a good basis, and a very good sense of her own inner and outer worlds, although she did not remember dreams. She'd had a number of varying illnesses but not very many, and a 'normal, average' life, as she said. The births of her children had been fairly straightforward. She was certainly a good-enough mother and she had been a more than good-enough wife in terms of her friendship with her husband.

And yet, at the borderland between life and death, she was struck by that enormous trauma. And she acted out the ritual of rage, of blasphemy. I have met many people needing to do that. At this place where life and death interact, in that moment, there's a sense of 'Oh God! Why should this be?' One goes into the crucifixion posture. It is the rage of, 'How could you do this to me? How could you leave me? Why should this happen?' And in our society that is terribly quickly glossed over. It used not to be. The rituals were played out by peoples in various cultures, where the rage and the tearing and the rending and the shrieking and the moaning were acted out by, expected of, the bereaved person. In acting these things out ritually, that energy was contained. Given containment of a ritual kind, a person then goes on through the sadness and the grief.

Now, although it is not so permissible outside, inside themselves people still go through those same rituals. Very often they have to take an apparently regressive form. Later on this particular client could easily, as we have seen, have become phobic about butterflies. But the butterfly is the psyche, it is the soul, it is very often the symbol of something vital; and the release of the butterfly may often talk about a death of something, inner or outer. If she had then chanced upon somebody who talked about butterflies, she might have been helped to get back again through that particular motif.

*IGB*: There is a difference between conscious ritual and that which is unconscious; then, rather than the rituals containing the energy, the ritual is itself invaded. Looking at it on a collective level, one example that comes to mind is where Jung tells how, when he was on a journey to Berlin in the early 1930s, he saw the ritual of Wotan the Wanderer being enacted by European youths. Suddenly he saw that many, many of them, from end to end of the continent, had taken to the roads. It signalled to him that something was very amiss in the general psyche. Probably this was the first time he was seriously worried about a second World War. The behaviour wasn't necessarily phobic, but it was unconscious – not a conscious, contained ritual.[55]

*BS*: And then later, listening to the sounds of those jackboots, listening to Hitler speaking (the way he phrased his words, the quiet beginning and the rising, and then the bringing down again, the torch-light) we can see an enormous, containing ritual being evoked: raising the energy, holding it, containing it and then taking it down.

In the same way we can listen to the conch-horns of the Tibetans, we can hear their rituals, we can see their flaming torches and their candles and the sounds, and the prayer wheels are going round, evoking the energy, containing it and taking it up, over and over and over. They are the same energies. There is a compulsion within those processes of ritual. Ritual can become obsessive at any moment. It is

---

[55] See Jung, 'Wotan', in *Civilisation in Transition* CW Vol.10, para 371-399, esp. para 373-375. Also Jung's letter to Miguel Serrano, Letters Vol. 2, pp. 593-4.

not necessarily something that has to be constantly played out. But the extraordinary thing about working with people who are obsessional is the energy. It is a huge energy.

*IGB*: Thinking of Hitler again: although there was a tremendous power evoked, it seemed that the ritual itself had become the dominant factor, rather than the support and container. The ritual ran the thing, rather than the life running the ritual. Take other examples (the coronation, say, or the wedding of Charles and Diana) and it seems that in Britain it is totally different. There is an enormous amount of ritual but it's not obsessive. The life of the process is supported and enhanced by the ritual, rather than run, dominated or controlled by it. Though it can sometimes be a very fine line. When Jung saw the youth of Germany on the roads acting out the archetype of the wandering Wotan, there was something about it that warned him. Perhaps the boy-scout efforts of this country at the time, camps for unemployed youth, was a similar impulse?

*BS*: Young people make their own rituals, with their own language and fetishes, their dress, amulets, routines, names, their experimentation with life and death energies. Again, it is this seeking for ritual to contain and to hold, and to have objects of holiness, and hellishness, which are bigger than oneself and will help one to contain these energies that are at war. If you want to be a diabolist and reverse the cross and worship the devil, it is still worshipping something bigger than yourself, and a way of handling an energy that is otherwise warring and sending individuals into their chaos. Individuals appear to have freedom of choice as to how they struggle to contain this energy, but ultimately it is the same energy. It is very neutral energy, and it can be raised or lifted, or dropped. Get the right orator, the right charisma, the right moment in time and it can go either way.

That's why it is desperately important. More and more individuals are facing the conflict and standing on the interface of their own nature. I think every individual who stands on the borderland of their own nature and deals with their own relatively small pairs of opposites is actually, at a very deep level, standing at the interface of things infinitely larger. We touch more lives than we can ever know, I think.

*A participant*: Another example of ritual is that classic adolescent book, 'Lord of the Flies'. The boys on the island keep saying, 'There are no adults, there's no one!' because suddenly there are no schoolteachers, no parents. They realise they don't have to wear their uniforms and can go swimming when they want to. The walls fall away and they immediately start to set up a ritual, which finally leads to their murdering Piggy and pursuing Ralph – to that confrontation with the outer, that chaos that is coming in on them.[56]

*BS*: And it is a cannibalistic ritual, which is internalisation of an external object. Penetrate these things and the same story comes up.

*Another participant*: I had a client with a tremendous split in herself. She'd been brought up by a very religious family, yet she had an absolute revulsion towards all the rituals surrounding their kind of Judaism. Almost phobic on the one hand, she felt tremendous shame on the other. An incident arose concerning the *mezuzah*, the small parchment of Torah verses which is put on the doorpost of every Jewish household.[57] A religious cousin turned up: 'But you *must* have the *mezuzah* above your door!' She went into a terrible conflict because of her phobia about such things. I asked her to take the prayer from the *mezuzah*, hear what it said and then translate it, first into English and then into her language of meaning, and see how she felt about it. In the end, torn as she was between the negativity of the ritual and her faith, she actually did it.

*Another participant*: Modern churches have become so chatty and 'good fellowship' and 'let's all shake hands' that the services have been taken away from ritual and made into very colloquial activities. Since a lot of the ritual has been removed, the energy has gone with it.

*BS*: And not just the outer ritual. It's the difference between poetry and prose. The poetic language of the King James version is for many the language of ritual, the container of an energy which is too big to be tightly structured. And yet I suppose, for other people born more recently, the Standard Version will speak and evoke big dreams.

## Words

The way words are used have tremendous power. When we use *wide* words – 'warm, loved, rhythm, ebb, flow, peace' – we use a different tone of voice from that which speaks a different quality of word. 'Chaos! Loss! Help!' – the same energy, the same person, yet within a few moments, a different body reaction. We can feel the change in the energies from: 'Now I'm for it!' 'They are angry!' 'They don't want

---

56  Golding, *Lord of the Flies*.

57  *Holy Bible*, Deuteronomy 6:9.

me!' to 'I'm safe here'. We often notice a change in their breathing and blood pressure.

*A participant*: Words – poetry – call very deeply in me; words immediately evoke connections. With 'anger, aggression', immediately there's a pulling-up.

*BS*: 'In the beginning was the word, and the word was made flesh ...'

### The preacher's son

I had a client whose father had been a Methodist minister, and strict. He went round to various churches preaching all the time. He preached at the dinner table, he preached everywhere – a peripatetic priest. This client just did not want to know. So he threw out his father, he threw out religion, he threw out the punitive behaviour, he threw out everything. Poor client, he used to come in and move things around, getting everything in order. He would move my pencils around all the time.

One day I heard my voice say to him, 'Why don't you bless those things as you move them?' In his quiet, obsessive way he blew up. In a very real sense, by degrees he began to practice the presence. He went on moving things, but he did it in a different way. What he was doing was very much Zen. By a widening, an elaboration, he went into what had been clamouring to be let through from within himself: comparative religion, the understanding and the blessing of the moment, that every act can be made sacramental. His compulsion was his way of handling the pressure; he'd tried everything else so he thought he might as well try this blessing of things. And so we got back. It was beautiful, and it was so much already *there* in his action.

If we stand at the interface with somebody, we may have moments where we hear it and, more importantly, they hear it. When he was moving those things, instead of thinking, 'Oh God, he's moving those pencils again!' I was watching the caring quality of his hand. I noticed that it was a very particular hand. I was more focussed on the hand than on the movement. I was standing with him at the interface. I think the words *why not bless those things?* came to me from him.

If the too rigidly-held tension releases itself in involuntary movement, why not bless that movement? Why not say, 'Yes, do go on making that movement', while helping the person to recognise that the movement itself can have meaning as a form of ritual. The exploration of the magical content of what is contained in that movement helps them to use ritual in a conscious way. Very often we can mobilise that tendency to ritualise by showing that there is creative ritual. We can help them devise creative rituals, the practice of the Presence. Through the compulsive moving of those pencils, through blessing them, the moment suddenly opens up the possibility of other dimensions. It is using the same energy, not taking it away, but helping to convert one kind of tension into another more progressive kind.

It is a very moving story; it is with all of this compulsion and phobia. We are looking into the mysterious heart of a divine creature acting oddly in the world. It can be very difficult to remember someone's divinity when we look at the particular things that are going on at the level of the flesh. That is why I have chosen to talk fairly clinically about these things; but always there is this underlying mystery which will speak, given the opportunity, in a poetic language: 'warm, loved, peace, flow, rhythm'. Their voices quieten.

*Another participant*: I worked quite deeply with a severely obsessive person who couldn't talk about it. It took me a long time to learn how riddled his life was with his compulsions and phobias. There were very many activities going on right through the day, preventing him from getting up in the morning, from working, from holding down jobs.

*BS*: I should imagine that following the line of any one of that apparent multiplicity of compulsions or phobias would have returned him to the same point. He sounds like somebody working exceedingly hard not to have to perform something. It may, at the deepest, profoundest level, have been a rejection of life. It may, at the highest, be that he was right, because what he was about to do was in answer to somebody *else's* expectation. If we can work in through the phobia and find out what it's about, we may get into the language of that essential seed, that person's language, and replace it (by degrees) with what is, for them, a different way of looking at the same thing. You can then use their obsessive behaviour but put a different tone on it.

*IGB*: A simple definition of a phobia might be that it is a distortion of our relationship to whatever it is that we're phobic about.

*BS*: It is love arrested, which goes back to become hate. While the bonding of the 'good-enough' parent allows us both to love and hate the same thing at the same time, here we are caught into an either/or polarity. This is because relations have snarled up. The person *either* loves or hates; they either become phobic to, or fetishist towards, something. It all comes back to relationships and love.

## Counselling people with phobias

A phobia does not easily give way under counselling; in some cases I've seen better and quicker results with aversion or behaviour therapy, both of which I think are exceedingly valuable and effective. However, instead of going to work straight away with these, we might (not always, but frequently) start talking to the phobia. The hope for counselling is that if we get to the bottom of the fear, it won't move into another area, as it may with behavioural methods. The counsellor needs to get at the roots of the anxiety, not at the symptom itself, knowing that the client does need to impose order on some threatening area. The frightened child, the primitive in them, is trying to find a place of security. We help them by degrees to build up a safe feeling, till they may little by little start letting go of the phobia.

The *paradoxical injunction* may be suitable for mild phobias, anxieties that are not too profound. For instance, if a person is somewhat afraid of going on buses, then we might say, 'OK, then, don't go on a bus.' And *de-conditioning* is often very successful. Dentists, for instance, can de-condition dental phobias, which also means parenting the patient and, even more important, giving them security. This usually works.

## The value of the phobic-tending personality

A very good counselling suggestion is to see the phobia first as a prison and then, from a different viewpoint, as something on which the person can grow. This opens the possibility of the transmutation of exactly that same energy into a wider aspect. For the individual (and for the collective), the anxious, compulsive behaviour is regressive and life-denying. The break occurs when the same thing can become life-enhancing. We look to see what is the life in it, what is the energy, what is its detriment, what is its transcendence. We let it be played out and transformed. If we can help our client to stand at the interface on the map at Figure 2 (page 9) and see both sides, inner and outer, then we see not the crucifixion cross but the equal-armed cross.

And the good-enough therapist loves the client, and loves themselves

despite what is said to them. And most of all, the good-enough therapist loves the Self within that client, the god or the devil which is
reflected within that Self.

Web of Life

# CHAPTER NINE

# The Anxious Personality

## Barbara Somers

*Courage is self-affirmation despite our anxieties*

Anxiety is a necessary part of being human, and one test of the mature personality is the wherewithal to face reality with courage and determination. The anxious person is more than usually sensitive to the threat of non-being. He cannot have a full encounter with reality because he daren't be open to doubt. Courage is self-affirmation despite these anxieties.

The usual 'medical' viewpoint has seen pathology in anxiety and even blamed the terrified person. In fact, someone chronically afraid may have been told that his anxiety took one of three forms: 'Firstly, you are afraid of fate and death, though these are universal and inescapable, and the neurotic' (he may have heard) 'avoids these fears by avoiding living. Secondly, you fear emptiness and meaninglessness, which you have avoided by building up rigid systems against them. And thirdly, your fears of guilt and condemnation are misplaced: you see guilt where there is none'.

I take a somewhat different slant on it all!

### Anxiety neurosis

This includes phobias. In a true anxiety state, we are always afraid. Our free-floating anxiety is there all the time and, when we are taken over by our anxious bit, the fear never goes away. In fact, we are glad of something real to fear.

This is different from what happens with *obsessive* people and from the *paranoid*, with whom the bad and feared thing is seen as 'out there'. The paranoid person's reaction is to direct hostility towards that thing out there. But the *anxious person's* reaction is to flee it.

Anxious people also differ from *hysteric* personalities who, when they react to fear, are saying, 'There's something wrong with my *body*'. But the anxious person is saying, 'There's something wrong with *me*'. The hysteric takes relief in a physical symptom, which solves the problem short-term. Actually they take very little interest in their bodies, but rely on other people. They are Feeling types (in Jung's terms) with Thinking repressed. But anxious people dread physical symptoms, trying to avoid the tension, the pounding heart, the chest pains. They panic. They limit their activities. They fear madness and death. They run away from people, preferring *things* – much safer. These are Thinking types, with Feeling repressed.[58]

Like the hysteric personality, the anxious personality sees the good and desired thing 'out there', but where the hysteric's reaction is to devour it, the anxious person's is to take refuge in it. What the symptom, the panic, the terror, is saying is, 'There's danger pending'. And the danger is that the hungry self may get out with its demands and furies. That is what is dreaded: the impending guilt for that.

*Anxious children* have nightmares and depressions. They can't mix with other children or express themselves; they live in dread of rebuke from other people, but they also dread the awful things within them that might get out. These are silent children, with strained faces, dark rings round their eyes, pale sweaty skins. They do not shine. They have tragic expressions.

### The value of the anxious-tending personality

Anxious people respond very well to psychotherapy. Patience is needed, or they will break off, but they are usually stickers. They do have considerable insight and are at home in their inner worlds, so our aim at first is to get alongside their minds in finding out what's within. In the end, they must realise they cannot do therapy in their own heads. Gently we ask, 'Do you ever get frightened by anything…?' Their depression is a cloak, an avoidance of feeling, a running-away from a pain and a truth, hiding first fear, then the anger and dangerous hates within, and below that, their thwarted love and need. It is a repressed love, the need to be loved and to love. A safe place has to be created where the person can explore these feelings and find that no awful results follow. Thus he or she comes to be free of a weight, and becomes lighter and more free.

---

58  See 'The Four Functions', Gordon-Brown and Somers, in *The Raincloud of Knowable Things*, pp. 48-59. Also see Jung, *Psychological Types*, CW Vol. 6.

We ask ourselves, which fear is it? Is this person from a chaotic background, staying within rigid guide-lines as a taboo against the frightening outside world? Or was the background rigid, prohibiting subjective freedom, and are they fearing their own inner, subjective world? Again, we can't label the person. We can say, 'Here is a depressive tendency', but not, 'She's a depressive'. The same goes for people with anxiety, or people with phobias. We are looking at a whole person.

## Panic at the weekend

*A participant*: One of my clients has symptoms of panic every day, and especially at weekends, and when she panics she often rings me up.

How can I tackle that movement (upward in her case) of rising panic? She has maintained communication and slowly changed and shifted, but the symptom has not disappeared.

*BS*: Have you looked at the symptoms of the panic itself, how it comes to her? To hold it at the level of the psychosomatic, you would explore the statement being made through the panic. What type of panic? This is obviously a 'psychic' panic if it only happens at weekends. What is it about weekends?

*Reply*: It happens on both Saturdays and Sundays. She's married and divorced, with two teenage children.

*BS*: You can go right into that by getting at what the panic itself does to her. Take her back into the feeling of it, and then *ask the panic* what it's about. The god Pan is in panic. It is the threat of chaos, and the anxiety level is extremely high. Ask her, 'Why the weekends?' and continue that exploration. 'What does that feeling remind you of? Yes, loneliness?' That's one thing. What does that feeling of loneliness at the weekend remind you of?' There could be many things: the natural anxiety of the single parent with two children faced with an empty Saturday; the sense of loss of what used to be the established family. Follow the cycle with, '… And what does *that* feeling remind you of?' and you will probably reach back well into the area of her marriage. It may take you to a pattern of weekend anxiety in the parental home as well. Stay with the symptom all the time and keep taking it from different angles.

*Reply*: It's every weekend, always, unless she has something particular to do or is being taken out. Then at least she has something to wake up for. It's when she hasn't got anything to wake up for....

*BS*: And that in itself is something which you take up: 'What do you mean when you say "something to wake up for"?' Then you can work with, 'What does it feel like to have something to wake up for? What does it feel like *not* to have something to wake up for?' You do not have to use the word 'panic'. Rather, explore what has come up out of it and then continue the dialogue.

### The anxious man

*A participant*: I have a client who has rather severe what he calls 'anxiety symptoms'. He's been put in hospital for them. His background was tremendously structured: home was chaos and he was sent to boarding-school at the age of eight. He later went into the Navy, where he stayed until he was thirty. Then, both his marriage and his time with the Navy ended. He altogether broke down and at that point he went into hospital. He's now found himself a new structure: doctors and drugs, and the medical profession. His anxiety-symptoms are now physical. Also, he recognises that his depression is about, 'You two against me'. He's seeing a psychiatrist who drugs him up heavily and who works specifically on repressing the symptoms. I am finding it a real battle to work with his symptoms. I keep saying, 'Tell me about the anxiety, tell me about what your body's saying'. but his whole focus is on whether to increase, or decrease, his pills. He wants to deal with the symptoms by reaching for the structured, organisational approach as represented by the medical model. It's hard going....

*BS*: It is very difficult. There's no doubt, this is what a lot of drugs are meant to do: obliterate the degree of anxiety. Do you know what form the anxiety was taking?

*Reply*: He's latched onto the word 'anxiety' and so he uses it for everything; but it's fear, it's panic. It tends to be respiratory. In terms of elements, it's airy, I would think: Fire and Air – Fire.

*BS*: If it's airy and fiery, there's just the hope that there may be some aspiration in him. I would certainly look to the possibility that he may really need the organisational side. There do have to be drugs, though they may need to be modified in counselling and of course the monitoring has to be done by a doctor. The client may have to have this holding by drugs within this climate at this time. We need to accept that maybe they give the structure which helps to impose a framework on the chaos. Could you ask what he hoped would emerge from this, to open up the possibility of the future, of somehow getting in touch with what lies beyond? It would have to be very delicate, not to push him ahead of his stage, but if somehow you can keep it there: 'What would you hope will come out of it, what will grow out of it?' It's about getting at the possibility of the emergence; sometimes it will go through, even above the drugs.

*Reply*: He certainly knows he's under-employed, and living with someone who neither challenges him nor gives him joy, and he knows that in time both of these are going to have to go.

*BS*: Does he have any hobby, or did he have?

*Reply*: Yes; sailing, skiing and windsurfing are all terrifically important. He's recently had two very successful holidays, both challenges. One was ocean sailing for a week with a few other men....

*BS*: The Air element, and the element of movement.

*Reply*: We've done a lot of work on trying to anchor that, going out and sensing, where and when he's ready, what this might be saying.

*BS*: You can only reinforce that, in the hope that at a certain point it will convert, as an energy.

## Counselling people in anxiety states

So we are asking,'What purpose does the fear serve? How would it be without it?' When the person is ready, we aim to bring back the original anxiety for facing. It is very slow. There is panic in the interface and they may feel worse for a time. In fact, counselling usually does make it worse at first, because now they internalise the fear. The equality of the relation with the counsellor may be the first such equality they have ever known. The hope is that then their parity with the outside world may begin to increase.

Our intention is that the client become more and more conscious. We aim to make him aware of the nature of his fear: is it masking some other anxiety? We map the history of the symptom, inviting him to picture and visualise it, to be able to touch the visualisation of it. We ask: 'How does it feel with you? Get back into the last time you felt it. What does it remind you of?'

### The girl with the teddy bear

Many of us still have our own teddy bears. I knew a girl whose totem for coping with her fear was a teddy bear which always came with her to the sessions. As time went on, the teddy bears she brought became increasingly large, till they were almost as big as she was. There followed a process of weaning her from her need to be so befriended. In the end the bears became smaller, and finally she settled for one tiny, talismanic bear on her key-ring.

Reflections

# CHAPTER TEN

# Adult Sexuality

## Barbara Somers and Ian Gordon-Brown

*Many people go through agonies (in their own beds, out of their beds, in marital beds, in other people's beds) because they feel,'Everybody else has got it roughly hung together except us – except me!'*

## INTRODUCTION

*A whole series of confusions are involved in sexual difficulty*

*Ian Gordon-Brown*: On this subject we are all in some degree experts. Even if not experts in the sexual act, we are experts in our incompetence. Also, we may have a special knowledge which no one else has ever had, or even heard of.

*Barbara Somers*: We shall look at sexuality and its early roots, the emergence of the sexual impulse in a 'normal, average' human being as he or she is brought up. Later, we consider some of the so-called 'sexual variations', seeing that such variations are still in the pursuit of love. In contemplating our symptoms as symbols, we are looking at these 'clinical' conditions from a Transpersonal perspective. I am suggesting that some of these variations, however strange their outward form, are in fact efforts of the psyche to readjust, to redress some imbalance from an earlier stage, and readapt itself to its own normality.

### Sexual maturity

What is 'sexual maturity'? It has been defined as 'the ability to have full orgasm', full release, full letting-go. However, I would consider that to be an extremely partial reading. It seems to me that, at all levels of intercourse from physical to spiritual, sexual maturity has everything to do with the ability to relate as an equal to an equal. And a child who has truly had the opportunity to emerge into their own sexual gender finds that they can relate sexually as an equal to an equal. That is probably quite rare.

### Confusion

*IGB*: This simple word comes out most strongly. A whole series of confusions are involved in sexual difficulty. We may be confused about the difference between sexuality and sensuality, about our identity, by the fact that we love and are attracted to both men and women. We are confused because we do not know whether we will ever find out which of our parents was Mother and which Father. We are confused about our own and other people's expectations.

### Of what is sex the symbol?

Sex certainly is a universal and fundamental symbol, going far beyond the bed and the sexual act. Explore mystical literature, look into philosophical systems, and we find some event which philosophers and mystics would regard as a union of opposites – or of likenesses. Clearly there is a relationship between the individual experience of sexuality and the collective. Sex is creative for both men and women because it not only produces children but is a sign of virility. We are creating our successors and building a family. We are making it possible for the tribe to continue in existence, establishing our own line, creating the future, and all this creativity comes into the whole business of sex. Obviously love is in it too. The coming-together happens on a number of different levels of consciousness: certainly at an instinctual level, certainly and very obviously at a body level. Emotionally? A great many relationships are difficult not because of the actual physical sexuality of it, but because the emotional side of the union is incomplete or inadequate.

And beyond this, there is the element of union in the fullness and roundness of sexuality. It is not only the union of two partners, it is the union of a return to one's origins, a union with the Self. There is an *inner* marriage, a contra-sexual union between the male and the female within each person. The union, the love, the creativity, all of these are in the broadest sense sexual. This is not just theorising. When we get down to rock bottom – to bedrock – down to sexuality at the level of physical expression, these factors come in and affect a person's performance and their satisfaction. Again, the love that enters in is not only a love of the partner. Very often it has to do with the love of the Self. Those who are unable to love themselves will very frequently have a problem when it comes to sexual expression.

## THE NURSERY

*The parents' 'good' and 'bad' become the child's good and bad*

### The phallic quest

*BS*: As far as we know, before the major part of its development begins, the foetus in the womb is female. It takes quite an effort in the later stages of pregnancy for the male genes to become dominant. Given this predominance of feminine nature in human beings, and given that the first five years of life are very much under the aegis of the feminine and of the maternal, the whole of human consciousness has had to make a strong phallic thrust towards emergence. It has been a fight out of the womb of the unconscious, out of childhood dependency on the environment. Drawing on their ability to go into outer reality and take action in the world, humans have struggled to make the externalising journey. This 'phallic quest' is part of the search of human consciousness as it gains control of the outside environment and pulls further and further away from the control of the unconscious.

The same thrust is there in individuals: the need in both men and women to break away from the original womb. A woman coming up into maturity moves into taking responsibility for, and control of, her sexuality via her own womb; while a man needs to take command of his own sexuality *away* from the womb of the mother, to penetrate the higher womb of his own creativity, to find another womb. So humans are struggling away from the mother. If they are on a spiritual journey and do not involve sexuality in that, but choose celibacy, they are still going to a higher womb of religious and spiritual homecoming. But always there is that struggle 'away from'.[59]

### Touch

We all start life weak and dependent, needing attention, caressing, nourishment and love. Touching and being handled are most necessary

---

[59] See Appendix 5, a discussion about being 'touched by the archetype'.

for a good start in life, as well as food and warmth and comfort. If an individual is to have any sense of an *outline*, then touch is very, very important. Having our body held, actual hands caressing its outline – this most puts us in touch with our flesh, with our five senses. Feeling ourselves accepted as small babies through sensuous touch is vital in helping us to accept ourselves. It frees us later to get in touch with our own sexual nature. It provides a sense of identity, a sense of how we are *felt*; it outlines an initial self-image, drawing the boundary between ourselves as people, and others, and the environment. In the first few months, certainly the first couple of years, what is given to the child in this way is extremely important.

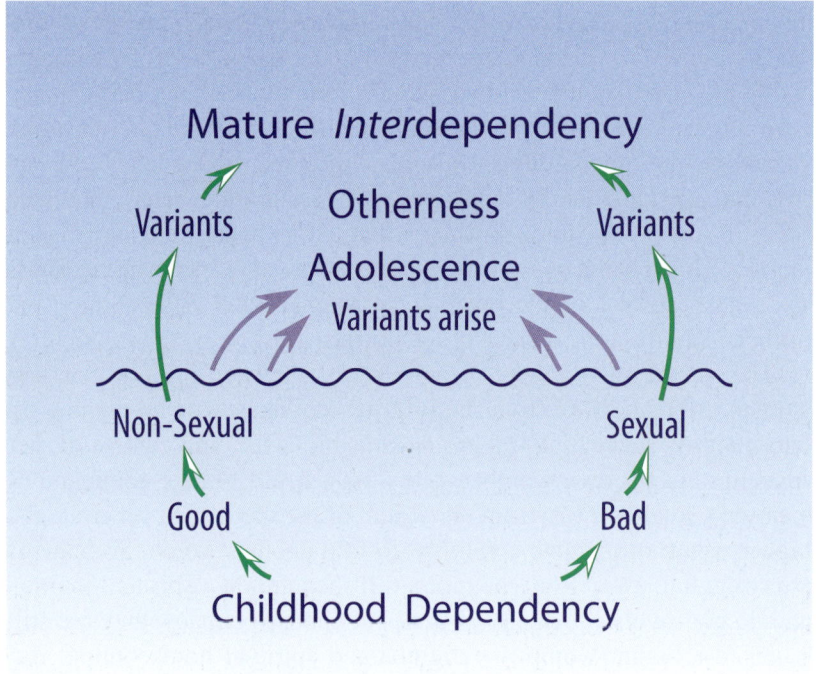

Figure 7. Adult Sexuality

Read from the bottom up, this map shows how individuals emerge from their inevitable childish dependency and grow towards the ability to make mature relationships, which would be the crown of this particular tree. On the left side is GOOD and on the right is BAD.

## Sensuality and sexuality

The ability later to distinguish between sensuality and sexuality has much to do with this early touch. Many people confuse them, treating sexuality as if it were in a watertight compartment. If there is this split between the sensuous and the sexual, though they can make love sexually they will not be present in their bodies. It is the touch, the hold, the sense of being defined by the touch of another human being that they are after, as much as the release of their own sexual nature. So, going into sexual relationships, they are really looking for sensual ones. The basis for confusion over this fundamental and critical distinction is laid very early on. If the infant experiences supportive, creative, warm touch, if touch is a spontaneous and natural thing and the child itself is allowed and helped to learn to touch others in an acceptable way, then the basis for the fundamental distinction between sensuality and sexuality will have been laid.

## Splitting good from bad

Even before the child is conscious, this pattern of what is good and what is bad is becoming present within the psyche. However well-bonded, well-held, well-handled, well-related to the sense of its body the child may be, with good-enough parents both intact, inevitably there is going to be this early splitting into 'good' and 'bad' behaviour. It is absolutely unavoidable in all cultures. It happens. It is how a child survives and adapts to its environment. Certainly from about three on, when the ego begins to make a big thrust for itself towards development, the *mores* of our people and our times are taken within and imprinted, 'introjected', to become part of our own patterning. Every one of us rapidly learns what pleases or displeases the major figures in his or her environment. Apart from what is in the culture, the setting, what the child takes as right and wrong is obviously much affected by its own family relationships and particularly by the mother. The parents' *good* and *bad* become the child's good and bad; their *acceptable* and *unacceptable* become the child's acceptable and unacceptable.

## Potting and creativity

I have in mind the potty-training period. Potting is obviously a very important thing, both for the seed being potted into its own environment, and the literal potty-training. This is often, certainly in the Western world, the area where 'dirty, untouchable, un-do-able' become very clearly marked. Think of the seed in the individual. Our very first creative act is to drop something warm and interesting out of ourselves into our pot. The impulse in all children, as it is in small monkeys, is immediately to turn round, to examine it, to eat it, smell it, wipe it around and generally enjoy it. And usually it's whipped away and shot down the lavatory. So that's the general feeling most children get about their first creative act, something that is out of themselves, tangible and tactile: 'Ugh, don't touch! Dirty!' Too many of us feel that roughly the same applies to every creative act thereafter. Anything that comes out of the body, out of the self, is bad, dirty, unacceptable, guilt-evoking. This tremendous split can be picked up very early on. Much of the later 'good-and-bad' around sexuality has to do with how those instinctual areas were first dealt with.

### *Body splits* (see Figure 4, page 34)

A great number of children, even before three, are conscious that the acceptable side goes from the genitals upwards and the non-acceptable from there down. In that split, we often experience what is the good and what is the bad of our environment in a very direct way. 'Good children', having potted acceptably, eat well, speak well, wear the right expressions, make the right gestures. They respond properly. 'Bad children' eat loudly, make rude faces and noises, are dirty, touch their genitals, demonstrate pre-sexual impulses, can't, don't or won't control their bladders or their anuses. Variable though this may be in different cultures, there is nearly always some form of this division, and the child picks it up very quickly. It will be particularly clear and obvious and conscious in the third and fourth years, but the ground is being laid earlier at an unconscious level.

*IGB*: The child is led to realise that certain areas of their own body are less good than others and are not to be touched, at least, not in public; and certainly you do not touch those bits in other people's bodies. There are things you know that you do not mention. This splitting of upper from lower body can, if it's very deep and very early, be one of the major problems in later sexuality. Good-enough parents will usually prevent it from becoming a large split. With them, the child is loved, good or bad, and a distinction made between loving, which of course is a very important part of sexuality, and the goodness and badness of the child. It knows that it is loved for itself, rather than for its behaviour. This is of fundamental importance because it provides it with the security that will allow it to develop into a well-bonded individual who can, a little later, begin to establish its own identity. The world may be split, but this child will later be able to tolerate inner and outer and remain whole.

However, there is a different kind of parent, one who imposes a pattern on the child. Then, we are loved and all is well *if* we do the right thing; but we are not loved, we are punished, if we do the wrong thing. We feel rejected. We can't poke and puke and finger and fart, all of which should be lightly treated and children encouraged to use all these naughty words. That is one of the keys. With the good-enough parent, what is forbidden and the feeling-tone that goes with that, and what is in fact allowed, all seem to go together. There is no heavy, punishing quality to it. There may be a verbal reason given if the child can understand it, simply: 'We don't do that because Granny doesn't like it'. We all know that Granny has her moments, but 'not when Granny's around, now!' And children understand; they're very rational and reasonable over this kind of thing. They know it's all right to pee in the corner of the garden when it's just Mummy and Daddy: 'Well, the dog does. Why shouldn't I?'

## THE GROWING CHILD

*'You mustn't say things like that!'*

### Emerging from the nursery

BS: Classically, the fifth to the seventh year, starting from a fairly critical point around the fourth birthday, leads to a mini awakening, an emerging sexual thrust, and an innocent interest and exploration of the sexual parts of the body. Till five, our childhood dependency has been primarily on Mother. Now that symbiotic relationship needs to be broken. We have seen how Father is required for emergence, as a bridge out from the over-emphasis of the feminine of those first nursery years. Toys and pets and playmates have helped to give outer reality a tactile consistency, with their transitional power to hold inner and outer, touch and sexuality together. Now, the function of the father in relation to the boy child is to enable him to separate from the mother and establish his own identity. His function in relation to the girl is to allow her to continue to grow with her mother, and yet recognise and see herself as a separate female identity. This is quite critical. If his role in helping both boy and girl to establish an identity in this way is not met, sexual and gender confusion arise and, at a slightly later stage, the failure to 'become their own identity' will be confused and tangled up with the development of their sexuality.

### Gender uncertainty

For you as child, the absent, or dominant, or over-present father or mother is going to throw your perspective out - your sense of proportion - to the detriment of the opposite parent. You will be very unsure of your own gender. The transition which helps to hold subjective and objective worlds together comes when you start to play. What do you play with, if you are unsure of your own gender? As a boy, you might want quite naturally to play with dolls: Batman, Spiderman, for instance. However, you may like dolls because you do not know whether you're a girl or not. Then you're told, 'Boys don't play with dolls' and 'Girls don't play football, or fall on their heads out of trees'. More confusion. And if your mother doesn't herself know who men are, or what the man within her is like, a fine old muddle goes on.

These uncertainties about gender do not always come from the much-maligned parenting experience; they can also come out of the good side of bonding. A muddled child can be born of muddled parents who happen to be people struggling with their own gender problems and relationship needs and had parenthood thrust upon them. The child is enormously sensitive to the way in which the non-verbal and the verbal fit together, spotting immediately any inconsistency in the adult attitude, the feeling tone, what is said or not said.

And there is also the parents' own wish-life. They may have wanted a child of a different gender. The boy or the girl will know they are not acceptable as they are and try terribly hard to be what they are not. Many's the girl I have met who is her father's son, and many the young man who is the confidant of the mother (which is actually the daughter's function). The mother makes him into the young lover and holder of her secrets, which can be a terrible thing.

A general freedom to dabble with the environment, exploring with our senses, sticking our fingers into things, picking things up, eating worms, is part of the exploration of life. It helps us relate to the outer world. We remember how hard the child must struggle to break away from the subjective, symbiotic relationship, first with the mother and then with the nursery, reaching to the objective, touching the world in oneness with nature. The two worlds meet in that interface where the child now plays. If it feels acceptable there, both in its good and in its bad side, knowing it is not going to be unloved because it does what is bad in its own culture, then it can begin to grow up with a sense that the subjective and objective worlds are friendly, not threatening, places.

*IGB*: There is a sweet story of a little boy and girl who were friends. The boy was a Catholic and the girl was not. One hot day, they went off into the country and they came to a wood, and in the middle of the wood there was a pond. Quite innocently they both thought, 'Let's paddle.' So they took their clothes off and were just about to go into the water when the little boy, looking at the little girl, said, 'Oh, now I see the difference between Catholics and Protestants.' Their interest is quite innocent, and the sexual side is quite innocent. God help them if their parents have a hang-up about it. 'You mustn't say things like that!' and immediately the thing is overlaid with disapproval and tension. If there is within the parents a difficulty about sex, if it is impossible to talk about it; if there are unnecessary taboos around it, then that will have been the atmosphere in the home and at any moment two or three ill-chosen words will bring it to the child's consciousness.

Good-enough parents will handle it quite naturally and the children will be allowed their innocent exploration. If they have been well bonded and conditioned as far as touch is concerned, touching becomes, in the critical three-four-five-year-old period, something that is good and to be enjoyed. It is acceptable, and any part of the body is all right.

### The incest taboo

*BS*: From five to seven, the child's own pre-sexual energy, which will become very much stronger later on, makes a particular drive forward. We start to relate to the 'otherness' outside our own family and our own tribe. The subjective and objective worlds begin to focus in terms of sexuality. This is where the incest taboo, which Freud strongly recognised as being such an important unconscious component of the human psyche at around this age, begins to come in. Certain taboos are set up before we are twelve. Who are and who are not 'sexual people'? This is made very clear by the environment. It is to be hoped that the child will discover that their own relationship with their parents is a loving but not a sexual one. 'You don't make love to Mother, you don't make love to Father, you don't make love to Aunties or Uncles.' Mother, for both boy and girl, can be touched, and she can touch you. But she is not an object of your sexuality, she's the *subject* of your sexuality. In the same way, Father may touch and hold, and you can touch him, but not genitally nor in any intensive way.

Also, from five to seven you learn that you do not have sexual play with your brothers or sisters – not, at least, in public, though you may have to be forcibly parted and put into the guilt cupboard. Quite often clients, male and female, tell how they had their first sexual experience and exploration with brother or sister or cousin. Yet the clear taboo stands: sisters are not to be touched. I think this is not a natural split, but a taboo of our peoples and of our times. It has to be learned. It may also be a biological taboo. Quite a number of the higher animals also do not relate within their immediate family. By making sure that there is not too much inbreeding, nature may be safeguarding against de-formations, ensuring the carrying-forward of the strain. However, psychologically speaking, peers *do* naturally relate to each other, which is why these taboos have been put upon us, giving us patterns which may not necessarily be even human, let alone natural to us as individual human beings. Yet the human species has had to take them aboard in order to survive.

By contrast, for the child, the taboo involving the *parent* is natural. And it is a two-way thing. Adults will guiltily admit to feeling stirred in their sexuality in the company of children, sometimes saying they are upset by it, especially with a child of the opposite sex. A woman breast-feeding can be quite disturbed by the sexual stirrings she feels in herself, particularly with her male child. A number of men will admit to being sexually turned on if a child pees in their lap, nice warm comforting pee. This taboo is probably instinctive and natural to us, but it is an untouchable area. It takes a long time and an environment of trust before it comes out from your client. We are deeply conditioned into our tribal customs and cultures and a lot of sublimation goes on.

So, while the child very rapidly learns at a quite unconscious level which people are *not* sexual objects for them, later they recognise that other women, other men, *are* permitted. Many men grow up believing that their mother, or any mother-figure, comes as untouchable Madonna, while any other woman, even a sister, is in the prostitute class, a sexual object. Hence the Mary-Madonna and the Mary-prostitute split so well exemplified in the Bible. In the same way, some women go frigid with a man who for them represents the father, even if he is not the father; while they can be tremendously sexual and playful with someone they consider to be their peer, even their brother. It comes up over and over again. 'When I was five – six – seven, I began to realise.... ' There is a very real splitting here. And later on, that taboo runs out like a transitional object, helping inner and outer both to separate and come together in a healthy, normal way.

In any society, what you can do covertly you cannot do openly. Greek plays and tragedies are encapsulated human experiences, as are all great works of art. People's attitudes change, but incest is in all literature as a reality of relationship. Certainly it is in the creative myths of early periods and it is also there in much twentieth century writing: Tennessee Williams, D.H. Lawrence and many others have written about this taboo.

So more guilt is built on. With the good-enough parent, this too is accepted as normal and natural and right. There is nothing wrong in being guilty. In fact, it's quite a good thing to own up to something you have done. You're probably given a present or a sweetie, not necessarily punished. But with the not-so-good parents, who themselves have their sexual problems, the child is sensitive all the while to the environment, knowing the fundamental attitudes, knowing what is *not* being said. Thus a whole series of minefields is being laid which can burst through at critical stages later. The latent guilt goes underground. Nothing may happen till the next major surge of sexual and emotional awakening, when all these things come together to the surface and the confusion and the adaptation difficulties begin to express themselves at the purely sexual level. It can happen.

### Oedipus and Electra

*IGB*: Freud spoke of the Oedipal relationship for boys and the Electra relationship for girls,[60] saying that at this point the boy has the internal desire to kill the father in order to assume the mother. So inevitably he has to become the aggressor. The girl equally has to come in conflict with the mother to lay claim to the father. The Oedipal myth was chosen; though I can think of a number of other myths that could have been suitable, this was the one. Oedipus does indeed manifest himself among children at this age. Jung very much agreed, as would anyone who deals with them.

*BS*: Though I have the highest possible admiration for the pioneering work of Freud, whom I enjoy enormously as a pioneer, I think he over-stressed this. Certainly, Oedipal and Electra fixations do normally occur round about three to five. While Freud held that most later mature problems with sexuality grew out of these 'diabolical triangles', or from the original trauma of seeing one's parents in the sexual act, Jung later parted from him on the matter, holding that it was not the whole story. It leaves out a great deal. The child is altogether dependent on the parents' love and understanding and if *that* is seen to be given to another (the other parent, or another child) and is not experienced as coming in to this child, there lies the root of the trouble. The Oedipal thing drops into a natural perspective in the light of the feeling that *I also am acceptable*.

### Archetypal influences

*IGB*: From the Transpersonal point of view, it may *also* be that the archetypes of male and female, of Earth Mother, Mother Spirit, now begin to make an impression. Going back in anthropology through the various cultures, we find initiation rites that quite clearly made that mark. From four to seven, the boys were moved over to the men's world and the girls into the areas of the women, in order to help them re-identify their gender in relation to the archetypes.

*BS*: Frances Wickes writes of dreams told her by child clients which coincide with my own experience: that at around this age there is much division into male and female within the dream content of the child.[61] 'Who is Mother? Who is Father?' Any polarity or ambivalence or contradiction in the parents, and questions will arise about how Father

---

[60]   The Oedipus complex: a boy is fixated on his mother and competes with his father for maternal love and attention. The opposite, the attraction of a girl to her father and rivalry with her mother, is sometimes called the Electra complex.

[61]   Wickes, *The Inner World of Childhood: A Study in Analytical Psychology.* See for example p. 234.

handles his sexuality, how Mother handles her gender-identity. And if the father's task in helping the children establish a separate identity has not been performed, then the archetype will have to take over. The Self itself must somehow begin to express its energy. Even with children who have been with a good-enough parent, the first movement of the contra-sexual nature and the gender-definition of the archetype begin now to be mediated through the Self. It's a matter of identity.

I think that this is what Jung observed: it is this way round. Believing that the libido was much wider than sexuality alone, he held that, though it was possible to make a 'nothing-but' approach from the Oedipus-Electra idea, it was really secondary to this archetypal side. Freud would presumably have accepted the word *archetype*: first came the archetype and everything followed from that. But for him the archetype, the God, would have had to be built in so as to explain everything as being sexual. Taken to the extreme, the Electra and Oedipal myths can make a person de-value their sexual identity, or feel guilty about their own sexuality, which is then set up as a taboo area of guilt and shame.

## Childhood masturbation

At around four to seven years old, both boys and girls tend to move quite naturally and spontaneously into masturbation, as an exploration of the body. I look at it as self-handling, a self-loving, self-identifying self-touch, in order to help establish the outlines. But if touch was one of the taboos, if hugging and holding didn't happen, or only behind closed doors, then it would have been left to the imagination as to whether it was just a gentle sensuality, or whether there was something 'dirty' or 'bad' or 'sexual' about it, of which one should be guilty. The child is too young to make such a distinction so there is confusion. Now, touching as well as sexual exploration, sensuality as well as sexuality, become something that you must not do. And, later, a warm embrace means you are expected to follow through.

Within the first five years any child, if it sees a hole, will want to stick its finger in it. But the environment may have been such that the ordinary normal exploration of the child (and the nature of the holes is less important than the exploration of them) is taken on and they are made to feel bad. 'No!' they're told. 'You mustn't put your finger into wall sockets.' However, you do put your finger into the fingers of your gloves. You don't explore the holes in your own body, or anybody else's. But you do put your leg into this sock, this stocking. It's a crazy world, looked at from the child's point of view.

*IGB*: It is immensely damaging, this total confusion arising from such poor initial understanding. The ancient Greeks were very clear, as far as we can see. It was quite permissible to touch where touch was appropriate. They had divisions and forms of love: *caritas, philias, agape, eros*. But the average middle-aged Westerner of our own times, our own society, has had many problems. Touching was something that rarely if ever happened in the youth of many men in Britain in the twentieth century. For them, there was a massive confusion about sensuality and sexuality. Until well into their forties, a lot of them were quite incapable of having a relationship where they could hold somebody warmly without experiencing it as highly sexual.

*BS*: So any development inevitably involves a splitting off. It seems to be a natural part of the instinct for survival. We have seen the need to go along with it all in order to be acceptable to our setting. Very few small children, at least in the first five years, have the internal strength to stand out against the mores of their times, against their scripting, and to risk cutting off the bough on which they themselves are nested. But as we move up into adolescence, and most of all into adulthood, it becomes essential that we begin to stand out against things which are not who we are, things inappropriate to the seed of our own nature.

## ADOLESCENCE

*If the parent won't let you go,*
*you can't relate sexually to anyone else either*

Someone stuck the name *adolescence* on the phase between ten and eighteen. What is called 'adolescent hysteria ' is likely to be uncontained life-force, natural, instinctual life which is not being given alternative channels in a benign way. It is rising at a time when it is entirely appropriate, yet it has nowhere to go. There are too few channels into which to turn it. Rites of passage would hold all this at an internal level and certainly, in other times and places, the priest or shaman, male or female, would have been around, and the image of the god would have helped hold people through this inevitable stage of growth.

## *The culture*

Culture has an enormous effect on the expression of sexuality. Though some cultures do set up alternatives which are valid, in the West generally this stage often involves trauma because neither the adolescents nor their parents can *wait*. 'Let's get through this awkward and uncomfortable moment in favour of real living.' This in itself is trauma-raising. It is trying to erase a relevant, inevitable stage of awareness. It's going from caterpillar to butterfly without the chrysalis.

Somewhere around the age of ten to twelve, that which is 'good' and therefore gets acceptance and affirmation in our society, and that which is 'bad' and therefore constellates guilt, are quite strongly polarised. Again, if the background has given the child a sense of self, and if that self has been found to be acceptable, they go on with an affirmation of their sexual gender. As the body outline changes and their own sexual energies begin to emerge in a big way, it is to be hoped that they will move into adolescence with a sense of the inner and outer worlds coming together. They will, ideally, be able to relate to the otherness of another person. They will have a reasonably clear-cut sense of the difference between sexuality and the sensuous boundaries of their own body. They will begin to explore, through the senses, the outer world and other people's bodies, and be able to accept those sensuous boundaries – their outline – in a normal, healthy, accepting way. Then they can come later into their own full maturity as sexual beings, as well as becoming the people they are.

*IGB*: The start of adolescence is a threshold period, a transition when we cease to be children. Adolescence is a learning to be an adult. It is not only a sexual awakening, when the major hormonal changes take place, but also a major emotional awakening when we become self-conscious of our feeling nature in a quite new way. And very frequently it is a spiritual awakening too. Something comes in. When there was a reasonable amount of religious culture around, boys and girls would suddenly undergo emotional experiences which had a spiritual connotation. They might begin going to church, whether or not their families were church-goers. This was quite spontaneous, a natural expression of an impulse which does not always come out and usually doesn't last very long; but it is there. For Roman Catholics, Confirmation at around thirteen years old was very appropriate and, among

Episcopalians, so was the First Communion that followed it.

There is a modern anti-hero approach in young people. They will choose their own insignia, their own language, their own dress, go through the 'dirty' stage, letting everything go. And it does not matter that much, because an aesthetic comes in which, though not necessarily religious, has a quality of ritual about it. The obsessive rituals of later years are linked to this particular period. There is a sensate, sensuous adaptation to the world, as well as a sexual one.

## Menstruation

*BS*: If there is a problem at this stage, the blood flow of the girl may well be affected. Perhaps she has amenorrhoea, where the periods do not happen or are interrupted in some way; or they may happen and then there is a holdup. If later we are bringing her back to the acceptance of herself as a sexual being, of herself with her blood flow, we say, 'Look at that symptom as a symbol. What does that remind you of?' This may take her back to an earlier stage, when she was very unsure of what it is to be a woman: 'Is being a woman acceptable in my society?' Is it accept-able in relation to the 'otherness' of the male, or to the sameness of the female? It very frequently relates to how both mother and father handled the earlier matters of psychological gender, and later of sexuality.

*IGB*: For the child of good-enough parents, things are difficult at this time, but manageable. Sensuality and sexuality are clearly distin-guishable. They may both operate together, but they do not have to; it is recognised that they can be different. The young person's self-iden-tity is being established on a firm base. There is a clear distinction between what is masculine and what is feminine. If they are lucky, they will be helped to understand and accept that male and female energies exist in both boys and girls. Their normal desires will be regarded as entirely natural and acceptable and to be enjoyed in a mature way, not just thrown all over the place. And support and advice will be available.

Perhaps I should add that this hardly ever happens, even with good-enough parents.Only pretty good people can make that kind of thing happen. Maybe the next generations will do it.

But with 'problem parents', the distinctions are not made. Confusion is there. Guilt is experienced for every natural impulse and there is very considerable conflict. As the adolescent tries to work out what it's all about, up comes a replay of many of the parent's own problems. What is the son at this stage trying to do? Has he managed to be detached from Mother yet? Is there still a confusion as to who is Mother and who is Father? Is he seeking to emulate Father, or to overcome Father? Is the problem the assertion of his own identity alongside his brothers and sisters? And how does he deal with all this?

### *Anorexia*

*BS*: Anorexia manifests in girls more than in boys. The starving side of it very often involves somebody who has gone too far up the 'good', conforming line in Figure 7 and has not felt acceptable at the 'bad' side. So the anger and the rage and the guilt have been pushed inward and the young person has a very poor self-image. She may make a split between her body and her own inner being, her very soul, trying to diminish the body to the point of its disappearing so that it shall not be seen. Boys will do this too.

*A participant*: I've heard that anorexia can be to do with a death-wish. Also that it often goes with low self-esteem. I know someone with anorexia who says she wants to obliterate herself. However, if you met her, you certainly wouldn't think she had any lack of self-esteem.

*BS*: No, but if, together with the client, you look at how they are outwardly putting up such a very different appearance, you can often penetrate to the low self-image. Given such a lack of self-regard, they can come to the point where they do try literally to obliterate themselves from the scene. Anorexia has very much to do with that. After all, this person does have the anorexia. I am not so sure about a 'death-wish'. Obviously there is such a thing, but I think that what looks like a death-wish is very often a fear of life.

*IGB*: It needn't be the wish to kill oneself totally. Very often the death-wish is the unconscious desire to kill that part of oneself that is causing the difficulty. I have worked with somebody with a very powerfully destructive side to her nature. It was partly mental from the 'thinking' function, partly emotional, and it was always bugging her and getting in the way of relationships. She just hated it. She was therefore trying to destroy the part that was so messing up her life. Oh, the shock and amazement when I suggested that! After two or three sessions, having got to the point where she could see this pattern in what she was doing, she said, 'Well, how can I deal with this? What do I do?' I said, 'Well, first of all you've got to start loving the destructive bit.' Total incomprehension. That kind of self-destruction is, I think, extremely common and may appear as a 'death-wish'.

On the other hand, with the so-called 'greedy', over-eating side of anorexia, the girl may have set up a demand in relation to her sense of deprivation at a deep emotional level; she is being fed on the wrong emotional food. Or it may have stemmed from being literally over-fed by the parents. Fat is a defence against over-feeding, against having something thrust into you that you do not want. Very often, fatness is protection against what turns out to have been like a rape of the soul. The early handling was so bad that, later, the young person wishes to die of it. There was no sense of being defined as a body, or of the senses being acceptable.

### Lack of touch

We know that if children, like Rhesus monkeys, have no handling, it doesn't matter how much nourishment, shelter and warmth they may be given, they will actually die from lack of touch. Anorexia has a lot to do with the effort to die because one hasn't had the opportunity to receive an outline through being handled. A colleague told me this story:

*I worked with a residential group of youngsters aged between seventeen and twenty-five. They had been kicked out of their homes and were mixing up a lot amongst themselves, going to bed with each other, and we had quite a bit of discussion. Almost all of them said that it was the touching that was the most important thing. Most of them said they wanted to curl up together, it didn't matter which way round. They wanted to be children but, because of their older adolescent bodies, they got into sex. They insisted that they often didn't want to get into sex, but it was difficult not to. There was this tremendous confusion. It was good that they could talk about it at all. They had simply never experienced that holding, that bonding process.*

*However, it was very difficult for us to hold it. It was seen and we had to close the place down because of public opinion. There was so much stuff going on that we couldn't work it through without many more staff and it all became too much. If there had been a lot of adults there who understood, we might have got much further.*

*Confusion, touch, holding.* We know how terribly important these words are. They form a progression marked by impulses of the individual, whether in 'normal' or 'variant' forms, as we try at various stages to find some outlining. On that interface, we are seeking *definition* between inner and outer. We seek the outlining of the body (being out of touch – in touch – later doing it through the touch of others) if not through somebody else's touch then trying to do it with our own. If that is successful, it's going to lead to sensual definition, then gender definition, then sexual definition, then maturational definition. But if a split appears, it will build on a split that builds on another split and, at the end of that, we are quite desperately searching for – whatever.

### Teenage fantasy and masturbation

In both boys and girls, masturbation is often related to imaging and romanticising. It comes naturally, and will naturally drop into an appropriate proportion. Most *adults* masturbate at some time or other, and though not all *adolescents* do of any age, it is still a very normal pattern from about ten onwards. If it is handled well within the environment, if the child feels not too heavy an amount of 'bad' and 'guilt' around it, they will quite spontaneously do it and then pass through it.

Here, on the threshold of puberty, what has gone on previously shows up clearly. At around twelve to fourteen, masturbatory fantasies and impulses in both boys and girls surface together. They come in as a way of exploration of the self, of getting a sense of our own spatial boundaries from within, and they can be held by somebody who's had the right hold and a sense of their own gender. Romantic idealism comes out also, a poetic side of us, an interweaving, a plaiting of spirit and matter, sexuality and spirituality which is quite often a very real religious or spiritual impulse.

Not only can the way a girl's periods are handled at this interface very much affect her whole sexual life but, in the same way, starting at around ten, how her masturbation is handled. Both of them are transitions over to some more mature stage. Boys particularly turn to the sublimation of sexual energy into masturbation. There is nothing else to do with it, and it is a way of handling their energies very naturally. However, the masturbation side, the handling of himself and his phallus, may well be so charged with guilt that it will have taken the side of his covert rather than his overt, natural life.

The difficulty comes when the masturbation and the romanticised imaging become a replacement for relating with the outside world. Then, the attempt to relate is all taken back to the person as subject, and not taken forward into the objective world as a natural stage on the way to relating, and eventually to intercourse with another body and with the outside world. Quite a number of men emerge into adult life with it all still held back at this level. The fantasy side and the masturbation are for them more real than the reality with another body. It is only then that it passes over into becoming a difficult area, having many ramifications with people of the opposite sex. This might well drive some people towards relating with their own sex, not because that is something inherent in them, but for them unnaturally, as a way of handling it.

### *Independence from parents*

Sexual guilt and the failure to become independent are one and the same thing. If you cannot get free of your parents, if they will not let you go for some reason, then you are bound to suffer from sexual guilt. Under the taboos in all cultures, you cannot usually relate sexually to the parent. So now, if the parent won't let you go, you can't relate sexually to anyone else either. You are stuck half in and half out, in a state of suspended guilt.

If a man or a woman is suffering from a great deal of guilt, if that is one of their great problems in relating, then we need to check the degree to which they are still dependent on their parents. The guilt is so entwined with the nursery, so often do the two coincide, as to make two sides of the one coin. However, the unavoidable struggle to emancipate the small ego-self, and ultimately the Self with the large 'S', from the ground of the nursery is the story of human growth. An acorn has to go into the ground if the oak tree is to appear. If it's kept cramped in a small pot for so long that the root can't grow properly – too confined, or too over-extended – then naturally the oak tree is not going to occur.

We have to have the splitting. But it can all be held together by the sense that we are affirmed.

And so, together with sexuality and sensuality and the joy of exploration and the love of aesthetics as well, we move towards adulthood. Now it is to be hoped that sexuality can drop into a different perspective, becoming a foreground at one time and a background at another. Can we not go into relationships with a sense of the joy of relating and the beauty of relationship?

## YOUNG ADULTHOOD

*Are we going to leave home?*

### *Relationship*

Coming up to fifteen to eighteen, we begin to relate to the other sex or, quite confidently, to explore our own. It is during this period that, through bonding and mating, touch and hold with another human being, we are helped to grow up. Some person from another tribe comes in and helps us move away from our own immediate family, from our own tribal customs, to relate to the otherness out there. If we cannot find that other person, becoming independent is that much more difficult. This is a real testing point. Have we in fact moved away from childhood's dependency on the original nursery? Are we going to leave home? This will determine the kind of person we choose as our mate, male or female, other or our own kind.

In every pair, heterosexual or homosexual, one will have a predominance of masculine consciousness and impulses, and the other of feminine. How we express our sexuality is determined by their balance. Even somebody fairly clear, coming from a supportive environment, will be very much conditioned in the partner they choose by the extent to which they are living out of this aspect of their nature. Leaving our adolescence with a reasonable sense of our own gender, a familiarity with and acceptance of our own body-outline, we won't have that muddle between sensuality and sexuality. The first touch, hold and bonding will have un-plaited the two, put us in touch with our senses, allowed us to befriend our sensuality and made it quite easy later on to extrapolate out to sexuality.

But how many of us get it wrong? We go forward into relationships and now the expectations are not just parental. All sorts of other bombardments are coming in from the environment. Young adults can find themselves very much prey to their own times, very uncertain of themselves. Life is difficult. Problems with their own sexuality are for many a cause of great distress, and may take time to come out. Is adolescence really behind them? Now, at a subliminal level, it is the adolescent within who is most vulnerable to these pressures.

*BS*: Anthony Storr commented that both advertisers and adolescents (I like that) imagine other people as having supreme sexual confidence. A 'dreadful Utopia' is portrayed in the media, where handsome men stride through life secure in their masculinity, and beautifully undressed women possess a nonchalant elegance, a sophisticated assurance of being feminine. Never at a loss, serene and poised, each faces the world in the calm certainty of their own supreme desirability.[62] A lot of adults are still trying to live out their own form of sexuality and relationship on the basis of such images built up and ingested in their own particular youth.

However, the more intimately we become acquainted with even the most sexually successful of human beings, the more we realise that these men and women are not real, and never were. Don Juan is a little boy; highly promiscuous people are incapable of love; the most ravishingly attractive exterior may conceal the profoundest inner uncertainty.

### The marriage bed

It is extraordinary the problems that people have, in their beds and out of their beds, and in other people's beds, and how they very seldom talk about it until they really trust and it starts coming out. I think it is wise to bear that in mind, because many people go through agonies about all this. And the pain they suffer is because they never know for sure how the other person functions in all this. They feel, 'Everybody else has got it roughly hung together except us – except me!' Their feeling of sexual adequacy or inadequacy conditions the whole of their lives and their sense of potency or impotency can affect and erode every aspect of living in a most extraordinary way.

*IGB*: For the early experimental periods, our choice of partners is often fine; but what about the people we bed down with for a long

---

62  See Storr, *The Art of Psychotherapy*.

period? We may choose them to contain our excess or to express our inhibition. Sometimes we find those very people who will, we feel, help us to be good children – or give us permission to be naughty children. Then two naughty children, each seeking something, end up together, neither able to fulfil that function for the other. And so they get angry with each other.

*BS*: One man told me: 'I am being raped by my wife!' It's not easy for a woman to rape a man, but emotionally he can be raped by a woman's *expectation* of him. This man came to realise that, yes, it was the expectation that he felt coming from her. The question of potency and impotency arose. How far had he emerged from childhood? He had begun to dream of trains coming out of and going into tunnels and the dream motif led him back to these expectations of 'the marriage bed'. Was the phallus still embedded in the mother-rock of the nursery-ground?

Whether someone is married or not, they need to get out of that bed. Some people, up-tight as anything in their own bed, can perform marvellously behind the sofa or in the garage. And some people *should* make love under the kitchen table, in the middle of the day, after a good and cheerful lunch and a couple of pints of beer. That may be what the psyche requires. Only when they are away and out of that bed of the stereotypes are they freed, finding dimensions of themselves they never knew they had, dimensions of each other. Perhaps they once had to share the family home and were worried about noises coming through walls, and over the years they have modified themselves into a set pattern. Now, given a little bit of insight, they might ask, '*What* is it that was so modified?'

While we were exploring his sexual imaging, another client (who works with the body and is very conscious of his own) noticed that the muscles at the backs of his thighs were losing strength; his legs were going completely weak. When I asked, 'What does that remind you of?' he said it was of having his legs lifted up to have his nappy changed. By following that through, we reached to his mother's attitude. She had touched him quite a lot in the upper part of his body but as she'd raised his legs he'd sensed a sudden ambivalence. He went and talked about it with his mother. She told him that when his father, away in the army, had come home, she had become very aware of her husband's jealousy of this boy.

'Were you potty trained by then?' I asked.

'I haven't the faintest idea. I seem to remember having to have my nappy changed. Did that happen rather late, I wonder?' The mother now told my client that she had deliberately held back certain stages of her child's development so that her husband might feel connected with his own baby stages. Just look what that raises in terms of ambivalence. The suggestion now was simply that he change his direction in bed. Was there a foot-board? 'No, but there is a head-board.' So, he could turn to the other end, put his feet against the head-board and give himself a sense of some grounding under his feet. This possibility of a grounding under his feet, this perfectly obvious, normal, natural suggestion, made a tremendous difference to him.

The ebb and flow, the timing, is very important with sexual energy. Women's major complaint concerns lack of time. They are being rushed, there's not enough sensitivity. Quite frequently a man *needs* to rush or he's never going to get up his head of steam or whatever. People need help to tie in the rhythms of their dance much more effectively. They get into terrible habits and can be so blocked over sexuality and sensuality that they don't experiment at all, with changes of posture or with anything else.

A lot of work is done with sexual therapy and in groups to help with this. It is a long process. We are all a bit unsure in this area and counsellors can compound the taboo if they're not careful. It needs treating just like any other energy.

## RELIGION AND MYSTICISM

*Some do it through sexuality; and some do it by trying*
*not to do it through sexuality*

In any culture in which body and soul, inner and outer, love and the senses are split apart, a god 'up there' will be needed. A god up there is not in the body, so then you will have to have a devil 'down here'. Whereas if God is immanent from the beginning, and in the joy of the senses, we can say, 'I salute the God in me, I salute the God in you. God is *here*.' It's no longer, 'Forgive us miserable sinners, there is no health in us', which is all we can say when God is cast into the shadow from out there. We no longer need heaven and hell, brimstone and punishment and guilt. The puritan ethic is a result of that, a symptom of this splitting apart. So we end up with as our symbol the crucified Christ, instead of the Lord Triumphant resurrected into His body.

In the complex life of any person, the maturing process may have been quickened when leaders and hero figures came in as well as, or instead of, the parent. Guides, masters, older people, the shaman, the priest, the hierophant, one's own dreams and synchronous happenings, all these may have been exceedingly valuable. I have known people who met a spiritual guru when they themselves were experiencing the earliest, most poetic, most imaginative of their own spiritual impulses. And the sexual impulse comes up at exactly this point in early adolescence and can later be deeply intertwined with the spiritual or religious urge.

## 'Rise above it!'

However, like the not-good-enough parent saying 'Ugh, don't do that!' my experience is that too many of these would-be 'wise' figures say to young people, 'That is not good. Sublimate it, go up the mountain, rise above it!' And that's just at the time when he or she needs to *come down into it*, to come to terms with their own sexuality. Any guru who says, 'If you're going to serve God, then you have to ignore your sexuality', and therefore takes young men and women into seminaries and convents – well, that is to split apart heaven and earth. I have met a number of dedicated religious people who have gone early into monasteries and so on, and then later are absolutely crucified (yes, little short of crucifixion) by the split that has been caused between their natural sexuality and their calling.

But didn't our own adolescence have as much to do with spiritual, religious impulses as it had to do with sexuality? It is in sexuality, very often for the first time, that we are overwhelmed by something bigger than ourselves. Perhaps it's the nearest thing we ever have to a mystical, religious experience. Is it an orgasm of the body, or an orgasm of the soul? This must be one of the reasons why mystics of all cultures speak so much in sexual language: no other language can so well express it. The two experiences are tremendously close together.

## Libido

What is the life-force, the libido? Jung saw sexuality as but one of the strong fibres in a many-stranded life-cord,[63] as important a strand as any, and deeply intertwined. If a person's creativity is blocked, if they are loaded with stereotypes, if they are not expressing this life-force, then the sexual side, which is as much a symptom as a symbol of their whole life's energy, is bound to be affected. The sexual drive is in exact proportion; it has as much importance as the religious drive, or the energy-drive, or people's drive to handle their money. But the trouble is that if other areas are blocked, sexual energy is either going to be overwhelmingly banging at the door to be let out, or is going to be diminished.

### Lack of libido?

Someone working in a sex clinic told me that people are routinely asked: 'Gauge your sex drive out of ten: zero, you do not have any sexual thoughts at all; ten, you are constantly thinking of it.' It would seem that sex is being seen here as a 'clinical' matter. These questions, useful in a general sense, may well tend to lose the individual. But he said one of the most common complaints was *lack* of this energy. People told, not that they couldn't get physically aroused, but that they were just not interested. Certainly some people who 'have no sexual libido' may not have much libido elsewhere either. Their overall energy, rather than going to a different place, may be running dry. However, might they not be in a state of profound internal change within themselves? Perhaps they are introverting and internalising energy and are not ready to act it out. Or again, might somebody who apparently has no life-force at all, never mind sexual force, not fall in love with an idea, or a project, or meet somebody different, releasing a sudden, unprecedented energy-flow? They could tick zero one minute and five, maybe ten, the next.

It is quite common for writers and sculptors and painters, when into their work, to have practically no sexual energy at all; and then it surfaces again. It is highly phasic. The birth of an idea, the birth of a book can often be the same sexual and spiritual experience as the birth of a child. There are many ways of 'giving birth to', and certainly the creative artist experiences that moment. You open your spirit to let in the creative flow and let it out again: you open your body to let in a child, and open your body to let a child out again. It is tremendously

---

63    Jung spoke of libido as life-force, with sexuality as but one strand in the whole cord. See, for example, Jung, *The Structure & Dynamics of the Psyche*, CW Vol. 8, para 54.

close, I think. And, through their senses, some people have to open to let life in and be 'raped by experience'. Many people keep their sexual and sense centres closed because they are frightened of such experience. Certainly those who, in adulthood, are still in the nursery do not have any such possibility.

## Celibacy

There are those who can choose either to take sex or let it go. They are not overwhelmed by it. They *choose*: that's the difference. They may decide that sex is part of the joy and libation and orison of life, and include it in their mode of expressing the energy that is in them, the wisdom of their understanding. Or they may choose not to. But very few, even among the truly wise people I have met, are in this position.

Though few people choose celibacy, yet for certain individuals it is true, proper and right to do so. These are the born celibates. We find them among reincarnated lamas, among priests who remain celibate because they have a true vocation to the religious life. For these people, not to be celibate would be a blasphemy against their nature. Meeting a person who seems to have 'no sexual libido' and wondering where all their life-force is going, we may be making judgements on libido in terms of sexuality alone. This is, as we have seen, to miss the alternatives. They may well be putting their energy quite naturally into some other area. For them, it would be outrageous to suggest anything else. We need to talk to the individual on the subject in a much wider sense. Yes, some of them may need to go out and do the sexual bit at another time. But there are natural celibates.

*IGB*: It is significant that the Roman Catholic church is *Mother* Church. You do not find that in the Protestant churches, while in Anglicanism there are rifts: only high Anglicans will refer to 'Mother Church'. And the body of Mother Church will draw men who do not wish to use their sexuality in a physical way. They are drawn to the *body* of something and the body they are drawn to is often clearly definable as a male or a female body within the Church. It is interesting to see which orders people are drawn into; the Jesuits differ from the Franciscans, for instance. We think of the heroic within the sphere of initiation. A boy with an absent father might commonly have found an older man, perhaps in school or church, to stand in for both father and hero. Often it goes further back still. The impulse that took the person into the order may be to do with being self-initiated into a deeper mystery. Some do it through sexuality, and some do it by trying not to do it through sexuality.

### The snake

*BS*: This time-honoured symbol of the life-force, the *kundalini* power, lies coiled at the base *chakra*.[64] How does the snake come into the dream or image? The horizontal snake is very often energy that was down in the instinctual life. All yogas, including Tantric yoga and all the disciplines, are about the stilling and controlling of the snake, and then the rising of the snake and the taking of it up vertically through the centres. Miss one junction and you have missed the connection. Nobody ever misses the sexual centre. The risen snake, with its great cobra head extended, is an example of the rising of the life-force through all the centres. The snake is a symbol at every level.

We have been given a fundamental slant from the beginning. The cultural and educational split of the West into mind and body, two separate compartments, has become the major split. But at an even wider level, which *includes* that split between mind and body, there is a split between body and soul. The mind, which needs to be seen as a wonderful *instrument*, is presumably meant to be a bridge and a transitional object between body and soul. The trouble is that body and soul are already cut too far from each other, and the mind does not know where to place itself. It boggles! But stand with your mind in the interface, and body and soul – or earth and heaven, inner and outer, objective and subjective – come together again in a different way. Whereas if you put your mind as one of the polarities, you lose the perspective of the interface.

So the mind boggles. But the imagination plays with all this. And of course it is when the senses are still and not getting in the way, when the body is not rampant, that the mind is most clear. I feel that the mind's is the right reaction to all this. It should boggle; boggling in the sense of awe. We are trying to live with a deeper understanding which, in this area at least, may in itself be wordless and therefore would hate to be translated from symptom into symbol. I suppose we are all 'variant' on this, but I would find it very difficult to hold a good

---

[64] *Kundalini*, see Gordon-Brown & Somers, *The Raincloud of Knowable Things*, Chapter 8, pp. 311-322.

mental conversation when I was enjoying the heights of love. It is a non-verbal moment, isn't it? Words bring it down. Death, life, rebirth, religion, non-religion, these are of the *tremendum* of life, and sexuality is certainly one of those areas where words fall short. As with all the big experiences, how to put it into words?

Nonetheless, in a desperate situation, counsellors need mental maps and models. We do have to use our minds. Many people are tied up with sex, their own and other people's ideas of it, and when someone comes in with a sexual problem we find ourselves *having* to talk about it. However, non-verbal therapy can be tremendously helpful with a couple having sexual difficulties. One of the very first suggestions may be that they don't sit there talking about it, but actually lie side by side and entangle their feet and their hands and let their bodies begin to speak. Often, the suggestion is not to go immediately towards or into intercourse, but to let that be a later thing. It is the touch of the body, the getting to know each other, the learning to trust again in order to be open at the sense level, defining and affirming the body. And it is about outlines. All that is absolutely non-verbal. It is like poetry, where words themselves evoke the ineffable. Or mystical experience. Is it not itself such a *tremendum*?

## SEXUAL MATURITY

*A quality of aesthetics and a love for and celebration of beauty are ... available to every human being*

Sexual maturity is the human history of the movement from childhood dependency on parents to mature relationships on an equal basis with another human being. It will include sexuality, unless a person decides that sexuality is not part of their life, and then their celibacy is by an act of choice, not by compulsion. And, conversely, a truly equal relationship between two people does, I believe, include a quality of mature dependency. A lot of people talk about being *in*dependent. But sometimes we wish to be seen to be vulnerable, to lean on the other person, and at other times we wish to be strong and able to help support and sustain the other person's vulnerability.

*IGB*: Mature relating does not consist in having a perfect relationship at every level. Sexual maturity is loving the other, coping with the difficulties and imbalances that one is bound to find, and not expecting the perfection of which one reads in novels, where the definition of sexual maturity as 'the ability to have complete orgasm' may often be left standing. A lot of people knot themselves up in every possible sense because of that definition. It is not any measure whatever of maturity.

*BS*: Many people are released into sexual freedom after the expectations of parenthood are gone or have been taken away from them. The man who happens to be a father (and it's that way round) is inevitably challenged by seeing his son growing up behind him. He sees a young stag coming up towards his full velvet and his first seasons. In exactly the same way, and this is simply how it is to be human, a great number of women resent their daughters' sexuality. It is always a threat to a woman who happens also to be a mother. 'No, dear, you *can't* wear a bra!' She's going to be challenged by this nubile young woman, fresh and clear. 'I do wish you wouldn't look like that!' she hears herself saying. Or, 'With your hair – your nose – you really can't wear those.' Both parents can hide and try to suppress this as much as they like: 'I ought not to feel like that.' But once they recognise that it is not a guilt-making thing, it's amazing how they can begin to befriend their own natures and actually be quite happy to let go and see these fine young people go out.

And with another person, or other people, maturely sexual people may explore their variations on the sexual and sensuous dance of life, and the childlike qualities of play may well become added to them. Many who have enjoyed sex and have had pretty good attitudes towards the give and take of it over the years will in their fifties and sixties (and sometimes their seventies and eighties and on) bring in a childlike quality of dance, which is a celebration of life, playing together in the most beautiful way. Being in touch with the senses leads them to the sensuous which then eventually involves the sexual. It brings to them a quality of aesthetics and a love for and celebration of beauty which are an absolute joy to behold.

People like that very rarely lose their sexual potency unless for some very good external reason, but come up as the years go by into a potency that they never experienced earlier. They have a freedom of access. I knew one lovely woman who was for about forty-five years without any sexuality, having lost her husband during the war. But she kept celebrating life and stayed in touch with herself. She had a number of outlets in the world which for her were sublimations of the sexual rather than replacements of it. And when finally she came into a relationship with a man in her middle sixties, it was with a vast joy. She was not out of touch; she had a body like a young woman and danced like one. And a number of men too, who thought perhaps in their forties and fifties that they were impotent, have rediscovered a quality of potency in themselves that is much wider than the strictly social. And, though not everyone stays in touch with it, it is available to every human being.

Inner Planes

# CHAPTER ELEVEN

# Sexual Variation

## Barbara Somers and Ian Gordon-Brown

*Sexuality belongs right at the heart of what we're doing.*
*It is very close to spirituality*

People are very relieved, after a while, to discover that someone is prepared to listen and to talk about the mode of sexuality and its variations. There is a tremendous need for all this to be involved and it is most important for counsellors working from a Transpersonal perspective to stand at the interface with this particular subject. The drive to sexual expression is very much woven with the religious drive, as we have seen. We are dealing with libido, the life-force in human beings. Sexuality belongs right at the heart of what we're doing. It is very close to spirituality.

Sexual variation is an extremely colourful area of the human psyche and Figure 7, Adult Sexuality (page 145) shows where it arises. Human beings show as much imagination in their departures from the so-called 'norm' of sexuality as in any other area of their lives. We looked earlier at the hysteric, depressive and schizoid positions that people take at the interface, adopting that stance in order to make some kind of balance, aiming towards a *modus vivendi* despite whatever may be happening to them. And at the interface, people are likewise very often drawn or driven over by the pressures of their lives into variations from the 'normal' sense of sexuality. They will, perhaps rightly, only let go of these if they can find another way of communicating. My own belief is that these variations are about an emergence into adolescence.

# SEXUAL UNCERTAINTY

*Sexual variations … are unconscious ways of trying to redeem
the gap between sensuality and sexuality*

*IGB*: Given good luck and good subsequent experience, any gaps
between sensuality and sexuality, inner and outer worlds, can be passed
over and healed and, later on, will lose their threat. But if the ground
for the distinction hasn't been laid during childhood, there is a very
shaky balance afterwards. If this inequality emerges strongly again in
adolescence, if there is another bad experience now, it can be very
difficult to redeem. Much work will be needed later on. This is a key
area. A lot of the movements people make that are called 'sexual
variations', are unconscious ways of trying to redeem the gap between
sensuality and sexuality.

The developmental processes of the child are powerfully relevant
here, and the patterning of the mother and the father. A client with a
sexual problem can almost always trace a very large part of it back, not
only to the initial patterning and bonding, but to the nature of the parental
relationship. What was going on between the parents? What was the
interaction between them and the child? A strong mother-tie may well
reflect, for example, that the father was weak or inadequate or absent.

*BS*: People who go over into the kinds of sexuality seen as
'variations' are particularly muddled as to what is sensuous and what is
sexual. They have not been given an outline of themselves, nor a sense
of the sensuous. Getting this muddled can make for apparently very
strange areas. But if one can go with their search, however strange or odd
the form it takes, they can be helped to recognise it is a search through
sexuality for an understanding of the nature of sensuality. Very often it is
a plea for some delineation of that. They can see that the two belong
together and that intercourse is communication. We help them link with
touch, the feel of the earth, ecology, beauty; and the tactile arts and
aesthetics can be thrown in. We are not trying to persuade them away
from the unusual form that their sexuality has taken, but to help them run
in something in parallel with it. Some people show great imagination in
their variations, and that imagination can be mobilised to help a different
form, until by degrees they choose one rather than the other. The old one
just drops away. It is quite extraordinary.

Pictured on the left of Figure 8 is the line of *sexual uncertainty*, which can lead to transvestism and transgender issues. Homosexuality can also stem from this uncertainty, though it may well be something else altogether.

The central *guilt* line of 'bad' (contrasted with 'good') may take us up into areas of sexuality which have more to do with things than with people. The person is still working on the continuous effort to relate objective and subjective.

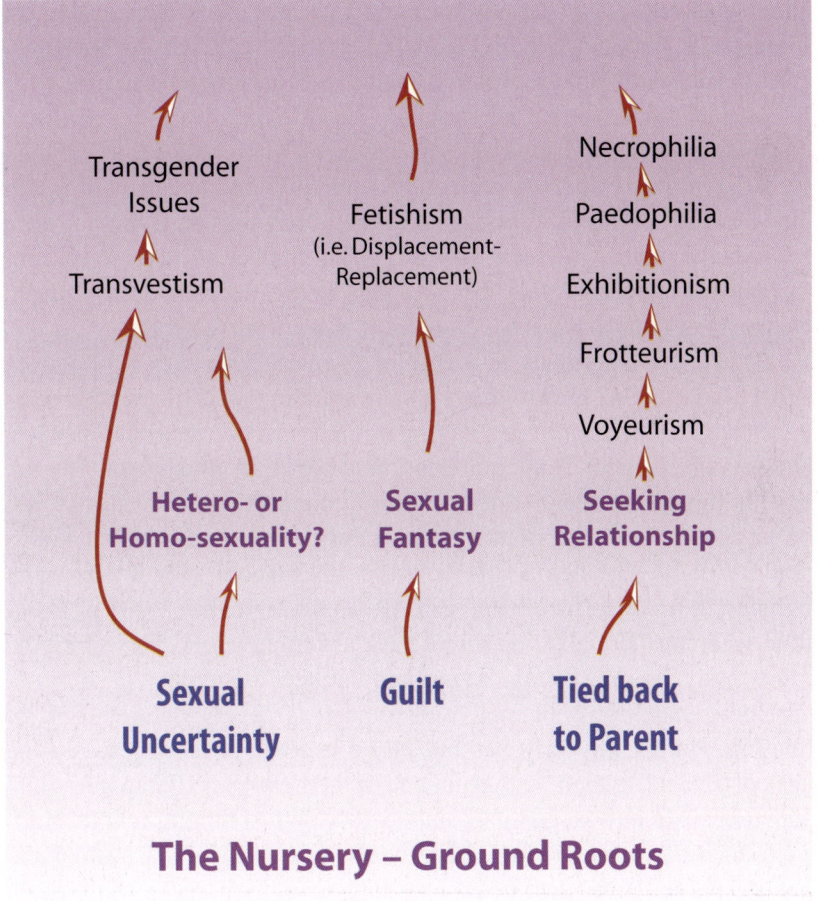

Figure 8. Sexual Variation

On the right, being 'tied back to parent' is an outcome of the early guilt of the person bonded, *tied back* into dependency. It might manifest externally as a symptom in the form of exhibitionism, frotteurism, voyeurism, paedophilia and so on.

## Homosexuality

So we get to know our client as a human being and a person and then aim to discover with them their psychological gender. It can be quite a journey; we cannot presume anything. When I first meet someone, I work with them on the understanding that I do not know their gender until I have explored with them for quite a long time.

Both men and women are having to discover new ways of relating to themselves and to each other, as sexual beings. Many women, as we shall see, are turning to other women for the tenderness and understanding that they feel they do not find in men. A woman may thus be trying to relate towards the mother in a new way. An equal number of men are relating to each other because they cannot stand being threatened by women. Neither might, otherwise, have related in a homosexual way.

'This client is living with a man' begs a very necessary exploration. What kind of man? How old is the man, what in fact is his gender, what is he like? Someone can be, say, masculine in body and intellect, yet emotionally female. That complication is not at all unusual, and it may have nothing whatever to do with the muddle in the nursery. It may just be how they are. One of the biggest, most 'male' men that I know, imaging what lay below his belt (he talks about a belt which he tightens in order to face life), said, 'It's a young child, a girl of about four, weeping.' Equally you might have a woman who is very feminine in her body, but her feeling nature and intellect are male.

Homosexuality, both male and female, is a very natural form of relating. Hardly anybody has not fallen in love, at least between the ages of ten and sixteen, with someone of their own sex. It happens quite spontaneously and is a natural and healthy part of human relationship.

*IGB*: Being attracted to somebody of one's own sex is a normal and natural phase. I was at a boys' boarding school where, in those days, there were no women around and there was a lot of homosexuality of a relatively innocent and relatively temporary kind. Older boys fell for younger ones, at least in that particular environment. If there was no young, attractive, nubile girl around, then there were plenty of new boys who still looked like them.

*BS*: How was it handled then? What was the original condition and pre-disposition for it? What climate did the person carry inside them, influencing whether they continued on that path? Did they drift into male or female homosexuality as the line of least resistance? Is it actually *against* their own nature in later life? Were they initiated at this very vulnerable stage into a form of relating that was *not* normal to them?

On the other hand, it may well be truly natural to them. Some people are quite normally bi-sexual or naturally one-sexed. We saw how the Greeks had their divisions of the forms of loving: *eros, agape, caritas*. It was taken as quite usual that men related to men up to the moment that they wished to become householders and set up a family. Only then did they relate to women.

But we are looking here at those who construe homosexuality as a problem, those forced into it by causes other than their own natural tendencies. There are a number of reasons why people may be pushed over into homosexuality *against* the grain of their own natural seed:

*Neither boy nor girl is helped to find their own sexual gender if, during the period of childhood dependency, they are given poor patterning as to what is 'masculine' and what 'feminine'.*

*They may have had the sense that they were the wrong gender for the parents' wishes.*

*Or that there was a muddle between who was parent and who was not parent. Did the child have to 'parent' the adults?*

*'In your childhood, who was father, who was mother?' is a terribly important question. We cannot just presume that they are talking about the parent of that gender.*

*And it is not just what is said to them; what is implicit in the environment will affect how they feel about their own gender.*

*Psychologically, we may be speaking to a man who's naturally female, or a woman who is naturally male. We can presume nothing in this area till we know who we are talking to.*

If it is seen as a problem, the tendency to relate to one's own sex, male or female, is often regarded from outside as a flight from the opposite sex. 'He's running away from the feminine' is commonly heard. The young man's wanting to relate to men more than to women is perceived either as an 'unconscious pull away from the mother', the original womb; or perhaps as an attempt to get back into the original womb, the matrix.

But I believe we have to look at it in terms of a search for manhood which he could never otherwise have discovered because he was never free of the body of the mother. The young hero has to withdraw his sword from the earth and from water before he can go on the heroic quest. Often he does in fact discover his manhood through the body of another man, pursuing his own individuality, laying claim to his own phallus in a very distinct way. It makes him feel more male and less threatened by the female to discover his masculine drive through another man.

## Lesbianism

*IGB*: I understood from my sisters that the tendency amongst girls, in the earlier part of the twentieth century at least, was to be attracted to those slightly older – the typical schoolgirl passion for an older girl or for a member of staff. What was happening there? Though this can be a natural expression, it is possible to become fixated in it and, working in imaging, we can often get some notion as to what age the person was when the fixation started. Also, where a woman is drawn towards the love of women, she also may sometimes be trying to find a quality of relationship that was absent with the mother. Perhaps the mother's implicit view of men was not very good. The scripting she gave her daughter may have been pretty harsh towards men and her fear of masculinity was handed down.

However, as with male homosexuality, certain women are quite definitely and fundamentally drawn to women rather than to men. Work with them and we will find their psyche is very authentically lesbian.

Again, at twelve to fourteen, the draw towards her or his own sex may be a classic impulse to a further initiatory ritual, for the girl as well as the boy. Lacking initiation through the mother, she is seeking another woman with whom to initiate herself into the feminine mysteries. The moment of initiation into the mysteries of male and female is quite as much the eruption of an archetype as a sexual thing, particularly in people on a growth path. This is one way of looking at lesbianism.

*BS*: One of my clients said, 'I needed to have someone of whom I could say, "Well, that is a woman, and that is what I am." Because I couldn't look to my mother; she wasn't a woman as far as I was concerned.' Or perhaps the father himself was absent, or not strong enough, or punitive. We are all growing out of some inadequacy.

'I am the daughter of a lesbian mother,' said another, a woman who was also a mother. She was asking for help to let go of her sexual guilt and her failure to become mature. Wondering exactly what the pattern had been, and hoping to pick up the chain at some point, I asked, 'What is your feeling today about yourself as a woman?' Only by degrees was she brought round to recognising the question. 'I had a lesbian mother' wasn't enough; it wasn't useful, it was just a description. Why was her mother lesbian? What did lesbianism really mean to the mother that was now affecting the daughter? And, very particularly, what had happened to the girl in the years approaching adolescence when her own gender had emerged? What had she picked up by then which was now affecting her mature relationships? Only as far as my client could now relate to herself as a woman would she begin to relate to the woman-ness in her *own* young daughter. Only now, as mother, could she lose her commitment to the mother role, which is what holds daughters. Only then would she set her daughter free.

### Woman seeks the sensual

*IGB*: Generally, my sense is that a woman is drawn towards the sensual. What she is looking for is tenderness, is touch. Very much less often is she looking only for sexuality, unless she is truly and validly lesbian. It is nearly always that she's wanting hold and comfort for the senses. It is very much an emotional matter.

*BS*: And I hear repeatedly that a number of women choose to go with women because, as we saw, they do not find in men the degree of sensuous, sensitive, emotional understanding that they find in women. Which is sad. And it is very true, because so many men are caught into the male stereotype. There is a real problem here. Society is aware at last of the difficulties of women, but men have difficulties too. They have had to put up with at least two thousand years' worth of stereotypes of what men are supposed to be. That is a tremendous weight on them. Lots of them simply cannot be as sensitive as they might wish, which is why some women are having to turn to women. And that doesn't help men to feel more phallic at all.

Nothing throws up more how far we are in touch with our own sexuality than the way we deal with it as a subject in counselling. Certainly it is leaving out a tremendous amount not to include sexuality as part of a natural movement in our clients' lives. If there is a man or a woman with a lot of masculine energy in our counselling room, then sexuality is straightforward and eventually the subject should come up; and it needs to be looked at straight. Feminine energy too, of course. But with women, unless we are dealing specifically with female sexuality, we are nearly always talking more about relationships and interaction. She is very often searching for the sensuous, the touch, the hold, the feel. She is seeking the feminine principle, whether it be in a man or woman, rather than straight, direct, phallic sexuality. This applies to any hetero- or homosexual pair where the feminine principle is high.

In whatever way a person emerges into mature human relationships, it's to be hoped that they will stay true to their nature. The majority do know who they are. It is very sad if someone feels *un*naturally pushed over to the other kind of sexuality in order to handle it. However, I've seen some very rocky and peculiar marriages between a man and a woman, and I've seen a lot of single-sex relationships which are modes of adapting and which do work. Some of the best 'marriages' I know are partnerships over many years between two men or between two women.

## Transvestism

Dressing to a different gender is often muddled with homosexuality, but it doesn't at all follow. Transvestism, the desire to dress in the other gender's clothes, is something different. It is usually a way of relating to your own sex. Sometimes a man does dress as a woman for homosexual reasons but a lot of men are transvestite and it is not about that. Transvestism has a lot to do with the interface. It involves both men and women, it is a very blurred area and it is also to do with the culture. We think of the ancient Greeks, of Chinese mandarins and Arab sheikhs, the transvestite made legitimate. When priests are drawn towards their vocation they change into female garb, becoming, in women's clothes, servers of the god. In war, again, the changes of men's dress were totally acceptable and seen as being manly. Look at the kilts of the Celts.

## Phallic women

Sometimes a person has to be a phallic woman to break away from woman in order to relate. In wars throughout history, women have dressed as men. Look at fashion through the centuries and see the way in which women protected their wartime vulnerability by looking like men. This was also in order not to deflect the hero on his journey when he needed to be military. In times of peace, we see their dress changing back and tending towards the feminine again.

Even in these days, it is obviously much easier for a woman to dress in man's clothes than it is for a man to dress in woman's. And often a woman is more free to be female when she is wearing a man's clothes. A female transvestite will nearly always go for rough, male-type fabrics, tweedy, hairy, smoky, blankety, rough-feeling. Then she will, for example, sit with her legs apart, she will stride around, speak out for herself, claim her ground. Wearing that garb she is no longer under the weight of expectation that is put on her by feminine clothes. She feels she is out of the area of threat that goes with being dressed as a woman. Again, we cannot presume we are looking at sexual variation. It may actually be sensual adaptation.

## Transvestite men

I know several absolutely normal, healthy, well-adapted men who have this impulse to wear female clothes. In the gentler garb, some men most feel their manhood, their strength. I have known a number of men declaring themselves transvestite who have said they feel more manly dressed as women. That may seem unusual and yet it makes a lot of sense. When a man dresses cross-sexually he will go for the softer, filmier things: satin, silk, gossamer. Sometimes he will talk with me about how much pleasure he gains from the colour and the touch and the sensuous feeling involved in the change of garb. The texture he's wearing, the flimsy things in lilac, the feminine feel of the textile, will give him more of a patterning of the sensuous than he was ever given before.

As counsellors, we stand on the interface, which makes everything look different. From there we see our clients come in, and some of the most weird behaviour suddenly makes a lot of logical, if not poetic, sense. What are they trying either to hold apart or to bring together in an adaptive way? Is it an attempt at the interface to hold sensuality and sexuality, the subjective and the objective worlds, *apart*, so that they can handle both in a better way? Or perhaps to bring them *together* as an attempt at contra-sexual rebalancing? We can presume nothing; we have to discover what it actually means to them.

*IGB*: A perfectly ordinary man may go over to transvestism when some major thing is happening to him. This can be phasic and to do with hormones, as when, for instance, he goes into the 'male menopause' (when, again, some men have told me they feel more masculine in feminine clothes). Or, when he sees his son growing into adolescence, coming up to challenge his place, the man may feel he wants to contact some missing part of himself, to stop providing the masculine stand and get in touch with his own sensuous, feminine side. And he does it in this rather overt way.

### Transvestism and relationship

Transvestism is a symptom which may be seen as a symbol because it can show the point of blockage, of sexual wounding or sexual trauma that has occurred. People go for transvestism while still trying to relate. It is about relationship. The split has occurred and, good or bad, it has gone underground. Guilt has been constellated at some point, otherwise they'd just walk freely around, dressing as they want to dress; but 'It's wrong!' A number of men I have known have practised transvestism in private. Some were distressed by it; having children, it worried them enormously if they didn't gain sympathy or understanding from their family. Guilt caused them to split inner and outer apart, so that they could apparently relate quite naturally to the outside world by the norms of their culture. But in their internal world, sexual fantasy was beginning to take over.

## Transgender Issues

*BS*: I would not call gender change 'variation'. We have seen how we may come across someone who is not the gender they appear to be. We have to explore a person's actual psychological gender, and presume nothing. There are those who are physically and mentally male but emotionally female, and *vice versa*. I am not sure that, even if they have medical treatment and surgery, anyone actually *changes* gender.

It's probably more that their true gender surfaces, and at a certain point their body has had to follow it. Look at the person's body; it is already expressing something of this.[65] Some of them seem to have picked up the wrong body in the quick-change department. They are caught in a mass of stereotypes that are alien to their psychology and are unhappily housed in an alien place. It is incarceration. For them, the very idea that they might be inhabiting the wrong body comes as a release and a great joy. Having an operation is what they desire and ask for.

## A personal account

*IGB*: It is not at all easy. If we are all of us psychologically both male and female, there are bound to be problems. I remember my own reaction to a man I knew who became a woman, which I report because it surprised me. Before he had the operation, when he was going around as a man, I had a distaste for this person, though I tried to be normal towards him. But I was fascinated to note how different was my attitude after the operation had taken place. From being edgy around him – or her – there was now a feeling of total acceptance. Whether that was because *he* who had become *she* was now fully accepting something within herself and I was picking it up, I don't know. But it was sufficiently dramatic for me to register it.

*BS*: We often find it very difficult to imagine somebody actually *being* a different gender from their sex. We need to look at our stereotypes and ask ourselves, have we never met a man whom we felt had all the nature of a woman, even though in a man's body? I once knew a young man who *felt* he was really a woman, but in his case it was a matter of his experience. Together we found that when he was a baby he had been treated by his mother as a girl. It was not that this young man had been born the wrong sex; rather, there had been a confusion in his upbringing. This possibility may be easier to understand. Here again we have to explore the nature of the individual. It is very necessary to hold open the parameters, the limiting factors.

## How gender may begin?

However, I have certainly met more than one man who actually *was*

---

[65]  Jan Morris's book on this, *Conundrum*, 1974, is one of the very best. Assigned male at birth, James Morris had five children before beginning a medical transition in 1964. He knew from his earliest years that he 'should have been born a girl: not homosexual but simply "wrongly equipped".' His transformation into Jan, covered in her autobiography *Conundrum*, took many years, beginning with female hormones during the early 1960s and culminating in the final operation in 1972 in Morocco. Later she was re-united with her previous wife in a civil partnership and the couple continued to live together extremely harmoniously.

a woman. At a biological level, as we saw above in connection with 'the phallic quest', the foetus is originally female. It goes through stages, and later the male has to pass through a much more radical change to become male than the female has to remain female. I suspect that for some babies there may have been a cross-gendering muddle long before birth. Perhaps a trauma occurred at that particular stage of development in the womb. Might they have been either more or less female at that moment and become stuck there? In counselling, if we cannot get at the feeling just by talking to a person, imaging is a wonderful way of working through it. It comes up frequently if we flip back, asking: 'What does that remind you of?' A colleague told me this story:

### A woman who became a man

I knew someone who was a woman of about eighteen when I met her. She really hated her own sex, wanting very badly to be a male. At twenty-one she had become a competent child-care officer, very good with children. She knew, going into it at great depth with various psychiatrists, that this change would mean giving up her career and she would find it extremely hard to abandon her profession. She would also lose the place where she lived and have to start afresh, because the reactions of society were so strong. However, in her female body she had recurring bouts of such depression that in the end it was decided that she should have surgery. It was very sad. She adored children but also she didn't want to be a woman. So she had several operations.

As a man, he stood a tremendous amount of nasty behaviour in the hospitals, finding that a number of the nurses and doctors really hated his kind of person. The negativity he experienced in the wards was awful. However, he did have a girlfriend. She kept teaching him, pointing out for example when he was sitting like a girl. He hadn't realised how much body language, how many mannerisms he'd have to relearn as a man – an immense field. All these things took a long time. He took various jobs, one in a jeweller's shop. He was very artistic and painted extraordinary pictures; he cured himself of a psychotic breakdown through those paintings. Though he couldn't marry the girl (not at that time in our society), she was able to accept his name. And so they lived like a couple, though in a totally non-sexual relationship.

## *The man who wanted to change gender*

Someone else came to me with great concern. In discussion with his wife – and he had two children – he'd decided to explore his desire to change gender. He wanted to do this psychologically as far as he could, to see whether the urge was genuine. His father had not come back from the war until he was five years old. He had had both a mother and a nanny. The nanny was very feminine, mother not, and these two women were a couple. He had been brought up by them and rejected by his father on his return. With this man (who was also transvestite), the desire to change sounded more like an expectation than something true. We worked as far as we could, and then he went away to think about it. I don't know what eventually happened. My feeling was that, in his case, to have the operation probably would not have been justified, and I think he was coming to the same conclusion.

Physical sex-change is not made easy. Certainly one has to be very cautious about it. Many tests need to be made and questions asked. The operation is very well protected. Unless they go to disastrous clinics in back rooms in side alleys, where catastrophic things can almost surely happen, it is very, very difficult still for people to have a proper operation in this area. Currently, you are supposed to have lived as the sex you want to become for a year, without fail, before they will consider you. There have to be three doctors, three psychologists, and three others; three sets of three, and the surgeon has to be prepared to do it. The rules are very stringent. And it is a subject where stringency is much required, though this also pushes away some people who would be greatly helped by it.[66]

One man who did become a woman was enormously worried beforehand about the operation. But he so loved his lover, who was tremendously supportive, that he went ahead and it was a great success. There may be more social acceptance of men who want to become women than of women who want to become men. The latter are very much less common. Very few women are drawn to the physical playing out of it; it is more an emotional playing out, coming from the *feminine* principle. That may also be why it is not so marked, or so obvious, or so heard about, when women do become men. But obviously, there is a tremendous need for counselling. In deciding whether to have the operation, the thrust of the exploration is whether

---

66   This was in the early 1980s.

the person really is of another gender to that of their body. Many people are psychologically unsure of that, but would never go that far.

# GUILT

*The private, hidden, inside behaviour is liable*
*to get out and manifest*

Coming to the central line in Figure 8 (page 179), we see that this is about *guilt*. In adult life we can look back and see how many of our parents' notions of what *pleases* or *displeases* are still alive and kicking in our psyche, perhaps having a quite considerable effect on our mature ability to relate. Guilt comes to any normal human being when they recognise 'bad' impulses. A split inevitably appears between outside and inside, overt and covert. In a good family it can be tolerated and held, and not become divisive. But if a child feels that certain acts are unacceptable, not only to its feared ones but to its loved ones, then it is liable to go in for overt behaviour on the one hand, and covert on the other. Then the private, hidden, inside behaviour is liable to get out and manifest, constellating a fair amount of guilt.

We have seen how mature adult sexuality would be about inter-dependency, the relating of an equal to an equal. But there is not much equality; in fact, there is considerable inequality about some of the variant modes we shall now explore. They are, rather, about *not* relating as an equal to an equal.

## Sexual Fantasy

First, then, comes the split, then the guilt about the split, then the handling of the guilt through sexual fantasy. The split is quite natural. It is the same as that between 'good' and 'bad'. It is absolutely natural to have sexual fantasies and dreams, and to masturbate. In adolescence, fantasy and masturbation come in together. By degrees the importance of the fantasy will be replaced by relating with somebody else, when it usually becomes part of the overall relationship. And this is all absolutely normal, except where it begins to become a way of life and to displace the natural flow of libido.

That is the difference. Sexual fantasy is truly 'variant' only when it comes up at inappropriate times and *replaces* normal relating – when it begins to haunt a person and run their life. If the split into lower or higher, inner or outer, has been too strong and a great deal of guilt has been constellated, then, as in the schizoid position, the splitting-off leads people to seek relationships to objects, to the detriment of their relating with subjects. It's when they then begin to play out their fantasies in the outer world that we are liable to hit quite a bit of trouble.

A great deal of female sexual fantasy has to do with being raped. At an unconscious level, men may be responding here to something in women. And quite a lot of men believe that unless they are that sort of phallic male, they aren't male at all. It is so multiple. We can presume nothing; we have to ask the person about it. I know men who have raped (or at least, the way they related felt to the woman like rape) simply because they felt that if they didn't get in there in that way, if they came in a gentle way, they would certainly not be accepted. And that was because they felt themselves to be unacceptable. Which is very sad.

Some of the sexual fantasies that people come up with are amazing for the sheer genius of invention. What comes out when we are given some of the things they have been keeping within themselves? Faced with this earth-shattering stuff, we hold steady at the interface and look at it as a movement, a symbol of the symptom that they have. We map the fantasy, exactly as we would map anything else. 'What does that mean to you?' We treat it just as we would any other image. 'Where does it take you? What does it remind you of?'

When is it appropriate to ask in this way about the content of a sexual fantasy? Only, I would say, when it arises as a natural part of the work. But it is extremely helpful, because fantasy is very powerfully related to so-called 'normal' as well as to 'abnormal' sexuality. If the sexual side of a person's life is a major issue, I would definitely explore this quite early. 'What were your fantasies when you masturbated?' It may seem fairly cheeky, but I think this question need not and should not be avoided. Otherwise one is setting up the original taboo again, playing into the system which is already splitting them apart.

Though it can be more difficult for a female than a male counsellor to ask that kind of question, I take it like any other fantasy. Talking about relatedness, whether with a man or a woman, if it seems appropriate I say, 'And how is it for you in the sexual area?' I wouldn't hesitate to ask that question with certain people. That's no problem. 'Would you mind telling me the nature of these fantasies when they come up?' If I have timed it right, they often show more relief than otherwise. It is particularly important to remember that we leave it open for them to say, 'Mind your own business!' Which is, after all, true for any question, any fantasy.

## Fetishism

Fetishism is the falling in love with, or being able to relate to, only a part of the body. Falling in love with a part of something, or someone, is often because one never felt oneself to be accepted as a whole, but at best only in part. For some children, although the bad was not acceptable, the good was all right. But others were not accepted at all, good or bad. They fall in love now with part of a person because they never feel they are with the whole of that person. Men will say, 'I am a buttock man.' 'No, I am a breast man.' 'Well, I am a foot man.' All these parts! Some people take it so far as to fall in love with a shoe without a foot in it, or a bra without a breast. There are many secrets to this, but the various clothes people get each other to dress up in and wear will outline some particular part – the posterior or the breasts or the legs or the genitals. Think about the distinguishing marks of animals in the mating season which show that they are now available.

### Fetishism and taboo

We know that the area of the taboo is a wide one. Fetishism, like many of the variations of sexuality, can firstly be a way of trying to accommodate to the stepping-over of the boundaries of taboo. If an ambivalent message came over in the nursery (double binds: 'don't do this; but *do* do it'), the later confused 'child' will become unable to release him- or herself into freedom, or express their spontaneous instinctual energies in the form of sexuality, without their fetishes. People who have been looped back to some trauma may pick a fetish that reminds them of that stage. It enables them to go out into the world and helps them come to some kind of relating. They can't, or don't feel free to, make love, or make sex or whatever, unless the fetish is present in some form. So a man may be able to make love to a woman only if she's wearing black stockings or a rubber mackintosh or wellington boots, or has a whip or whatever.

These are the ordinary things that you see in pornographic literature, the everyday stuff where, through guilt, people have split off their inner fantasy from their outer conformity. 'I can only make love to a sheep under a tree under the full moon, and only on Thursdays ... ' and we still work with it in exactly the same way as we would with anything else. It is another way of adapting towards, relating with, the world. The question 'What does it mean to you?' applied to the strange-seeming thing that turns them on will very often take them back to a much earlier time when they were caught and made to feel bad for what they did.

Or again we have seen how, when a person's sexuality is developing, the relationship between fantasy and masturbation becomes fundamentally important. If a lot of guilt was laid on these things, one of the frequent results is that the fantasy and the masturbation can be infinitely more exciting than the 'real thing'. Then, in order to make the real thing exciting enough, the person has to bring in their fetish, which will be related to some of their original and very early fantasies. So we have to ask quite specifically, 'What sorts of fantasy has our client had at certain stages of their sexual development?'

Women are not usually as fetishistic as men. They rarely need to objectify in that way, being much more *au fait* with the emotional level. Nevertheless, a number of them do need to fantasise in order to be turned on: it's their favourite film star, their particular type of man, who is loving them. In doing this, many married people free themselves so that they can bear to relate to this person. They can each only ever make love to the other when it is put out on to a fantasy, or an object. This is also displacement, the replacement of a person by a thing. The fantasy itself is an object – a transitional object. It is highly complex, but it indicates an attempt to hold subjective and objective together in a new way.

One definition of 'fetishism' *is the displacement and replacement of a subject by a full or a part object*. I suggest this is an attempt to hold together good and bad, up and down, inner and outer, in a new way. We have seen how, for the child, the teddy bear is part object, part subject, allowing the child to relate to the outside world and escape from the subjectivity of the mother. It also has the companioning, it's-all-right-to-be-alone-in-the-dark quality of the good mother. The teddy bear moves between inner world and outer, a transitional object to hold back the fear and keep it at bay, putting it 'out there' from 'in here'. Just as it allows the child to be alone in the dark, to sleep, to get in touch with its senses without being frightened out of its wits, so this displacement onto fetishes is a very similar attempt by the psyche (maybe in quirky ways) to try and hold things together now.

Some of what I have heard from both male and female clients as to what turns them on, well, the imagination required can be staggering. So if someone says they can only make love when their partner is wearing, say, one boot, we may think, 'What weird area am I in here?' On the other hand, we may stand with them at the interface and ask, 'What does a boot mean to you?' It's exactly the same approach as for anything else. We stand at this interface and hear these things and we are in touch in a different way, given an entirely different viewpoint. We try to hold whatever is coming at us, discover what it represents. Our minds are reeling as our imagination is extended beyond its bounds. Given the very word *fetishism* – well, a boot is quite a normal thing to fall in love with.

Go right back to when early human beings stepped out from within the relative safety of their nursery, their people, their ground, their tribe, from within the camp fire's circle, to explore the unknown world of the Other. Venturing beyond to a world which was full of 'them' – full of ghosts and terrors – they took along a fetish which held the spirit of the god and of the tribe. And a lot of our male and female clients who use fetishism as a way of being able to relate sexually are taking that same step into the unknown, exploring the otherness of another body and doing it with the aid of this object. They are putting 'out there' the talisman which allows them to be free enough and safe enough to relate to that person.

### *The talisman*

Look how people drive that great phallic symbol, the car, with their St. Christopher hanging up, their dolly waving around. It is exactly the same thing. And the fact that some people fall in love with the St. Christopher or the doll is only one stage removed from the need for the fetish, the symbol that leads into the unknown. Is it not, after all, very close to how we give somebody a talisman if they are going on a journey into the subjective world of imaging, leaving outer reality to explore the world of their inner reality? The fetish is not just a fantasy talisman but an objective one, a physical object to hold onto. It goes with them to help them step out over the threshold of the known towards the unknown. The longer the journey, the more tactile and tangible is the talisman they may choose.

## TIED BACK TO THE PARENTS

*They ... need to relate to the child in them – the child that was,*
*when the Garden of Paradise was all around them, before*
*the gates were closed behind them*

The more extreme variations of sexuality, shown up the right side of Figure 8 (page 179), go with the degree of emancipation that we have gained from the parents. They arise when good and bad are split too far apart, lower body from upper body, inner from outer. We have seen how those less mature, still caught right back, have a great confusion between what is sensuous and what is sexual. The inside and the outside reality can be completely muddled, or so split that people put them into watertight compartments. And then they hit a real problem in terms of their later movement towards sexuality.

*IGB*: In men, an excessive tie back to the mother (which may well reflect, for example, that the father was weak or inadequate or absent) used to be thought to lead to three fairly normal and common reactions:

first, homosexuality (because, being tied to the mother, the man was thought to be seeking for a masculine identity in relationships with men);

secondly, the Don Juan reaction (every relationship with a woman was a conquest, and once she had been conquered and taken to bed, he could move on to the next one. This was seen as a getting-back at Mother and at the feminine for the damage they had done him);

and the third was impotence (where, in the face of a woman, it was not possible to express masculinity).

*BS*: However, though these probably are fairly common reactions, I would wish to modify or add to them. If people haven't left home, if they are still tied back, they will inevitably choose a partner who allows the parent and child relationship to go on relatively unimpaired. The shock comes when, in mating or marriage, they discover that what seemed at a semi-conscious level to be a good way of continuing the original enwombing of the parental home blows up in their face. They find they have married or mated with someone who's *also* still back home in the nursery; and now there are two children, each trying to find in the other the parenting they wanted themselves.

And for a while it may be provided. One of the partners may have had to become the parent themselves at a very early age. Their own parents will have still been back in the nursery and, having by no means come up into mature relating, given birth to male or female children who at a very early age were much more mature than they were. These children, seeing how the parents were themselves struggling with their own childhood dependency, had to do a role-flip. Now, they tend to go on searching for 'children' to look after, because that's what they understand relationship to be. So of course they try to parent the other sex, mating with them, relating with them, only to find that their own mature dependency needs are not being met within the relationship.

## Bonding and Bondage

Though bondage can still come up in healthy relationships, yet it takes a great deal of trust to talk about what is usually such an agonising problem.

### *Bonding*

Moving up the right hand side of Figure 8 (page 179), Sexual Variation, we find voyeurism, frotteurism, exhibitionism and paedophilia, to name but a few; approaches from behind, approaches from the front, but generally, approaches at our own eye-level. And they arise from this 'bonding'. The *symbol* is the earlier guilt of the person tied back into parental dependency, and it manifests externally as a *symptom* in the form of a bond or a bonding back to the parents. It leads to all these following variations.

So, on this right side of the map where the 'bad' has been rather heavy, we also find a lot of guilt. Here, it is not just uncertainty, it is actual guilt; guilt about one's own gender and about one's sexuality, which will have been described as 'animal, dirty, secretive, sordid'. We have seen how the child will have started out with many different prohibitions: 'Don't suck the fingers of your gloves, don't suck your big toe!' And later they don't touch, hold, feel, suck or generally inspect anything. It is all dropped into the lower part of the split. Guilt has tied the person back into parental dependency. It is not that they are actually held back; they have the possibility of breaking out. But they are *bonded* by ties of guilt.

## Bondage

Sexual 'bondage' – being tied with ropes – is part of variation. When someone is tied back but still seeking relationship, they might well move into this area, where to be held down in bondage means an erection or an orgasm. When is a bond a tie? Viewing it from a Transpersonal perspective, I am fascinated by how far this fantasy of being tied and held and roped is a way of handling all this guilt and beginning to find sensual freedom. It gives a sense of boundaries. It can grant somebody the freedom to experience and enjoy their senses because, by being in bondage, their body is given outline. It may be simply – simply! – that their experience of relationship in the nursery was one of submission or conquest. It was a polarity: 'placate or dominate'; 'be masochistic or sadistic'.

For some people who cannot make love unless they are somehow bound, being tied down can be a way of saying, 'Well, how could I take responsibility for what I did, or what was done to me, when I was tied up?' Or tied down? 'It wasn't me, I didn't do it, I wasn't in charge at the time!' Or could it be that the very ropes give them the sense of a body outline? It may be the holding they never had; now it has become the only thing they understand of relationship.

They need to learn a totally different language.

## Sado-masochism

Very often bondage goes together with being whipped or assaulted by someone more powerful. The person has the sense that it is possible to relate only from that position: victim or saviour, victor or captive. It is the same with many of the mammals: placate or dominate. Take a dog in conflict with another in a territorial matter. If it is not going to be able to relate equally, it will grin broadly, go over on to its back and placate. It is a natural survival method, and many people also use it. Those with the sexual fantasy, or the acting-out, of sadistic or masochistic forms of relating probably never had an experience of true relationship. Their understanding and experience of parents, or of any later parenting at school or wherever, meant they understood no other way – only submission or conquest. They have to be a victim in order to be free to relate. There is no equality; therefore their relationship to the world generally seems to be out of nick.

## Some Further Variations

### *Voyeurism*

This is an absolutely normal thing, judging by all the books and magazines on the stalls. It is quite natural to human beings, who are born curious and want to know what other people do in private. There are very few of us who do not feel stirred, directly through our eyes and visually through our imaging. It is part of the imaginative and creative process of being human. As counsellors, we find there are times when we are sexually moved by things that our clients say, or by a client themselves. As long as we befriend this, accept it and know how to handle it, that is all part of the body's sensing of the shape and pattern of things. Many people use voyeurism in order to become *more* potent, more connected to subjective relationships.

It's when, on the other hand, it gets in the way and begins to cut them off from life that it becomes difficult. Voyeurs are often very, very lonely and isolated people. The looking has become more important than the actual relatedness to the outside world and they can *only* be turned on from the voyeur position, watching other people make love and being all the less potent in their own relating.

Pornography, being turned on by seeing films and photographs, is again a way of holding it 'out there' in order to be free to experience it 'in here'. It's much easier to put sex at a distance in order to enjoy it, since guilt won't let the person enjoy it from inside.

## *Frotteurism*

This is quite rare. Yet, despite the lengths to which most people go to avoid contact with each other, it does happen on crowded buses and underground trains. Frotteurism is where someone will attempt to rub another person up, approaching from behind. It is the inability to come in full frontal and face someone else. They may also come in to play, to dance, to flirt in a way which can be very distressing. It quite often involves animals rather than people.[67]

## *Exhibitionism*

Most frequently, the exhibitionist client is male, usually hooked back into adolescence or childhood and wanting a response. In certain phases of their lives, many men have a tremendous impulse to exhibit, and it is nearly always because their sexuality has been blocked in some way, very often by their partner. Women don't do this so much, at least not with their genitals. They tend to do it by their physical action, pointing up certain parts of their body. The odd streaker does appear among them, but that is usually for some other purpose. Women tend to cover, and use body-language as their variety of exhibitionism.

So it is mainly men who exhibit their genitals in full display. It's their only means of communicating, because they do not expect to be heard in any other way. And to be seen to be phallic and to get a reaction, usually from a female child, is at least to get a reaction. Noting the eye-level, we see that it's often the need to relate in whatever way to some particular age-level. They often exhibit only to a chosen age group, needing to relate to the child in them – the child that was, when the Garden of Paradise was all around them, before the gates were closed behind them. Lewis Carroll, for instance, as a creative artist wrote for children out of the creative child in him, with the wisdom of the child. 'Alice in Wonderland' is a most marvellous story. Written by a guru for grownups and by a child for children, it is a very good example of somebody with the child's eye.

Very many women will have met a male exhibitionist – a flasher – at some time in their lives. There are a lot of them. Since it is done to get a reaction, rarely does the man follow it through. Like a child, for him any response is better than none. It is done in order to let him feel a connection of some kind. In the same way, all Samaritans will have

---

67 Frottage: 'abnormal desire for contact between clothed bodies of oneself and another.' (*Concise Oxford Dictionary*.)

had the odd heavy breather on the telephone doing such verbal exhibitionism. The call is made in order to get a reaction to the voice, make an attempt to relate and communicate. Exhibitionism is the commonest sexual offence and of course it is a police matter. People can get themselves into real trouble with it and some of them can be extremely distressed. But if we see it as a signalling system, we can try to reach behind to what is being signalled.

One of my friends and colleagues gave a marvellous example of this. A man came into her private practice room, exhibiting himself and playing with his penis for almost three-quarters of an hour of their hour's interview, and she took no notice at all. Almost nothing was said. She just went on listening to him, accepting it quite normally. And then towards the end she said to him, 'You've been communicating with me for three-quarters of an hour in your way. Now, could I try to communicate with you in mine, and will you listen to me?' And he burst into tears for the love and understanding that came out of her, that she saw what it was truly about, saw it as his way of trying to set up a rapport with her. It was a very loving thing to be able to say, holding her place so clearly at the interface and seeing it as a signalling system from somebody who felt there was no other way. A lot of work was moved from that and they really began to communicate.

## *Paedophilia*

*IGB*: I had a client some years ago, whose great problem was that he not only felt drawn to people of his own sex but was terrified because the ones he was most attracted to were boys of thirteen and fourteen. He had 'dressed up' at that age himself, when there had been crucial traumas. It turned out that he had always been made to wear clothes too young for him, and as he began to grow up, the major problem settled particularly around that age. The attraction was a symptom of what was locked in and undeveloped. Now, his great fear was of being unable to restrain himself. Would he one day find himself making a relationship with one of these kids? There had already been several really very traumatic incidents, one much earlier on. He would be caught and end up in prison, where he knew from experience that people like him get a very rough ride indeed.

But his great attraction to boys of that age represented the fact that he also felt himself to be thirteen or fourteen within. It was a projection mechanism. This principle of projection can make relatively clear a great deal of what would otherwise be strange in the pattern of sexual relationships. For instance, why do we 'marry our mother' or 'marry our father'? Likewise, as is true of many of the sexual variations, we are often attracted to people who make it possible for us to live out or express something in ourselves that is either locked back at a certain stage, or blocked and unable to express itself in what is regarded as the normal fashion.

*BS*: Though we are likely to meet paedophilia only where it emerges in a minor form, we usually need to pass people over to sexual coun-sellors in these areas of risk.[68] It can be very sad – and very dangerous, since they may become criminal cases. But the word *paedophilia* means love of children. Almost always it is linked with the particular age at which they themselves were locked back, usually when they were still in the bi-sexual era of the pre-adolescent state.[69] Their dreams and their inner imaging tend to be distinctly pre-puberty too. Hardly ever do you find a true paedophile relating to a whole age-range. When it is in a mildish form, they'll be quite clear about who they are relating to. The film *Death in Venice* was very much about the non-phallic, pre-pubescent, non-facial-haired boy being related to.

Again, nearly always, somebody who relates to small children will be aiming to connect to the child within themselves. When working with them, instead of thinking, 'Oh my God, how could they do that to a child!' we have to go into the interface. There, as with the exhibitionist, we ask, 'What is their eye-level?' We need to realise that they only rarely actually 'do that' to a child out there. But it is usually much more in the mind, where they are trying to make rapport with that internal child; perhaps indeed with the Divine Child. What is this child they are trying to relate to? We aim to get them to befriend it and take it back in. Then very frequently they will cease to have to do it in the outside world. They will put a loving eye out to the world but they will not have to act it out, because they are being helped to act it *through* in a new way. Again, I would emphasise that expert sexual counselling is needed where any risk is involved.

---

[68]  It should be noted that the workshops on which this book is based took place before all the revelations about paedophilia in its extreme form came out in public. Society at large is not aware that so many adult perpetrators of these crimes were, as children, themselves victims of atrocious sexual and emotional abuse. Though meeting many such survivors, both Barbara Somers and Ian Gordon-Brown were here referring to the inner landscapes of particular clients, not in this instance addressing the issues of victims nor considering how to deal with any confessed acting-out of crimes against children. Ed.

[69]  And often by tremendous personal trauma perpetrated against themselves at a young age. Ed.

## Necrophilia

Those involved in digging up the dead and then having sexual intercourse with them, or murdering somebody and having intercourse, are hardly liable to appear in our counselling room. Necrophilia means being able to make love only to something which is dead. Here we are going into the more psychotic areas, where people kill in order to be able to make love. Or maybe they can only make love to something that is dying.

To react with disgust, to recoil ... I would again point out that we can still presume nothing. What on earth and in the name of God does this say about the borderlands of life and death? What must they have experienced in the way of communication? Or perhaps they felt that they killed the thing they loved, so that's the only way they can relate again. 'You nearly killed me – I went into hospital – if it hadn't been for you, I would now be living the full life that I want!' Or, maybe, mother just went, or father just disappeared. Since, till they are about five, children are naturally enough the centre of their own universe, they may have felt that, as someone vanished off the scene, it had something to do with them.

However, we quite frequently meet with someone who is necro-philiac in the sense that they are in love with death, or drawn to aspects of death in a morbid way. Working on it, we very often find it is because they are afraid of life. As they are helped to relate more fully to life, they lose the love of death, becoming more affectionate and befriending of life. Again, symptom as symbol.

# SEXUALITY AND COUNSELLING

*Never be the parent; always be a sister
or brother who is also struggling*

Nature can resolve our sexuality all by itself. For a large number of people, it is that simple. We do not have to intervene. It is like our heart-beats: think about them and we get in the way of them. Given a good-enough environment, it happens quite naturally and spontaneously and in phases; mother nature knows what she's up to. Yet in mid-life, people often bring their relationships into the counselling room. The work usually involves an unplaiting, finding what is valid to the person. We stand at the interface and begin to open up the parameters of possibility. Beginning to talk at a deeper level with a person who has a sexual difficulty, out comes whatever is their apparent gender behind the stereotype. Behind that, we find what is their original psychological gender and behind that, there is a *person* who is neither male nor female. And they talk with the same voice.

Say they have had a row with their partner. 'Right; what was your eye-level?' This can give a very good feeling about how they are relating with the other person. If they are looking up, then this other is a parental authority, a 'big' figure, and they are smaller and their stature has gone down. If they are looking down, they themselves have gone into the parental position of authority, and that other person has diminished inside. We can help to adjust that eye-level. The aim is to become the artist who would make in all relationships an equality.

It is important as counsellor or therapist that we are in touch with our own sexuality. If we are at least reasonably aware of the possibility and range of it, we are not going to be shocked. We need broad, wide, imaginative parameters and, above all, not to repeat the 'Ugh!' of the parent. In this area it is vital never to be the parent, but always to be a sister or brother who is also struggling. In that position on the interface, we may not have sorted it out in ourselves, but at least for that moment we are wide enough to hear anything and dance with it. Because it is somebody telling their story.

*IGB*: Libido is a very powerful force which we meet at every level of our nature. In terms of relationships, sexuality (a symptom and a symbol of this force) is very often the carrier for a whole series of other and very much deeper difficulties which emerge at the physical level when people get together. I have had several clients who have experienced inadequate sex at the physical level. However, it is very rare that a problem is *purely* physiological. With one couple, it became quite clear that several links between the partners were incomplete. The woman had had a number of good relationships at the instinctual and emotional levels. Now suddenly she had gone right over and chosen a 'spiritual' man, very thoughtful, compassionate, gentle, caring; but he was completely absorbed in his research study. She loved him deeply at the mental and intuitive levels, but it was fairly difficult for her emotionally and only rarely was it adequate physically. It was a very incomplete union.

When we begin to explore what is going on physically, we are almost immediately drawn to what is happening at all the other levels: what of instinct, emotion, thought, intuition? Ideally we would presuppose that each level is nurtured and nourished and met by the coming together of the two partners. And what in fact is the relationship at the level of the Self? A great many unions founder on the fact that, at the deeper level, the two people have different paths, different energies, different qualities, and can no longer meet.

Another client told how the physical side had been amazingly successful with a former partner. 'It was like the combustion of two chemicals. Whenever we got within a few hundred yards of each other, there was an explosion.' But the relationship hadn't lasted because there had been no union, no meeting on any other level. He later married a different young woman. Here, the relationship was fine in terms of emotion and intuition but somehow it never worked sexually.

Take the Emergence map (Figure 6, page 104). The coming-together of the partners is rather like the meeting of the two centres: the personal ego and the Self. At the ordinary everyday personality level, they may get on well during the relatively early period of life together. In their twenties and thirties there is an emotional or physical union, though perhaps not a great deal else. And then, one of the partners begins to grow and the other does not. As they change and other aspects of their natures come in, it is very difficult for those more superficial links, satisfactory before, to hold the relationship. Often, they keep the union together, but only for a period. Time will eventually run out, and not only will the partnership begin to founder because the parties are growing apart, but sexual problems will emerge.

We recall the difficulty of the 'container and the contained'.[70] One is the contained person who is fully met within the relationship, and the other is not. Eventually this is bound to affect the partners' coming-together at the sexual level. The Self has come in and their paths have begun to diverge; their problems are coming from the archetypal energy and line of the Self.

*BS*: But when people are released into their sexuality and begin to play together as a pair, then they can respond to the mood-music of

---

70  'Container and Contained', see Gordon-Brown and Somers, *The Raincloud of Knowable Things*, pp.96-98. Also, Jung, *Marriage as a Psychological Relationship*, CW Vol. 17, para 331-337.

their play. Then their love-making frees them from stereotypes; the man can take the female role much more and the woman the male. A great deal of inhibition and expectation and predisposition is released and falls away as they play together. The recognition comes that the mood can change. So they can happily dance together over one night's love-making, or twenty-nine or fifty years of living close together.

Blossoming

# CHAPTER TWELVE

# The Meaning of Illness

## Barbara Somers

*There was a time not all that far away*
*when to be hit by illness was seen as a visitation from a god,*
*a goddess, a divinity*

I feel very small in the face of such a challenging and gristly theme.[71] I think of all the millions of men and women through the centuries who, through their souls and their bodies, have wrestled with its problems. And their answers have been only partial. There is an encouraging story about a Little Priest, so small that he couldn't be seen over the lectern. One Sunday morning, he began, 'Brethren, my theme today is the Light of the World.' With which a voice at the back piped up, 'Well then, you'd better turn up the wick!'

And there are as many different answers as there are people. What we share in common is that when illness hits us personally, we see it as a threat, an affront, an invasion of our individual identity. We have to be pretty balanced not to. 'Why should it happen to me? What did I do to deserve this?' In youth, surging with energy, rushing forward into life, we can very happily ignore illness; but in the middle years, if not in ourselves then in our ageing parents or our contemporaries, the moment inevitably comes when someone is laid on their back. Then we are reminded of our own mortality.

## Ageing

Growing old itself tends to be viewed as a disease to be averted, denied, dreaded. We deal with it cosmetically. And ageing brings crises in its wake: loss, failure, redundancy, bereavement, separation, loneliness, rejection, poverty. A lot of these crises come from outside,

---

71 Most of this chapter came from a talk with the same title which Barbara Somers gave at Dartington in 1985. It was published as 'The Meaning of Illness' in Somers and Gordon-Brown, *Journey in Depth*, Chapter 9, pp. 157-172.

and if we lived in a sane society, a lot of them would be remedied from outside. But illness, whether or not we pick it up by contagion, always seems to come from inside; an attacker, a disturber of our internal peace, an invader from our own inner space. It's much too close for comfort.

## Crisis

We have looked already at what happens when a person is hit by an external crisis: divorce perhaps, or redundancy. The crisis hits us with impact in the present, and the natural response is to regress, go back on ourselves, recoil. We hope it's a recoil in order to advance. But now we find that, together with the present crisis, we have picked up a whole back-memory, a photograph-album of other times when we failed, felt lost, rejected, defeated. And on that back foot we catch the full impact, not just of the present but of the past, and of fear for the future. This is very natural; rather as, when we go back to the parental home, we regress and feel small in exact ratio to the time we spend there.

If the crisis doesn't knock us totally flat, we come from the place of recoil to the place of gathering. We 'pull ourselves together', we get on the move. 'It's going to be all right!' we tell ourselves. And the time-lag from recoil to gathering, as well as the time spent in the gathering itself, does give us the chance to move on. Crisis grants the opportunity to do so with a changed view, an understanding that we cannot be exactly as we were before. But a lot of us go on unchanged by the experience and, within the following six to eighteen months, we very frequently pick up an illness.

## Illness

And what when illness strikes? Again, we are hit in the present, and in the recoil we very often search for help. The mechanistic approach of allopathic medicine steps in very boldly and largely here. Somebody who already feels fairly regressed and on a back foot may now also be infantilised. *Infans* means 'unable to speak'. 'Me doctor, you patient' too often becomes, 'Me God, you infant. Leave your body to me, don't ask awkward questions, don't discuss your illness, even your dying, with anyone but me or the hospital staff'. Some patients are able to accept this – in fact, they want it; thank God it's there for them. But many more find it an affront to their personal identity and integrity. As someone cogently put it: 'So doctors pour drugs of which they know little, to treat diseases of which they know less, into human beings of whom they know nothing.' Knife-happy surgery may follow: 'If in doubt, cut it out, just in case'. One woman who'd lost a womb, one and a half breasts and a lymph gland said, 'I'm not simply a surgical case, I'm a just-in-case.' 'Cured to death' is too often the result.

The best of doctors also rage. Thank God there are many around; marvellously healing, therapeutic doctors; true physicians ... but they are raging too. It is saddening that many of the best are leaving their profession, looking for alternatives which may take them away from the very vocation and calling which most needs them. If they do stay, they can remain stressed and prey to fatigue, disenchantment, drink, drugs, suicide; things of which the statistics too hideously inform us.

## The alternative approach

This is why many doctors and patients and healthy people turn to more holistic and imaginative ways of looking at things. The holistic approach is so exciting that I would sound a cautionary note: we must be very careful of polarising or we'll go too far in the other direction. In moving towards alternatives, away from the allopathic, mechanistic approach, there is the chance that we become over-enthusiastic and, as alternative practitioners, try to make our holism too whole, too complete, too healthy. As a psychotherapist, I see a disturbing number of people who, deciding against allopathic approaches, have gone instead towards alternatives. They have had all sorts of treatments and diets, yet their symptoms are either unchanged, or have moved somewhere else in their body or system. Not only do they still have their original illness, but now they carry an extra burden of inadequacy, shame, failure and guilt. We have to watch lest we simply move the symptom around.

As alternative practitioners, it is dangerously easy to be as thrilled by our patients and clients as proud parents are of their adolescents. We see them growing, becoming more creative, moving on, and we get so glad about it that we start denigrating all the allopathic approaches. Then, 'Me God, you infant' becomes 'Me proud parent, you my child'. In Japan or China, a craftsman or artist who made something too perfect would put a flaw in it – to make it more real, more human, more usable. If our holism, our wholeness, is too perfect, too complete, it has nowhere to grow to. We need not the complete circle but the broken circle, the little gap still to leap, and something may come of it; even, one day, a spiral.

## Chronic illness

What about the stubborn illness, the unshiftable, recalcitrant symptom that we carry around and cannot move? Importantly, it may be telling us that we live in an imperfect state of being, an imperfect world, a world in process of becoming. We may even be under the loving eye, or whatever, of a god who is also growing and in process of becoming. These questions have been asked from the beginning of time. They are still worth asking.

Men and women loved Jim, a very special guy. Aged fifty-seven, he was a successful lawyer, an ace skier, a good mountaineer and an absolute charmer. He vastly enjoyed all aspects of his life and all the things he did. And he had stomach cancer; when I saw him he'd been told he might have six weeks to live. He'd tried diet, acupuncture, homoeopathy, autogenic training; he'd been given potions, diets, exercises, massage, meditation; he'd put off smoking, drinking and sex. And still he had cancer.

In the course of all this, he'd been told that he was 'not a typical cancer case'. He did not have 'the right psychology'; the illness must be a stress reaction to his very busy, very much-enjoyed life. And he was told, 'It's that you must be afraid of death.' By now he felt fairly inadequate, and increasingly guilty and frustrated. So he came and talked. We discussed this 'fear of death' he was supposed to have. And he went inwardly to a place of gathering, the place of quietening, of going within, a place where there is the possibility of absorbing and assimilating the impact of life. And there, quietly, with his eyes closed, he came to be a bit more in touch with what he felt this 'fear of death' to be. At first, pictures came up, mediaeval mind-images: Old Father Time, Dante's 'Inferno', corruption, worms, Hieronymous Bosch's nightmare characters. None of it felt right. And so, in that place of gathering, he began to let go his mental assumptions. He went deeper, quieter still and allowed to come to him pictures that had to do with what he really feared.

And the first thing he saw was his wife's face; then his children playing in the garden; a dog from his childhood; his stereo-deck; his skis.

He was surprised by the experience. Through discussion, he realised his fear was not of death, it was of life, of love and commitment. Death he'd been playing with for quite a long time, taking all sorts of risks. Life, love and commitment were his major fears.

And life gave him time. The provisional six weeks became eleven months, during which he began the process of relating, talking with his wife and his children. Most of all, he began to commit to himself, which led him to commit more to the family, and finally a little more to his illness. At last, his wife telephoned me: 'He died with a smile on his face, and his precious paper in his hand.' He'd shown me the 'precious paper' some time before: a translation from an ancient Egyptian papyrus, very old, but for him very new. He was excited about it. This is what he was holding in his hand:

> *Death is before me today, like the recovery of a sick man,*
> *like going forth into a garden after sickness.*
> *Death is before me today like the odour of myrrh,*
> *like sitting under the sail on a windy day.*
> *Death is before me today like the odour of lotus flowers,*
> *like sitting on the floor of drunkenness.*
> *Death is before me today like the course of the freshet,*
> *like the return of a man from the war galley to his home*
> *when he has spent years in captivity.*

Did he find the poem, or did the poem find him? Do we have symptoms or do our curing symptoms have us?

This gathering; we come to it when the present has hit us with illness, when we have recoiled, when we have tried many things and still have to address our sickness. At this place of gathering we are held in linear time, unable to go forward or backward, having only the choice of addressing our illness, our dis-ease. And it is here that we most need to pay attention to the language of symptom.

## Symptom as symbol

People are marvellously symbol-creating creatures, and have been from the beginning of time. It is there in our art and our poetry, our painting and dance and literature, and in our dreams. And I believe this wonderful symbolic language that a human being can create is here in our symptoms of illness. By listening and attending, here at this gathering-place, we can see how the symptoms had been building up for quite a long time before surfacing into the body. They are an early-warning system signalling a disturbed homeostasis, an imbalance between who the person really is, or who they need to become, and their own chosen lifestyle, or the environment in which they find themselves.

A great deal of the time – not always – it is when the symptom's preliminary signalling system is ignored that disorders and stress-responses become either acute or chronic. And if the symptom is masked, whether allopathically or homoeopathically, alternatively, it's liable to displace itself and, as we have seen, manifest somewhere else. For example, asthma cases are often treated in a way appropriate for allergy, and in some of those cases I have seen the symptom move away and then recreate itself. With one person it came back as claustrophobia, and the exploration of the claustrophobia led back to what originally set up the asthma. (Asthma tends to have to do with early holding that is too tight, with invasive hands that don't allow for identity; not loving hands that touch and give a body-outline.)

I knew somebody who went to an osteopath and was cured of a frozen shoulder. Now, osteopaths are very brilliant people; don't mistake me, this is in no way putting down the treatment. But I am suggesting that we perhaps treat too hard, too quickly, before we have listened to the symptom. When the shoulder was better, this person developed a very serious sinus problem. Working with the sinus problem, we reached her tears, which took us round again to the frozen shoulder. And that led right back to the small child. She was standing outside the room where her mother was feeding the new baby. Her face was buried in her arm. Already, at three, this child had a pre-history of feeling locked out from mother and father. At school she always felt the outsider. She used to comfort herself by crying and sobbing into her arm. And now her husband had set up another relationship. Once more her face was in her arm. And it became a frozen shoulder. But that was cured. And so it became a sinus problem, and then she could attend to the tears.

### Addiction

We must listen to the signals, or we work against the body and not with it. At this place of gathering, I have heard many fascinating dialogues between the person who has the symptom, and the symptom itself. Take addiction to smoking: let's try now to go with what the smoking may represent, with the action of it. Yes, it can be the desire to remain oral, to be at the breast, to replace the dummy; not in all cases, but in quite a lot of them. But it can also, or alternatively, be a way for somebody to desensitise themselves, to play for time, to centre – to steady the flickering world.

Different people do the same thing for different reasons. Some people drink to blot out, regress, be non-responsible, return to the original womb. But many do it because they have a thirst for meaning. In pursuit of a new vision, they are seeking a new spirit and they do it through the bottom of a glass of spirits. Over-eating may well be to pad out against life, to muffle, to act as a buffer, to hide. But for many people it has more to do with adding weight, substance, dignity. If we treat someone in a way that takes even more dignity from them, we collude with the original problem.

## The language of the symptom

My experience is that some cancers may come from the demand of the internal psyche to grow. It is sometimes said that cancer is about 'fear of growth, fear of self-expression, bitterness, a strong, powerful feeling of anger in-turned'. Yet, in many people, it may not be that. It may be the demand to expand, to be recognised, to emerge. And perhaps the person inside the body needs to know about that possibility.

During one year I worked with three different people suffering from arthritic feet. All were in line for surgery – three pairs of feet attached to three very interesting human beings. We explored what was for each of them the image for their feet, what the problem was linked with, and what the exploration of the symptom led to.

The first person's image for the action of his feet was: 'I'm groping to find my way'. It was linked with eye problems: 'And I can't see, either'. The exploration led us to look at direction, purpose, motivation, and his need to get on the move.

The second person had as image, 'I don't want to budge; I'm gripping the earth'. The link was with hypertension, a secondary if not primary, symptom: 'I'm too rushed, I can't get a breather'. The exploration was of the need to steady and stay still, reassess, be much more alone.

The image of the person attached to the third pair of feet was: 'Trying to belong somewhere'. It was linked with problems of the inner ear and with vertigo; that too was about trying to belong, after early fostering. The feet were now beginning to act out the need. The exploration had to do with her relationships, her housing situation and the deep need for connecting.

Three pairs of arthritic feet, three totally different people; all the feet in some way in touch with their own solution. I also know three people with heart problems likely to go for treatment, if not for surgery.

For the first, the image the heart threw up was 'a soggy sponge'. This was linked with 'taking in too much', with greed and eliminatory problems. The exploration had to do with the tendency in every relationship to keep on taking in like a soggy sponge, and then – cut!

The second had similar symptoms, but the image was of 'Parmesan cheese, hard as marble, won't give'. It was linked by the patient with his own personal boundaries and space. And the exploration had to be of what he called his 'bloody-mindedness'.

Number Three saw the heart as 'a leaky bucket'. The link: 'I can't say "No"; I'm always placating'. Here too the exploration was of space and boundaries, and the right to say 'No' instead of being a leaky bucket.

Three hearts, three individuals, three very different solutions, and they might all have had the same type of surgery or treatment. I find three a good, shapely number, so here are three clinical depressions, all of which were going to need drug treatment.

For the first, the image is of 'coming over the abyss of hell'. This woman linked it with 'boredom; wanting as a child to be an actress; needing colour'. Nobody would have guessed it from the look of her – as grey and grim as it's possible to be, and a dark wash over that – but the exploration here was the expression of her colour-range, her emotional palette. Depression was masking the very vital emotional colours that she needed to express. She said she'd rather go into depression: 'At least hanging over the abyss of hell makes me feel alive'. There was something dramatic in that; not just being bored out of her mind.

The next gave as image for her 'clinical' depression, 'a blue-grey mohair shawl'. It was linked with warmth, the need to be held. 'I don't want to let it go.' She knew this was not the moment. She was not yet ready to get rid of the depression. She had to go into it, stay with the nature of it. Somehow it was giving her the chance to explore the depths. Like a seed in the ground, she could allow that she wasn't yet quite ready to touch the surface. She needed a little more time to stay with it, work with it. Later, looking at it more, she came to see ways of dealing with it other than depression.

The third person's image was of 'being rocked in a new moon under all the stars in the sky'. It was the dreaming child, the story-telling child who, ashamed of being different in a highly intellectual family, had since university been in all the 'wrong' jobs. 'Rocked in the new moon under all the stars in the sky.' And this was 'depression'?

Might not individuals who can create such striking, rich, varied symptoms and imaging also have a deep sense of their own feeling requirements? The internal knower, the internal healer (not in everyone, but in many more than we think) knows more about the person's life than anyone else can. Many people have never been asked the questions, but at this place of gathering, given the right quality of evocation, people will come out with suggestions over and over, for themselves, to themselves, as to what they need and how they might set about it.

## *Listening*

People are coming from all directions with this fantastically alive, rich material to be worked with. We need practitioners multi-skilled and flexible enough to be able to help them. We need to put the symbol-creating, richly diverse patient back into the centre again. Individuals often know more than they themselves can recognise about their own processes of sicknesses and health. Never know first and never know better is Jung's principle for dream work, and it applies for our first (and for every) meeting with another person. We have to remind ourselves that we need to work with the power of love, and be cautious about the love of power. It is so easy to drift, forget, and set up a new polarisation exactly like the old but with different terminology. To put patients back in the centre, acknowledging the artistic nature of what their symptoms may be bringing, is to help them return to self-authority and self-respect, help them back into life. It is not only listening, but hearing. We practitioners should then, but only then, apply our multi-disciplinary skills – in response to what they need, not to what we assume.

## COUNSELLING SYMPTOM AS SYMBOL

*The body is as good a place for a temple as a temple itself*

So we remember the map of the Inner and the Outer and the Interface (Figure 2, page 9). Knowing that the map is not the country, we recall the two levels of tension between them: the regressive tension that allows somebody to have psychosomatic factors; and the other tension that changes their approach to life in hysteric or depressive or schizoid ways or in some of the other ways we have looked at. We have seen how as counsellors we try and create the interface in order to hold Inner and Outer together in a new way. We know that counselling is not about standing opposite a person, shouting from inside our own space to reach through to them in their space. Nor is it listening to what they from their space are saying, but hearing it only from outside, from what, as far as they are concerned, is the world of outer reality. Somehow, rather, we take a psychological stance by trusting the basic Self within (the Self with a large 'S'), trusting that, however outrageous, kinky, odd or strange the symptom may be, it is trying to communicate something. It is a symptom which is a symbol of something much more profound.

As we begin to recognise that, we move more and more to sit alongside our clients, sit with them. Remember the man (page 131) who pushed the pencils around in that very compulsive, obsessive way? By physically moving to sit beside him, as well as trying to do it psychologically, I was able to observe not only the movement, but his hand making the movement. So I could say 'Why don't you bless those pencils, those actions?' This is speaking from the interface.

So we get in there with the client and listen. We listen to their inner and outer reality. Then, if they cannot hold it together, if the tension is too much for them, by being beside them, by being with them in the interface, by listening and gradually giving them the courage to listen, we can help them begin to explore the interface. Knowing that somebody is with them in that place of chaos, that order-threatening area, they can take a stance which will allow a conversion of energy to take place. They are in the regressive step, the recoil that follows the crisis (see Figure 1, page 8). But whatever is happening to them, however caught, frightened, traumatised, devastated they may be, if we can keep the movement of the dance between inner and outer always in mind then somehow it will get across to them.

By degrees it will give them the courage to step forward. We take a stance in the 'now', at the interface, holding both their inner and outer for them if we have to, until such time as they can stand there. Then both of us can look to see where the energy will take them, see the meaning of this crisis, the symbology behind this symptom that they are experiencing. Again, the more we can stand at that interface, taking a posture with our client between their inner and their outer reality, the more we can listen to this quite extraordinary language. It is the interplay between the symptom, whatever it may be, and the symbol which lies behind that symptom – the most incredible, wonderful dialogue.

## The place of gathering

Our gods have become diseases. Was Jung right in this? If so, perhaps we need to dialogue with the gods and the goddesses – with the divinity. And that would take us to the remembrance of a time not all that far away when to be hit by illness was seen as a visitation from a god or goddess. Then, the place of gathering was seen as the place where one taught and listened, parleyed and dialogued with that divinity, so bringing in a different dimension. We try to handle things in linear time; but maybe, for the visitation of the god, we need also to work on the vertical dimension, allowing the opportunity, even in our lives, for eternity to intersect time.

Then we may begin to see illness as the place of gathering, place of healing, an internal Epidaurus [72] for ourselves. That love is the greatest therapy was recognised in Epidaurus, the greatest Greek healing centre, which must have been a sanctuary for people in trouble. Among other practices, the priest healers used herbs, diet and surgery; and also, as part of the therapy, sleep was induced, and the healing of the soul led to the healing of the body. Dreamers were evidently put into a small, deep place over running water and there left to dream their dream. Then when they awakened from this incubation (or maybe this lonely vigil), the priest-healer was there waiting for them, listening to them. The dream sometimes suggested the correct treatment and sometimes the god appeared in it to great effect. The speaking of the dream is what healed them. The *therapeutes* gave them time to go into their inner

---

[72]  See also Gordon-Brown and Somers, *The Raincloud of Knowable Things*, p. 96.

landscape and talk with the figures they met there. So they came out to greater wholeness, seeking it in the world.

The illusion of the one-time Noble Savage in a state of total health is perennial, though it seems particularly marked in the twentieth century. 'If we ate the right diet, just as our ancestors did, we'd all be healthy.' I am sure there is a great truth in that, but it cannot be the whole answer. Each generation, as far back as one can read, believed the one before it had better ways of dealing with health and illness. Yet disease and deformity have been found in the remains of bodies from earth-burials and ancient tomb-burials. The plagues of the Middle Ages became the consumption of the last century, and have become this century's cancer and heart trouble. Perhaps we should attend and listen more, treating illness less as the arch-enemy, the arch-betrayer. While not wanting to hang on to it, at least we can explore its implications in our lives before we try to treat it out of ourselves and others.

It has been said that it is possible to look upon every illness as a measure of protection against a worse fate – such as an inappropriate life? Carl Jung said that when we submit to our fate, we are more likely to call it the will of God. If we put up a hopeless and exhausting fight, it seems more like Devil's work. The seminal work of James Hillman reminds us that we have always had imperfect gods, sages and heroes: Chiron, wounded, unhealing, yet wise; Aesculapius, god and patron of healers, so successful at raising the dead that Zeus struck him dead; Hephaestus, divine smith and artisan, skew-footed and broken-legged, yet supreme craftsman of Olympus; Achilles, Trojan hero, strong in war but vulnerable; In the Odyssey of Homer, poet and story-teller, we find Teiresias, blind yet insightful, the powerful blind seer, blinded person (and eye problems, often backed up by our dreams, may have to do with a change of vision; just as the initiates were blindfolded before they took the challenge of passing over a threshold of new consciousness). And Prometheus, fire-bringer, with his perennial liver problem.

I would add here the Goddess: raped, traumatised, having to forgive or take revenge, carrying the dark face of Olympus; dark-faced Hecate; Sophia, so hated, so feared; the dark face of the moon; witchcraft and evil things. Yet originally it was the goddess who taught mankind how to find herbs and heal with them.

## *The wise woman*

My favourite character from fairy tale and life, from the villages and the slums, is that unassuming elderly woman who mysteriously appears at just the right moment, both to midwife the babies and to lay out the dead. She is earthly-wise and bread-making and healing. Not quite universal aunt, she is universal presence, turned to when people have nowhere else to go. This Wise Woman would say, 'Dig a hole in the earth; tell it your problems.' She's not fussed, but where she walks things start to happen and people begin strangely to grow. She reminds us of touch and caring and nurturing, of the seasons and the way of the heart, of the times to take up and the times to let go, the times to be born and the times to die, the times to give and the times to receive. She is re-membering us. In the fairy stories, and in reality, certainly in dreams, she often comes out as a rheumaticky old crone, but also she may be very round, almost circular, distinctly overweight. What would happen to her now, given the usual treatment for rheumatics, or the current attitude to that sort of roundness?

## *The journey*

Listening to people dialogue with their symptoms, I am struck by the sense of a journey: that we come from somewhere and we go to somewhere, and illness is but part of the process. Light and shadow belong together, and pain and joy. Do illness and health perhaps belong together also? Privileged as I have been to sit in on the telling of many lives, I'd say that the crisis, perhaps the serious illness, that hits in the present has its value. It blows our assumptions and our expectations, showing how very ill-equipped we usually are for life's experience, and also how appropriately, or inappropriately, we are living. The place of recoil lets us protest and rage, try to placate, buy our way out of the situation, avert it, seek help from others, anywhere, everywhere, to make it not happen to us. We seek cures from our present and we fear for our future. This is not necessarily regressing; it may be a very necessary first step towards becoming child-like instead of childish, being vulnerable and open, not knowing the answer to everything nor neatly putting life into boxes.

The place of gathering is unquestionably the place to remember ourselves; to re-member, to gather in those disparate parts of ourselves that have been scattered everywhere. Every moment of insight, every 'Aha!', every sudden realisation which seems to be new, feels like the remembering of something old, something we'd only just forgotten. So lest we forget who we truly are, or live without the experience of being alive, I believe we should attend to this gathering-place where linear time intersects, or is intersected by, the timeless. If we are made in the image of gods who are the true background to human life, then our sickness is divine in origin. It is not merely sent by the gods but is the foreground and the background we all conform to. As James Hillman said, we can only do in time what the gods do in archetypal eternity. If this is the place where the god appears, where one speaks with the god, then this is also the point at which the god withdraws. And the one who has come through that process is allowed to move on from the gathering place, perhaps more fully into life, perhaps more fully into death; and it's to be hoped that we see these as one and the same reality, doing that which we must.

Our symptoms and illnesses have been seen for a very long time as our sharing of the pain of the suffering God hanging, loveless, on a cross of grief and despair. But are they really that? Do we necessarily have to follow that, in the imitation of the dead god? Or are we, in our sickness and our health, participating in some profound mystery, the very blood and breath of our bodies being transformed into living spirit and fire? In health and in illness, are we taking part, through life, death and rebirth, in the celebration of a divinity already active in the human body, the human life? In our tension and struggle with our personal illness and disease, are we taking part in a major redemptive process? Are we helping, as the alchemists tried to do, to release the living gold that's already in the prima materia – the divinity already within matter? Are we, through the process of our struggle and our tension, assisting that collective and vast process of raising earth to heaven, and bringing heaven down to earth? Is it that the uncompleted wholeness, staying with the gap to be left in the circle, with everywhere to go, is a new earth in the making? I very profoundly believe that this is exactly so.

The Source

# CHAPTER THIRTEEN

# The Transcendent Function

## Barbara Somers

*Find a motif of light, and take the light down*
*to explore the darkness*

And so we are seeking for the Transcendent Function.[73] It is always remarkable when it appears. What is it? Everybody has within themselves the paradox of their own nature. Over and over we find ourselves caught in a tension of opposites. There is a pull between spirit and flesh, order and chaos, masculine and feminine, head and heart, doing and being. If one end of this opposite pair feels negative and the other positive, it's extremely difficult to handle.

Suppose that in a relationship we feel both acceptance and resentment. We both love and hate the other person. There will be times when it is possible to hold our ground and move towards the area of love, with the resentment down in the unconscious. But then suddenly we get caught into the opposite pull, and the more we try to be accepting and loving, pushing back our irritation, the more likely is the resentment to burst out and a battle begins. On the other hand, it may be the resentment that we're conscious of, acting out all the time. Then it's the love and acceptance that go down into the unconscious, where they in turn pick up energy. And that bothers us too; we cannot hate, dislike, loathe, resent this person constructively and creatively and energetically if we also love and accept them.

So it's well nigh impossible to stay at the centre, and we're in trouble again. If we are to be in any degree conscious, we'll be faced with these equidistant poles within our own nature. The more conscious they are, the more difficult to handle. The person in the middle does not know what to do. The ego, the everyday self, simply cannot manage. The will that once held up one of the ends is withdrawn; it can no longer hold.

---

[73] This chapter also appeared in Somers and Gordon-Brown, *Journey in Depth*, as part of Chapter 10, 'Polarities and the Transcendent Function', pp. 173-187.

We lose libido, our energy is drawn *down*, drawn back, as Jung says, to its source, back into the unconscious, activating it, taking another form.[74] Now it comes up in dreams; perhaps it takes the form of a depression, perhaps of a psychosomatic illness.

Continuously throughout history the battle between spirit and flesh has been waged, and it is still being fought out in each of us. Every one of our positives has its counter-face, for every light its shadow, for every shadow its brightness. It is in the nature of human experience that we all wrestle with these polarities. There are many examples of this struggle between an equidistant pair of opposites, two apparently equally-matched powers, and Western religion has simply split the poles apart. Luther still fights it out with the devils; St. Anthony struggles in the desert; Faust and Mephistopheles are caught in the tension between heaven and earth.

## The transcendent function

There has to be some other way of handling the deadlock. How is it done? Out of the unconscious there now emerges another factor, which holds within itself the energy originally contained within the two polarities.[75] This is the transforming symbol, the transcendent function, which includes the pair of opposites and takes them to a higher level. The resolution lies in our hope that it can be resolved.

Osiris, dismembered by his brother Set, was put in a lead coffin, enduring the period of scattering and the descent to the deepest before the gathering, and his raising as a god. The young Buddha struggled with Maya – illusion. He followed the Noble Middle Path, exploring life and death, to arise as the Enlightened One, the Buddha. Jesus, in conflict with Satan in the desert, was caught in the struggle between the powers of this world and of the next. His crucifixion was between the intolerable tension of spirit and matter. Then came the descent into hell, his giving up and submitting his will. Out of that struggle, after three days there emerged a new transcendent factor, the Christ – and that resurrected Christ has been resonant for two thousand years.

---

[74]  When the opposites are exactly equal, and the ego absolutely involved in both, there is a suspension of the will. When every motive is balanced by an equally strong counter-motive, the will can no longer operate. Life cannot tolerate a standstill, so there follows a damming-up of vital energy. See Jung, *Psychological Types*, CW Vol. 6 para. 824.

[75]  Jung goes on to say that this would lead to an insufferable state, unless out of the tension of opposites could come a new, uniting function to transcend them. Since the will has been completely divided, no progress can have been made; so the vital energy streams backwards towards its source. Thus the opposites give rise to something new which has arisen out of both the thesis and the antithesis. Compensating each of them, it becomes a middle ground for the uniting of the opposites. See Jung, *Psychological Types*, CW Vol. 6 para. 824--5.

## Inner alchemy

The transcendent function lies at the heart of Alchemy. Jung pointed out that it unites the pairs of psychic opposites in a synthesis which transcends them both. This is very close to the definition of the Transpersonal as that which includes the personal but also transcends it. The Transpersonal is very much concerned with this transformative symbol, this transcendent function with its synthesis of opposites.

There is a tendency in Transpersonal and spiritual work to try and push people too quickly towards the synthesis of a polarity, before they've explored the nature of the polarity itself. That cannot be done, because of the pull of the energy down into the unconscious. The polarities cannot be dealt with by consciousness. That's why the libido withdrew into the unconscious in the first place, there to gather energy and to bring out a new transcendent symbol. The mind can't do it. We

can't *decide* to let the energy withdraw, we can't direct it down into the unconscious and assume a symbol will arise, nice though that would be. It is an entirely spontaneous happening. Often it comes through dreams, whose images and motifs help ease out the intolerable tension and bring in some third point between the pair of opposites.

Speaking of the degree of consciousness and individuation which we can begin to reach – at least a little – Jung observes that a problem which, at a lower level, had led to wild conflicts and panicky emotional out-bursts, seems from the mountain-top to be a mere storm in the valley. The storm is real, but instead of being in it we're above it.[76] People who have been in tension, taken down into their own darkness, made to face the reality of their own responsibility, have over and over again had the transforming, transcendent function emerge out of the darkness to lead them to a different place. Now, they are seeing from the mountain-top.

This is the secret of Alchemy.[77] It is a mysterious process, and it happens endlessly, drawing to our attention that there is some great Alchemist at work and that all life is alchemy. While working with somebody, trusting the process, allowing time for the incubation to happen and the cooking in the alembic – the alchemical flask – to occur, we begin to see the transcendent function emerging. It is then that the original conflict comes to seem like the storm in the valley.

---

[76] Wilhelm & Jung, *The Secret of the Golden Flower: A Chinese Book of Life*. Also in Commentary on *The Secret of the Golden Flower*, CW Vol. 13, para 17.

[77] Jung said clearly that the transcendent function is the secret of Alchemy. In its light the noble and the base parts of our personalities, both conscious and unconscious, are blended and fused, as are the most with the least differentiated of the four functions. Thus the personality is transformed. Jung, 'Individuation', CW Vol. 7, para 360.

When this transcendent function, this transforming symbol, appears, the balance between the ego and the unconscious is restored. And then, of course, a new imbalance will begin and we'll have to go through the same thing all over again at a higher turn of the spiral. However, many of us haven't yet had the transformative symbol which would carry us up the mountain track. We have to climb it ourselves by steps and stages, however much we feel dragged down by the conflict of the polarity. But as we ascend above the valley, we can work with it more and more consciously, helping ourselves prepare the ground. We may keep a dream book, a notebook, explore our dreams on tape, allowing time for the cooking to occur. Then, even if the transformative symbol hasn't yet appeared, we hope it will come and take us up the mountain.

### Little bull

Two figures came up for me in imaging, one male, one female. I intended to discuss with them the problems they were posing, but instead these two figures took me firmly by the hand, led me out into a meadow and *they* discussed *me* – as their problem! I became happy with that and accepted it. But in the middle of their discussion, a little bull wandered by. He meandered around, Disney-style, sniffing the daisies and holding a buttercup under his chin. I looked at him and thought, 'There's nothing in me that has anything whatever to do with this bull!' It took me seven years to see it. The laziness – 'I'm not allowed to be like that!' – the idleness, the love of just being, dozing around all over the place. He was the perfect counterpoint to my polarities and my tension, a lazy bull just doing nothing. He was my transforming symbol.

### The gypsy girl

Here is an example, a man terribly caught in a polarity. He came from an upright, Scottish, very rigid, Puritan-ethic background. Over the fifteen years of their marriage, his wife had been 'the feeling one'. She did all the flowing, while it was accepted that he did all the thinking, looking after the structure and the mapping. But now his own feeling side was emerging. As it spontaneously arose, their roles and functions were badly thrown and the nature of the relationship changed. 'Don't be silly,' she would say, implying, 'That's my area.

You don't know what you're talking about! Keep off my grass!' He started to speak in a slow, blurred way, with a time-lag. A familiar story, as one of a pair begins to change and the roles and structure are blown. This was his dream:

'I am looking after the gate of a palace when a gypsy girl comes and asks if she can give me healing. At first I ask for whom she is collecting money and tell her to go away. I go into a field where figures like Mummers are enacting a symbolic dance in the shape of a figure-of-eight.' He drew this as the shape of infinity, sideways rather than upright.

'A fight breaks out between a strong man and a weak one who has apparently insulted him. We all watch transfixed.' The strong one hits the weak with a club which the dreamer describes as 'a roll of hollow paper'. The fight becomes symbolic, like a dance. The strong man is changed by the weak and vice versa. 'I rejoin the dance, which turns into a sexual orgy. I don't stay, but go off in search of the gypsy girl. She's transformed into a beautiful woman whom I know quite well. We discuss how this can be, and she reminds me that I saw her at Belsen at the end of the war. She was the only one in her family to survive the gas chambers. I feel that we are to be united and that the union is shortly to be consummated.'

Now, here is the transcendent function coming in. You couldn't force this dream. We waited upon it. We looked at the various motifs; at the young anima-figure of the gypsy girl, representing the feeling side, close to nature: an instinctual, intuitive motif. We noted how he told her to go away – he said that was his tight-sporraned approach to money and energy and libido. But then the dream brought in the figure-of-eight and the ritual quality of the dance, the traditional, distinct steps of the Mummers dancing. Next, the fight broke out, the strong man hitting the weak with the 'roll of hollow paper', exchanging energy, the strong man being changed by the weak and vice versa. He said this had a good deal to do with his sexuality; his penis was like a roll of hollow paper – and in terms of what his wife said about him it unquestionably was. We recognised that the roll of paper and the exchange of energy pointed to a change of function.

Next, the girl was transformed into a beautiful woman whom he'd seen at Belsen at the end of the war, the only one in her family to survive the gas chamber. 'What did happen to you at the end of the war?' I asked. He hadn't been to Belsen, he'd been at university. But that was the time when, with a complete change of mode, he'd switched subjects – from the Social Sciences, which had been his original choice, to Law. He'd gone against his own feeling nature at that point (it was the feeling side of him, the side tending towards the Social Services, that was re-emerging now). Just at the end of the war he had married a 'feeling' wife in order, he said, to flesh out the polarity within his own nature. But now he was unable any longer to hold apart head and heart in himself, or to project it out on his wife or his daughters. And this tension within him was facing him with the reality of his own predicament. He had all sorts of symptoms: the typical stiff neck and rigid shoulders that follow when head and heart are split.

He did not know what this lovely dream meant, but he felt a lot better after it. It had carried the transcendent function. It came up out of the unconscious with a dance, a flow, a figure-of-eight which could unite at the symbolic level the pull of the polarities. The roll of paper exchanged the energies, and head and heart came closer together. He had previously been driven inwards, holding all the tension down in his body and trying to project it out to his marriage. Now, a great release of energy came. The body, as Jung said, has to be in the experience too. Going down, we draw up the instinctual side. The transcendent function includes everything. It goes down and it goes up; the horizontal struggle is put at peace, brought together, making the perfect, equal-armed cross, and Earth is taken up into heaven.

The gypsy figure began more and more to play a part in his life. He was made to look at the difference between a 'weak man' and a 'strong man'. In the view of his Scottish background and his paternalistic clan, the older-style 'weak man' meant a feeling, heart-based man. And his wife was of course expressing her view of what a 'strong man' should be.

That one dream stated the situation, led him, gave him his transcendent function, linked the two ends of the polarity and began the healing of the split. I am almost overwhelmed by the quite spontaneous way these graphic examples emerge. We look at our dreams, the motifs that crop up, the things that happen in our lives – the people we bump into, the film we saw last night, the book that falls into our hands. It may take a very long time, but after a period of tension and withdrawal, after enough time in the unconscious, that redeeming factor emerges to take us through. Here is another example.

## The yellow flowers

She was young, American Jewish, brought up in the most appalling circumstances in New York. Her mother had been left pregnant after a one-night stand and she never knew who her father was. When she was three, her mother married someone who brought in two step-sons, one ten and the other six. She was raped by her new father and by each of the brothers just about alternately. There was hardly a time when this was not happening. Not surprisingly, in these dreadful conditions, by the time she was in her forties she had a very marked anxiety neurosis.

All the way through she remembered one thing. She had been hiding one day in a doorway in the windswept streets of New York, curled up in a corner not knowing what to do (she didn't want to go home and there was nowhere else to go) when she'd seen a splash of yellow in the darkness of the street – some half-dead flowers lying there. These flowers were the one motif she could hold on to.

Sexuality loomed enormously large in her life. Every image, every dream, came up as distorted sexuality, and it had begun to obsess her, though it became apparent that it was tenderness rather than sexuality that she was looking for. As do many people with a very wounded background, she became a social worker. By the job she chose, she was unconsciously seeking a transcendent function, looking for a way of pulling together this split in herself. She was fully aware that she was trying to do for others what hadn't been done for herself. Such a movement in the unconscious often leads us to adjust our own healing. She became a sexual counsellor, both fascinated and repelled by her work.

Together, we looked for something in her job that would hold her and by degrees draw her up. People cannot go straight up the mountain. One of the dangers, as we have seen, is to rush them, not letting them penetrate their darkness, not allowing time for the healing factor to emerge, pulling it out too rapidly into consciousness. Where people have too suddenly come up to the light, there is nearly always a throwback. Better rather find a motif of light, and take the light down to explore the darkness.

We also sought some anchor-point in the outer world where she could begin to express herself. She kept a notebook for a while, then she began to 'dabble in paint', as she called it (she'd never touched a paintbrush in her life). Art was spontaneously emerging. Her first picture was of the dead flowers, with a red ball representing her sexuality as it had now become. The picture showed the new relationship between this ball and the flowers – a remarkable thing to have emerged from somebody so incredibly wounded. It wasn't just on canvas now, it was in her life: her own redeeming, salving motif. It had been with her in that doorway when she was about seven, and it had stayed with her all through the years. Again and again people come out of the depths of their hell and it is as if somebody has said, 'Lo, I have been with you all the days of your life.'

Five years later she drew a final, enchanting picture. It's when she broke out of the egg – one of my most-beloved emergings: a chick with one leg in the air, standing in a puddle, not very footed yet – and very, very beautiful.

### Gestalt with objects

When someone is struggling, when they cannot hold the tension any longer, they're going to glissade down. Therefore we cannot wait for the transformative symbol to appear. I work *as if* it were on its way. The art is to help the person become more conscious, so that they can at least hold the balance as they seek the integrity of the Self. And over and over, in their dreams and images, there comes a sudden 'click' and something appears. I've found a good method of working towards this. I use a Gestalt technique, letting objects rather than chairs or cushions stand for the issues of choice. I add another object to be alongside the person, which stands in for the integrity of the Self, the Soul, the spirit. Here is an example.

### The man in the middle

There was a man who drew 'chaos' and 'peace' at the two ends of a pole. He said that at one time he'd been unable to tolerate any upset or anger anywhere. He'd adjusted to the impossible pull by going for peace at any price. But after a while, he became aware that the peace was set against the chaos of his original background. 'When they get into trouble with each other, my wife and my son,' he said, 'I dive straight in the middle – and then they *both* come in and bash me.' A member of a partnership of three at work, he would leap right into the fray when the other two went for each other, and again they'd both bash him. He saw how often he had leapt into the fracas and always been hit (reminiscent of the sketch of the husband and wife caught in a drunken brawl. One small policeman is hanging on-to the two of them, they're both bashing him, his helmet's dented, and he's shouting, 'Help! help! Somebody do something!').

We used this 'Gestalt with objects' to explore his family problems. I put on the table things to stand in for family members. I began with a rock crystal: 'That's you. Now, here's your wife. This is your son. What's happening here?' By this Gestalt method we got the feeling of the energy-flow between the three of them. Next I said, 'Now, here's you, at one end of the polarity. What's at the other end? How do you respond to your son and your wife? What out here makes you react so to that scene going on between them?'

'Fear of being the outsider!' he said. This visual Gestalt, these three objects, had enabled him to see it. A memory: he'd been evacuated away from his family, while his younger sister had been kept at home, and when he was brought back after the war he'd felt he belonged nowhere. We talked about the chaos of his parents, and himself as the rejected little outsider. We used these objects now to stand for mother and beloved baby sister, and for him being put out. His family seemed complete without him, a set-up family from which he'd been pushed out. Longing for a way into their containment, he didn't know where to relate. It hadn't just been love of peace: 'I was afraid of being the outsider'. The rejected child pushed out of the family, he'd tried to become the insider by being peacemaker and harmoniser. And it had worked very well. The family indeed called on him when they hit problems, so he did feel to some extent included.

The visual movement of objects on a table had enabled him to see it. I asked, 'If you could handle things differently, how would you do it – if you had the choice?'

'I'd like to be able to stand in a different place, see it in a different way.'

'If you could stand there instead of here, and not be drawn back to the earlier stages, how would you like to handle it, now in your maturity?'

'Well, I can see my wife's point of view – she has a lot on her side; but I can also see my son's – yes, there are some positive things between them.' Eventually he said, 'But it's their business.' As he moved the objects around the table, we could see the energy-dynamic going back and forth. At last he understood what he was doing when he leaped into the middle and tried to handle things from there. He realised it was because he was that fearful child (frightened of chaos and disorder, frightened of the breaking-up of the harmony of the family) trying to get in. Leaping in without a transformative symbol took him continually backwards and forwards and down. Together we tried to rebalance. He saw how far he split off; he was so afraid of reactivating that childhood chaos that no price was too large for peace. He had to recognise that in speaking his truth he risked being an outsider.

His dreams suggested that a transformative symbol was about to appear; but until it did he started to act as if it had, *as if* there were the possibility of a new harmony. He took the positive values of the peace-maker, and also the positive values of allowing chaos to happen. 'What is the energy within chaos which you can use creatively and constructively?' No longer feeling he personally had to 'do something about it', he found that he could tolerate a lot more chaos both in the world and in his personal relationships. He'd never allowed himself to look at the nature of his own chaos. The peace and the chaos each lay within himself. From that moment things improved. 'Peace has got to start in me.' In the bringing-together of peace and chaos, he discovered his own usefulness and his own transformative symbol.

### Using Gestalt

I may use the more conventional Gestalt here, with chairs or cushions rather than objects. Giving a place to each of the critical feelings as it emerges, moving from one position to the other, getting into the two that seem to be conflict, may lead to a sudden clarification. Or we may give a personification to two figures, finding perhaps that this one is conventional, traditional ('My partner's not behaving very well – it's time he was punished!') while that one loves the partner. Till now there is been no clarity. Using Gestalt will bring the split into consciousness in a most remarkable way, identifying the poles that are fighting. Then of course we have to move on towards the transformative symbol.

Some people, needing to be in control, would refuse absolutely to move themselves around in this way on cushions or chairs. But, seeing the table as an energy field, they'd be willing to work with objects, which they can move about in the middle of a conversation. We need to use both methods: first the polarities need to be identified, and then a tableful of small things can in an extraordinary way give people the sense of having a choice, having alternatives, being able to move things around on the board of their own life.

## Hubris and inflation

All these symbols are containers of energy. We may have a sudden emotional conversion and believe it to be a transformative symbol. We may go wild, go into hubris, fly up, lose contact with the ground. Catholics become Communists and Communists become Catholics overnight. But the groundwork hasn't been done. We haven't been through the suffering and tension of opposites, the struggle to raise that which is unconscious up into consciousness, and there can be a very dangerous sense of inflation. If we're lucky, it dies away; otherwise it can take hold of us and make us into fanatics, cosmic boy scouts.

## The transforming symbol

St. Francis, very much enjoying life, was obeying a sudden inner vision when he built his little church. What he'd seen as just a small building turned into a whole movement, because it brought with it the energy of transformation. The truly transformative symbol changes our attitudes, our lives, because it brings with it the energy required in consciousness to transform the whole situation. If anybody had described my little bull to me or given me a reason for him seven years earlier, it might have meant quite a bit to me at the conceptual level, but it would have meant absolutely nothing beyond that. We have to be very, very careful of interpreting for people. Let them do it for themselves. Otherwise, as well as the problems they come in with, we send them out with the burden of our interpretations. We need to wait upon life. The transformative symbol comes to each of us when the moment is ready. The transcendent function is its own explanation.

It is said that the prime energy of our lives gets lost in the system. To be caught into the mass is to be caught into the shadow side of the group. We come into incarnation and embody ourselves in the mass, but many of us know that it is not quite right; the unity in the group means that the shadow side is not experienced. It was necessary to be born into our families, be enwombed in the womb of unconsciousness. Many people are enwombed again, but this time in the womb of consciousness, to be reborn.[78] Before that, we muddle love with desire. What we call 'love' is very often the need for possession of the other to give ourselves a sense of identity, a desire that comes from the solar plexus. However, out of the upper region of the heart comes love of the whole, love of the One, the love which enables us to go back to the original group – but consciously, having had the experience. The individual journey is to find the line home to the original place we came from. We come from the One, we return to the One – the faces of God, the faces of the One – and the energy of the One is life.

---

[78]   See Stage 6 in Figure 6, Stages of Emergence, p. 104

# APPENDIX 1

## AT THE END OF YOUR TETHER

Further discussion between Barbara Somers,
Ian Gordon-Brown and participants [79]

*A participant*: I had the sensation of a yoke over my shoulders on which hung two buckets, one with water and one with cement. I had to run somewhere in time to build a thick wall. The sun was hot and the bodily feeling was of heaviness in the legs and arms – surprisingly, not over the shoulders; and a pain in the head and over the eyes. I can't really associate that with anything. The memory was that when I was a child of four or five I had to keep going on hot country lanes with a group of grown-ups. It was boring, the sun was hot and I felt guilty because I was naughty and dragged my feet. Fire and Earth were the elements, I think.

*BS (to the group)*: A simple counterpoint for this imaging would be, 'Now go to its opposite. What is the release from this? Do you have a memory of such a release? When have you felt like this before?' The client can work on that; you have given them an alternative. Now, each time they begin to constellate that original feeling again, firstly, it is up in consciousness and won't ever be so unconscious again and secondly, you have given them the counterpoint, the feeling that they can work towards something else, have some degree of control over it. And so the pattern of health begins to build up.

*Another participant*: When I was 'at the end of my tether' I felt about to collapse, my legs were being stretched down. I also had a surprising sensation of amazing strength.

*BS*: And aren't you also indicating the antidote: mentioning the leg stretches but with your hand on your *heart*?

*(To the group)*: This is quite an important message for the client. You are watching out for him. It doesn't seem, and isn't, logical that somebody who feels their legs are being stretched down should have the antidote in the heart; but the fact that the client indicated just that by his own action suggests that's what you might follow. A kind of elastic band may go from exactly where your client indicates with his hand, to where he feels collapse is imminent, in this instance, where his legs

---

79  Appendices 1 and 4 consist of transcripts of further tape-recorded discussions between Barbara Somers, Ian Gordon-Brown and groups of their students. Like most of the rest of this book, they took place in seminars on the subject of 'Symptom as Symbol' held at the Centre for Transpersonal Psychology in London in the early 1980s as part of their two-year training in counselling and psychotherapy.

were 'being stretched down'. So, suggest some exercise which links the two. It may be different another time; but without their realising it, the person is likely to indicate with their body exactly what they need.

*Another participant*: My image was of becoming a corpse in Lapland, a huge, flat, totally blank white area of ice: the Arctic. And then being attacked by a black bird and not being able to move my arms. I wanted to vomit. I feel a sense of panic even now as I talk about it. Keeping the image, I felt as though birds were trying to attack my eyes – a corpse without eyes. I'm very short-sighted. I also have a lengthy history of depression, the feeling of being freezing cold and unable to move, of rigidity. I was sent to the doctor as a child with a psychosomatic stomach pain. My memory was of my mother being angry at me because I complained about it and was sick a lot. When I get that image she's always dressed in black, which symbolises the anger. It is all centred in Water; all that frozen water, ice and snow.

*BS*: And inability too, I suppose, to express and receive warmth? Yours is a good example of how we cannot presume that anger is always red.

*Another participant*: I got the feeling of a large tidal wave falling on me – 'drowning' or 'death' – mixed up with 'screaming into infinity', 'a cornered animal', and being 'overpowered by some burden'. Bodily, I felt I was being pushed in the stomach, and that was mixed up with a giant roar; it's a roar, not just a scream. That sensation reminded me not of a particular occasion, but of constantly screaming and screaming and screaming, and no one hearing me because they're screaming too. It may be related to some early memory. I can see the Water symbol as it first appeared, which is fascinating because I did have a life-threatening renal disease when I was ten. It was very watery and did nearly kill me, so I can understand that. There seems also to be a lot of Fire. The palpitations I get I've already come to terms with a bit, trying to make my life more rhythmical and flowing.

*BS*: ... Giving you the chance to absorb and assimilate?

*Reply*: Yes, but I don't know what the roar was ...

*BS (to the group)*: In the counselling process you'd explore the nature of the roar, and what the energy in it is. Where would the roar come from? You indicated with your hand ...

*Reply*: From here. Roars are meant to come from here, but this one doesn't!

*BS (to the group)*: And you as counsellor may well expect roars to come from *here*. But your client indicates 'roar' *there* and so you need to explore what for this person is *her* roar.

*A participant*: My graphic image was a feeling of being torn apart or fragmented. My body – it was like a head or heart exploding. The memory was of being left at school as a boarder aged six, my mother going away, and having to put on a brave front against all sorts of feelings. The elements were Fire, then Air, and the last was Water: a lot of bother with tonsils, throats, runny noses as a small boy, but really very little since.

*BS*: You have a nice combination of elements: inflammation and allergies, locked Fire hitting Air passages, and running Water. Thank you.

*(To the group)*: Looking back, you can often see a pattern of symptoms over the years, a medical history that might relate to the elements. People often come up with water, inundation and so on. Typologically, they are often being presented by the unconscious with the bit they haven't got. It is their 'inferior function', which is their redeeming principle and is very often mediated via the body.

For other people, their body is so vitally important to them, so much 'in the way', that it may well cut out. Then the unconscious may give them something completely different, where the body is of no effect whatsoever. Because matters of the body have come very easily to them, they are forced into a position where the body is no help. I've met this in a number of polio cases, or accidents which cause a paralysis of some kind. For example, I knew a young boy who was injured in a sports accident. His whole orientation had previously been to the body; all his values were of the body. It has had an extraordinary effect on him at a psychological level. It can be very painful but seems to be essential to the rounding out of our total nature. We need to have the experience of all aspects if we are to become more whole. Thus the benign nature of the symptom begins to become clear – or clearer, anyway.

*Another participant*: What came up for me was strongly connected to heating and temperature generally. Being at the end of my tether is like having hot steel bands tightened round my chest and stomach, and a choking sensation of steam-pressure in the upper chest and throat. It starts just above the heart and moves up into the throat and shoulders. I did have a heart attack, and that's what it did on the night. The doctor was impressed by that, said it was a very interesting fact.

*BS*: Would you like to say that more clearly: why was the doctor impressed? Heart attacks happen all the time. What was different about it, from his point of view?

*Reply*: I've seen that particular doctor several times. He'd always dismissed any illness I had on the grounds that I was a hopeless neurotic, therefore there was never anything wrong with me. He was also foxed when I fell off a ladder and smashed my right elbow; it confused him no end. I couldn't have a smashed elbow, I was so hopelessly neurotic. When he was called out at one o'clock in the morning to this thing about a heart attack, he marched in raring to go, with 'You're putting it on'. Although I could hardly speak at the time, I described the symptoms and he said, 'Oh, yes, well perhaps you are then.'

About temperature: I remember two things about being in intensive care. One was the contrast between feeling hot up here and having terribly cold feet; so much so that, when I was barely conscious, apparently the only thing I mentioned was my feet. The nurse said to me afterwards that at one stage, ridiculously, I had six or seven blankets on the lower half of the bed, and nothing on the top half; that was all wired up.

The first incident in childhood that came to me was being slapped by both my parents. It's my only recollection of their being unanimous. They agreed in their verdict of me. I was about thirteen and I got slapped for describing somebody as 'ruddy-cheeked'. That, of course, was 'disgusting bad language, people don't speak like that'. Again, 'ruddy-cheeked' seems to have something to do with temperature.

For the childhood ailments: the only two things that I ever had wrong with me physically as a child were hay fever and glandular fever, which again imply heat but don't necessarily have it. So it's Fire and Water, very strongly. I'm not sure whether 'cold feet' is saying something about my unearthed state, almost total for many years? It might be, but it seems rather a negative comment.

*Contribution from the group*: You're seeing that as psychological. But wouldn't it be natural that your feet would be cold in these particular conditions?

*Another contribution*: It certainly very often can be. If the circulation is as poor as that, it's pushing to get round anyway. You were wired up, weren't you, to a life-support system?

*Another contribution*: Also, if there are drugs involved and the blood is short, your body says, 'Well, we won't circulate what isn't absolutely necessary today'. Which would put your feet into that critical condition, and your skin and other things not vital to the circulation.

*Reply*: I was regarded as a bit soft as a kid because I needed a hot water bottle on my feet. Ironically, that was one of the physical symptoms I shared with my dad; it was all right him having cold feet, but it wasn't appropriate for me.

*BS*: At the psychological level, having the ground cut out early on from under one's feet very often leads to a loss of heart – of *coeur*, of courage. Thus there may well be a psychological link between heart and feet. It shows how graphic are the symptoms and the symbols when you work directly with them.

*Another participant*: From quite an early age I've had tension and aches in my neck. The pain shifts from the top to the base but it's always been in that region. My body has become aware of feeling as if somebody's pressing down on my shoulders. They feel quite tight at times, as if they were giving in to something. I quite often feel tired, like a washed out rag, drained of all energy. During this exercise I was yawning incessantly. There are times in the morning and the evening when I do seem to yawn an awful lot and I don't think that it's normal. I'm the only person I know who yawns such a lot. People laugh about it. It's not that I'm more bored than anybody else. The sensation reminds me of being held down to the spot, 'held captive?' I couldn't prove it, but it's easy for me to think that perhaps as a child I was held down by my mother? I was willing to be at home, she relied on me; and I still feel I have to be around, and feel guilty about it. It seems familiar. Perhaps it's Earth, being held down.

*BS*: Do you think the yawning might give you a clue?

*(To the group)*: It's terribly easy to come up with total theories: 'Oh yes, hyperventilation is the problem'. But it's not necessarily so with any particular client. When you are told that something like yawning happens every morning, yes, it may be that the body is trying to re-adjust itself in some way. You observe it, note it, explore it a bit more. Something may need to be corrected. Perhaps that much air shouldn't be drawn in, it's causing a carbonisation or an over-oxygenation or whatever, and all that may be absolutely accurate and help one person tremendously. On the other hand, for another person it may have nothing whatever to do with that. I don't think there is a panacea or an

all-round explanation for a symptom. What is important is to explore what it is for the individual, and to link the corrective yawn with that.

*Contribution from the group*: In long, guided daydreams I've often found that a change in the client's breathing, sometimes with yawning, can signal a shift to a different level of consciousness, particularly a deepening. The yawning seems to be a transition phenomenon.

*Another contribution*: Again, in doing meditative exercises with different groups, I've found that yawning can come in as a barrier when there's a fear of going down somewhere, perhaps into the body or into some deeper experience.

A *third contribution*: And yawns may help someone move *through* a barrier, through a resistance to moving into a different level.

*BS*: So here we have 'yawns signalling a deepening process' and, conversely, 'yawns showing a block against going deeper'. Also, 'yawns helping us go through such a block'. This is where one cannot say, 'What it is, is *this*.' For instance, one person might yawn during the prayers in church, putting their hand up just to try to smother it and look holy. For a different person, the yawn might give the opportunity to put their hand in front of their face because they are socially unsure. You never know what it's saying. You have to ask.

Or take addiction to smoking. I assume that it's become an addiction because somebody's done a lot of it. I ask people to act as if they were smoking. 'Draw on a pencil – or a cigarette for that matter – and get a sense of what it does for you.' That in-drawing and pausing ... so often the cigarette is a comforter. Or a social moment. Quite frequently it gives 'time to absorb and assimilate', time to help correct the breathing till it becomes natural, which may not be at all what one thinks it should be. But we aim to get them to listen to the body so that they don't need the cigarette.

*A participant*: I felt as though I were trapped in a dark pit, wanting to burst. There was an awful lot of tension but I was numbed and dead, shut off from any sensation at all, hardly seeing. The world was behind a membrane. Medically, being in the dark is paralleled by the fact that I don't see very well anyway. There was a tremendous tightness across the chest; the stomach was pushing it up and making it feel tight. This links with a lot of back difficulties and stomach troubles – having an ulcer bursting, that sort of tension. I associate the image with being suffocated, which must have been as a child? Did I get caught in something? Was it maybe even during the birth process? The elements were Air and Earth.

*BS*: This awareness of birthing comes up quite spontaneously again and again. First of all, we remember that it's generally current just now; people are being 're-birthed' every day of the week. But a *psychological* birth process very often seems to throw up symptoms associated with the *physical* birth, so check out the history of any symptoms that emerge. If there's one which has to be listened to, it may be that the body is releasing energy it has been holding back from that birth experience. The symptom may cause the person to seek help to release the psychological burden. Those drawn towards a therapist or counsellor with a Transpersonal orientation are quite likely to be going through some internal birthing or threshold – some crisis of opportunity, anyway – so birth symptoms might well be coming up again at that moment. Working on a client's psychosomatic history, I usually also ask, 'Do you know anything about the nature of your birth?'

*Another participant*: My graphic image was of walking through black treacle, trying to move, flailing around in it. I couldn't see in the black, was completely bound down. In the film 'Roots', a young African is caught by slave traders and writhes and howls against his loss of freedom. Well, I drew a parallel, screaming and throwing my body in all directions. Body reactions were very familiar and classical for me: a pain in the forehead, to do with not seeing, and a pain in the gut. The whole image was very much of Water and Earth, water being the treacle that I could neither walk nor run through. The body seemed to say, 'I'm fed up, I cannot do any more'. Digestion, the Earth. It reminded me of going through the birth canal, of not being able to see inside the womb, and various pains in the neck. I didn't know which way to turn, was all twisted up, 'cannot get round this corner and get out'. The image for that was Fire.

*BS*: If this were your client, you could now work on the actual birthing process. Again, bear in mind that you may be talking to someone who's going through a psychological birthing as well.

*Another participant*: For me, it felt as if I was being held down under the water, sitting on the mud of the sea bed. A tube allowed me to breathe but there was no voice, I couldn't speak. I was getting real pain in the eyes. I realised that if I allowed myself to cry it would be a release. I used to have an awful problem with my back. I'd traced it back yet again to that ghastly convent. I thought: 'Not that, everyone's so fed up with hearing about that.' But I had my womb removed when I was thirty-two, and blood was poured into me. I was a Caesarean birth. My mother's womb was entirely locked, I'd been held down in Water for a long time and only just made it. Between us, it's all four elements. My mother is a very Watery-Earthy person but I feel happiest with Air and Fire. I can usually cope with it all these days. When I went into therapy, all these symptoms started disappearing because I could talk about them or write about them or shout about them. The trouble was in the days before that. I don't know where I'd have ended up next.

BS: Held down on the sea bed with just a tube allowing you to breathe, unable to cry out. How dramatic can you get? The actual experience was of Water and Earth.

*(To the group)*: Although I do not like stretching maps too far, Jung's typology can also be thrown up by the elements. You have to look for where the functions are *not*. The body is often trying to present that as the necessary balancing principle to the person's view of the world. The body may be drawing attention to a need to concentrate, presenting symptoms that cause one to pay attention to the missing aspect.

In my own case, Earth (and to a degree Water) is definitely the missing factor in both my chart and my typology. The body pushes us all the time. It has continuously presented me with the need to slow down. I have to concentrate on the body, I have to get more rhythmic and flowing, to pay attention to emotion – to Water – in others and myself. So, linking the elements and the typology, you can very often see the homeopathic requirement, psychologically, to give that person either a touch of the poison that they've already got, or the complementary side. Their psyche will nearly always tell you what it is they need.

### Other comments from different people

'I had a feeling of being wrung out by an enormous pair of hands. This manifested itself in muscle tension, particularly in the arms, legs, shoulders and neck. Thinking about the birthing process, I recalled a symptom: I was a Caesarean baby, in no mood to be born at all. I was all over the place and had to be cut out. Maybe because of this, I had a twisted neck and had to have a muscle cut when I was five. I'd completely forgotten that. It felt like Air and Fire; there was difficulty in breathing.'

'This was a very profound exercise for me. I experienced a sensation of implosion, of my rib cage being squeezed, of splintering. Also of drowning; an inability to see or breathe, constriction and strangulation. My memory was immediately *felt*: apart from being premature and jaundiced, I was a breech birth and that accounts for quite a lot. I associate it all with Water and Air.'

'My graphic image was of drowning, which is clearly Air and Water. The symptoms were breathlessness, fatigue, panic, beating of the hands and feet in the water. And a headache, paralysis, open mouth. As for my health history, the pattern of any illnesses: well, I'm appallingly healthy. I've broken a few things in my time, a ligament in my leg. I had a psychosomatic ten days in bed with a temperature of a hundred and one, but that was Fire and doesn't seem to relate. However, I do have a clear memory of how, when I was an undergraduate, somebody upset our boat and pulled it over so that we all had to swim to the shore.'

'I felt as if I were being suffocated by an octopus; so obviously it was in the element Water, which is very direct. Followed by a sense of disintegration in all directions. The body symptoms came immediately: a tremendous heat in the solar plexus and sacral area. This certainly relates to body symptoms: my liver becomes enlarged, and I do have problems in the sacral area, as well as nervous palpitations in the throat. In childhood I had a lot of coughs. One early memory: my brothers used to send me in to confront my father to try and get gifts out of him, because we weren't allowed any treats. That used to cause tremendous feelings in the throat. A more recent memory: moving house, coping with family situations.'

'My graphic image was of being crunched in the teeth of a giant bulldozer. Yes, I had masses of symptoms: pain in the back of my neck, clenched jaws, dizziness, a restless feeling in the blood, creeping claustrophobia, heaviness in the head. As a memory, the sensation of being pinned down, held down by someone. My medical history is of anaemia. I clench my jaws and get pains in the back of my neck. I connect all this with Earth and Air.'

'… An elastic thread in front of me, extending further and further to the horizon. I feel it will be extended to the limits, but so far that's not possible; however, it will not be broken. On the Body level, I felt, "if it continues I will get another migraine" – a threatening migraine. It reminded me of being manipulated by external forces and I couldn't do anything about it. I was just a victim of everything that happened to me.'

'When pushed to my limits I feel frayed, in shreds, to be cut up. The symptoms: a pain in the chest and heart, a very tight throat, a pulsating head, my liver enlarges, my feet swell up and ache. That sensation reminds me of the longing to go to bed to rest and sleep. When that happens, I want to be unconscious. It totally matches my health history: I had my thyroid cut out because it felt tight. I had my gall bladder out. And my feet do ache. I would probably go for Earth because of the feet but I cannot really relate the shreds and the cutting up, or the frayed feeling, to any of the Elements.'

'My experience was rather like drowning, with a tremendous restriction and heaviness of the throat and chest. My arms were up, as though I were falling. It was very hot and I seemed to be gasping for air, with a sensation of deafness and suffocation; also of a lot of heat, but not being able to express it. I can remember, when I was very young, being shut in a garden shed. It was hot and I was frightened of creepy-crawlies. I was also frightened of being left, being walked away from. As a child I had a lot of sickness, and also tonsillitis. It feels like Air and Water, with a touch of Fire.'

'I think it has something to do with context. Your heartbeat's meant to be a basic fundamental rhythm. I've had the palpitations, and to me they are to do with regularity and timing and rhythms, trying to tell me something about being out of rhythm – that I should be in rhythm with what's happening around me.'

# APPENDIX 2

## TYPE A and TYPE B PERSONALITIES

Aiming to research the link between personality factors, stress and coronary heart disease, Friedman and Rosenman (1974) undertook a nine-year study of 3,000 initially healthy 39-59 year old men. On the basis of their responses about eating habits and ways of dealing with stressful situations, they were divided into two types: Type A and Non Type A.

*Type A individuals* tended to be ambitious, competitive, easily angered, time-conscious, hard-driving, and demanding of perfection in themselves and others.

*Non Type A individuals* tended to be relaxed, easy-going, not driven to perfection, forgiving and not easily angered.

*Findings*: 70% of the 257 who died during the nine years were Type A individuals.

*Conclusion*: People who are of Type A were seen as more susceptible to stress because of their behaviour traits, and consequently more likely to suffer stress-related illness such as coronary heart disease.

Though the study showed a strong correlation which suggests that there is a link between 'personality type' as assessed by the authors, it must be remembered that correlation is not the same as cause-effect. While it could be the case that Type A behaviour leads to increased risk, it could also be the case that the behaviour and the risk are themselves caused by a separate unknown factor. Also, dividing men into two groups in this way is somewhat simplistic.

---

[The rest of Appendix 2, overleaf, summarises some further research and study, undertaken since the material of this book was formulated. It explains a little more how having a Type A personality affects people, and how to deal with stress if you have one, or work closely with someone who does. Ed.]

## TRAITS OF TYPE A BEHAVIOUR
### Elisabeth Scott, MS., November 07, 2007

Since researchers started studying the Type A Personality several decades ago, it has become a household term. Most people now know that its characteristics have something to do with being competitive and work-obsessed, and can bring an increased risk of health problems. However, it is not always understood exactly what traits constitute Type A Behaviour, or exactly how these traits impact health and wellbeing.

### *Key characteristics:*

While the term 'Type A' personality is often thrown around, it is not always fully known what specific characteristics make it up, even among experts. For example, to some, the term applies to rude and impatient people. Others see workaholics as 'Type A'. Many see competitiveness as the main characteristic. According to research, the following characteristics are the hallmarks of Type A behaviour:

> *Time urgency and impatience*, as demonstrated by people who, among other things, get frustrated while waiting in a queue, interrupt others often, walk or talk at a rapid pace, and are always painfully aware of the time and how little of it they have to spare.
> *Free-floating hostility* or aggressiveness, which shows up as impatience, rudeness, being easily upset over small things, having a 'short fuse'.
> *Competitiveness*
> *Strong achievement-orientation*

### *Physical characteristics:*

The following physical characteristics often accompany both stress and Type A behaviour over years:

> *Facial tension* (tight lips, clenched jaw etc.)
> *Tongue clicking, teeth grinding*
> *Dark circles under eyes*
> *Facial sweating*

## *Negative effects:*

Over the years, the type of extra stress that most Type A people experience takes a toll on their health and lifestyle. The following are some of the common negative effects:

*Hypertension.* High blood pressure is common among Type A personalities, and has been shown to be as much as 84% more of a risk among those with Type A characteristics.

*Heart disease.* Some experts predict that heart disease by age 65 is a virtual certainty.

*Job stress.* Type A people usually find themselves in stressful, demanding jobs (and sometimes the jobs create the Type A behaviour) which lead to metabolic syndrome and other health problems.

*Social isolation.* They often alienate others, or spend too much time on work and focus too little on relationships, putting them at risk for social isolation and the increased stress that comes with it.

## *Fixed characteristics versus situational reaction:*

While many personality traits, such as extroversion, are innate, most researchers believe that Type A personality characteristics are more of a reaction to environmental factors, or tendencies toward certain behaviours, and are influenced by culture and job structure. For example:

Many jobs put heavy demands on *time*, making it necessary for workers to be very concerned with getting things done quickly if they are to get their jobs done adequately.

Some workplaces put heavy penalties on mistakes, so *efficiency and achievement* become extremely important.

Other jobs simply *create stress*, making people less patient, more tense and more prone to Type A behaviours.

Though some people do have a natural tendency towards being more intense, this can be exacerbated by environmental stress.

These effects can also be mitigated by conscious effort and lifestyle changes.

## PERSONALITY TRAITS AND HEART DISEASE RISK

### Dr. Martha Whiteman and colleagues
### The University of Edinburgh

The Lancet, London, August 22, 1997

While a number of studies have found that someone's personality can increase or decrease their risk of a heart attack (for example, aggressive, highly competitive people with the so-called Type A personality have been found in some, but not all, studies to be more likely to have a heart attack than people who are more easy-going, the so-called Type B personality), here the researchers report that another personality trait, *submissiveness*, may also affect a person's risk of a heart attack.

In this study, the researchers followed 809 men and 783 women aged 55 to 74 for five years. At the beginning the subjects were given physical examinations and a number of tests, including an electrocardiogram. They also completed questionnaires designed to identify people who tend to lack confidence and to prefer to stay in the background, people with so-called submissive personality traits. The questionnaires determined that on average the women tended to have more submissive personalities than men.

At the end of the study, about 10 percent of the men and 4.5 percent of the women had had heart attacks. The researchers found that submissiveness had little effect on a man's risk of having a heart attack. Among the women, however, the researchers found that those women who, according to the questionnaires, had more submissive personalities compared to other women in the study were nearly a third *less* likely to have had a heart attack.

The finding indicates, the researchers conclude, that it is important for scientists studying heart disease to look at a wide variety of psychological risk factors. 'Since the finding was particularly evident in women,' they add, 'it is clear that both sexes need to be included in studies of coronary heart disease.'

# APPENDIX 3

## WE ALL NEED HOMEOSTASIS:
## A CARDIOLOGIST'S POINT OF VIEW
### Based on a paper of P.G.F. Nixon, Charing Cross Hospital

From this cardiologist's point of view,[80] just as a thermostat protects the system against overheating, so the body protects us against change: too little water, we are thirsty and we drink; too chilly, we get goose bumps and put on more clothes. Equally, too tired and we feel exhausted. But we scorn to listen to the voice of fatigue. We do not rest.

The figure shows how we go over the hump and let ourselves be aroused long past the point of 'healthy fatigue'. Our functioning deteriorates; but still we try ever harder to compensate. Performance starts to dip but, because our arousal levels are still rising on a tide of effort, we don't notice how we are becoming less efficient. We can no longer do what we believe we should. As we struggle to close the gap we cease to sleep properly, considering this to be 'normal' even as we become more exhausted.

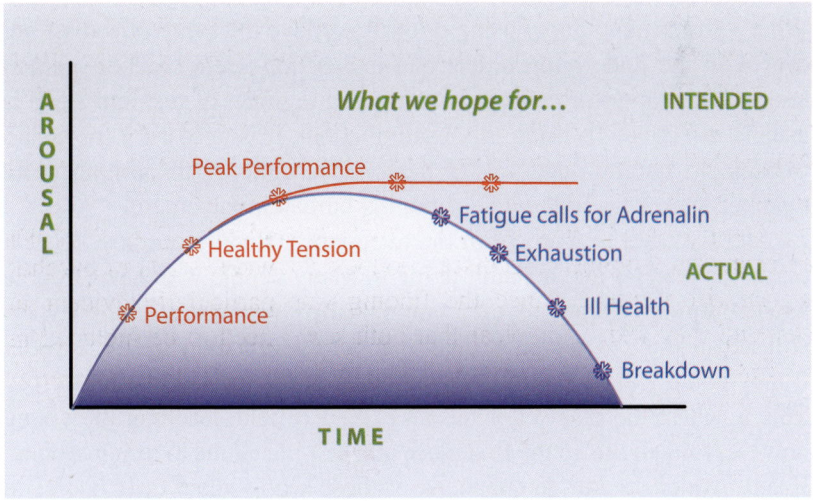

Figure 9. The Human Function Curve

---

80 Based on Nixon 1976, of Charing Cross Hospital, 'The Human Function Curve: with special reference to cardiovascular disorders'.

Chronic exhaustion is dangerous. It makes us less adaptable when things go wrong. We cease to be able to relax and enjoy the calm interludes of our lives. We cannot tell the difference between things we must do now and things we can leave until tomorrow. Our self-concept suffers; we become more tense and irritated until, eventually, we lose our tempers and begin to damage our relationships. We become impossible to live with. At work, there is no room for initiative, no energy for change. At the extreme end of this lie rage and, eventually, despair. We can't opt out, we can't continue; and talking is no help.

Exhaustion, despair, rage – a dangerous combination. We can neither control or understand what happens to us. Poisoned by people, pressured by time, resentful of changes imposed from without, we reject or deny our circumstances. Furious and frustrated, we soldier on, keeping going, but ever downwards, till (at the point P) things go seriously wrong. This is breakdown into illness of one kind or another.

The heart often suffers here, beating rapidly or erratically or becoming painful and inefficient. Our demands have exceeded its ability. Our blood pressure soars and won't come down. We cannot resist infection, we become accident-prone and all kinds of physical ills follow. A few tough people can battle on through all this for longer than most – the Type A individuals of Friedman and Rosenman. Most of us cannot.

The heart has been too badly used for too long and signals with pain. What restores us? Simply using drugs to remove the symptoms does not deal with the underlying defeat and exhaustion. Beta blockers cannot remove frustration or despair. An enforced regimen of rest and sleep is usually effective. To bring this healing about, it is necessary for health workers to commit themselves *personally*, rather than administering treatments from on high while shunning human involvement.

And we need to learn from the experience, finding out how to treat ourselves better – and actually doing it. Many people with heart trouble would improve greatly if they could learn how to stop being hyper-aroused and how to recognise their own sleep deprivation and exhaustion; if they could learn to be still, to know when they are tired, and to rest. This is where the counsellor has an extended field, teaching the young how to avoid all this in the first place and helping adults to turn it around. If self awareness can be enhanced, if those who violate their bodies in this way can be helped to transcend their troubles and at least recognise their addictions, then the over-stressed among us may get well, or at least become more peaceful in their affliction.

# APPENDIX 4

## SOME FURTHER SYMPTOMS

## Discussion between Barbara Somers, Ian Gordon-Brown and Participants

### *Alzheimer's disease*

*A participant*: When my father had Alzheimer's, I asked a doctor about it. He said that this kind of illness tended to happen to business-men, engineers, men who use a lot of maths and do a lot of paperwork; the symptom tends to go into the head. Whereas doctors, nurses, carers, tend to have heart attacks, congestion of the heart; the nature of their work is stressful to the heart.

*BS*: The cure may well be to stand at the interface and get a better rhythm of inner and outer, a better heartbeat and a better quality of being. It could be that using the two hemispheres of the brain in a more equal balance would help protect against Alzheimer's. The sequence of counselling, aiming to get inner and outer more well-synchronised, seems to touch in to these things: 'time for being, time for doing'.

*IGB*: It's still difficult to separate out those heart-based people in the 'caring' professions from many of the Type A's. However, those who carry a lot of responsibility in the professional sense do also carry very much in the heart. There is a psychic pressure, an expectation of other people, certainly a responsibility for other people. Often it's not part of the individual's psyche, it's collective. If you are in a responsible position within an organisation, it's one of the hazards for you at this particular time of world history. You are inevitably going to have to make a lot of decisions which will impose pressures on your heart-nature, whether you are conscious of it or not. People are inevitably going to project a whole weight of expectation on you and, if you haven't got a pretty tough constitution or protection mechanism, that's often where you will catch it. I think we are likely to see more of this in the near future.

And it's also to do with not having time for your own needs. Isn't the heart symptom saying 'What about me?' People in power, perhaps unconsciously, push organisations, be they commercial, educational or whatever, towards their vision faster than they can actually go with regard to the people involved. Those people may well be giving time to the organisation which they should be giving to themselves. They are pushing against the river.

## Cancer

The Simontons [81] suggested that severe emotional disturbance and rejection in early childhood might be linked with cancer. Poor self-image would be a significant element, since there might have been a lost relationship, or the image of having lost a relationship. There was often tension with one or perhaps both of the parents. Patients tended to be melancholy and anxious and had great difficulty in expressing hostility. They reported that their natural reaction, when confronting a difficult situation that might normally require people to be angry or to speak their mind, was to take it inside themselves.

*A participant*: Those who recovered under other sorts of regime than that which the Simontons were offering seemed often to get very angry with the treatment they were having. They'd say to the doctors, 'Well, to blazes with you, I'm not going to take any notice of that.' They were full of aggression against the medical practitioners, full of the ability to say 'No!' to what was offered. That this sort of thing seems to go with spontaneous remission and a high success rate has been well documented.

*Another participant*: According to the study done by Lawrence Leshan,[82] the loss of closeness often happened before five and was more associated with the mother than anyone else. To what extent was the mother actually there for them from eighteen months to three years old? Was the child allowed to be a child, or was there a demand that it grow up too fast? The picture suggested includes a tendency for the personality to fix on one primary love object in adult life. Then an experience of loss or grief usually occurred in the six to eighteen months before cancer actually emerged, a trauma that often included loss by divorce, separation or death. The difficulty for many of them in coping came out of their tendency to depression, to hopelessness.

*BS*: I cannot thank the Simontons enough for their work and for the use of imaging in this kind of study. Yes, the factors you mention are there. I have limited experience; I haven't done cancer counselling as such. However, in our work we also need, and are able, to discriminate a bit as to the *type* of cancer, and its location. There are different types.

---

[81]    Simonton, *Getting Well Again: a Step-by-Step Self-Help Guide to Overcoming Cancer for Patients and their Families*.

[82]    Leshan, *Cancer as a Turning Point: A Handbook for People with Cancer, Their Families, and Health Professionals*.

There is the take-over cancer – extremely fast, a rebellion through the cells and an absolute annexation of healthy cells – which would go with a fiery imaging. Then there is the slow-burning cancer; probably too much energy is, for any number of reasons, going through the system and not being properly handled by the organism. Finally, there is the very slow, erosion cancer, which seems to point to energies of earth and water.

Cancer is a big word for a number of different types of illness. Cancer of the womb or genitals is different from cancer of the throat. I'm sure the use of imaging in a very discrete way ('discrete' in the sense of discriminating out certain areas and working with them) makes a very major statement. Earth – Water – Air – Fire: yes, we can bear them in mind; but the localisation is terribly important. So ask where the cancer is, what organ is being hit, and why it has located itself there? The exploration of that will often throw up the person's history.

If, for instance, the cancer appears in the lower part of the body, it may well be taking you back to a trauma in childhood which had to do with rooting and with parental loss. If then, say eighteen months ahead of the actual cancer, some fresh trauma keys that in, it may develop as a symptom that pulls you down into a regressive tension, back-footing you on to the basic loss of root. Then it will probably have hit this lower part of the body.

Cancer of the tongue or throat seems, on the other hand, to have a lot to do with expression, speaking, being heard, communication; and it can be found in somebody who is not at all badly rooted or bonded. It's the inability to speak. If the trauma that rises before the cancer appears is of the 'wanting to speak and can't vocalise' kind, it's more likely to hit the upper part of the body.

*IGB*: We can try to clear the *chakras*, particularly asking which centre is being energised. Is the energy flowing through, or is it blocked? Is it affecting the subtle body, the energy-field underlying the physical body? The Simontons said that in the attempt to explore the personality types it's the general soil that counts, the soil in which the disease would happen. If the general soil is of a particular kind, it's cancer you are likely to get, whether it be an Air/Fire cancer or a Water/Earth one. If the general soil is different from that, the symptoms may well come as rheumatoid arthritis or migraine. If a depressed, inhibited individual cannot express themselves, their difficulty of expression may somehow go within and, because it does that, the predisposition is to cancer.

*BS*: Looking at the difference between the galloping types, such as some pancreatic cancers, and other kinds, we can only talk to the affected organ to find out why trouble has chosen to go there. We could ask which *chakra* is associated, and in this case it would be the Solar Plexus, the seat of the emotions. Among people I have known who have had the very fast, overtaking cancer, or remissions from it, it repeatedly comes up with people who have quite a strong energy-field, a lot of rage and anger and unexpressed fire. The speed at which it overtakes gives a sense of that rebellion against. It's as though anger turned in on one's own body begins to rage through the system.

### Schizophrenia and diabetes

*IGB*: It's interesting that people who have schizophrenia usually have reasonably good physical health. Instead of working as a totality, they are so split that the body remains on neutral ground and goes on functioning as a factor split-off from the psyche itself. I remember, way back in my Industrial Psychology days, we were interviewing a diabetic person who often failed to take his insulin. His symptoms were schizoid; not taking insulin, he would begin to go into a schizoid split, a dissociated state.

*BS*: Well, consider fasting. Often, if people want to change their state of consciousness, they will fast. It changes the blood-sugar level and this begins to affect the functioning of the brain; thus it can sometimes look very much like schizophrenia. There is probably quite a considerable link. People are beginning to believe that schizophrenia has some somatic causation.

*IGB*: Certain types of schizophrenic episode have been traced to an imbalance of the adrenal cortex. I would suggest that there may be some sort of energy relationship at a subtle level, as well as a straight chemical relationship.

*A participant*: I've been working with someone who is a diabetic, and tremendously passionate. He'd had a rather chaotic life, the 'too loose hold', and he said that the diabetes was the first thing that had given him any structure in his life. During the last three years he has had to get up at certain times to inject himself and he has had to eat at a certain time. His whole career has changed immeasurably. He's matured mentally. One wouldn't want to take that away from him.

*BS*: It's a beautiful example of a symptom emerging to help create an interface to hold chaos and order at bay.

*Another participant*: I've got a client whose father's whole personality changed from the time he became a diabetic until he died: he became very self-absorbed, self-indulgent, very worried about himself, shouting at my mother, 'You didn't weigh my carbohydrates properly!' But it seemed to be a self-nursing thing. Are these the people who perhaps haven't been nursed or nurtured? And I wonder if a slowing down is not part of it? He may want that at the same time.

## Multiple sclerosis

*IGB*: Someone I knew had been diagnosed as having MS. She had all the typical symptoms but they seemed to be highly selective. For instance, I discovered that just the left side of the face and brain and the right side of the body were affected. This suggested that it was a masculine/feminine thing. When we mapped it further it was clear that the symptoms came every time the masculine side was over-stressed and had to carry too much weight. She'd left school at the age of fifteen and gone out to make her way in the world. Her first job was in an architect's drawing office. They'd said, 'Are you a trained draughts-man?' and she'd said, 'Yes.' She wasn't, but she was so quick that they took her on. She was now working at the level of an architect, and being paid as such, without a single qualification. And her artistic side was calling. She needed to answer it, but every time that side got over-stressed, the MS symptoms appeared, on the right side of the body and the left side of the head. It looked very much as if this was a stress symptom and not necessarily MS at all.

A colleague who also suffered from this told me that in his view a lot of 'MS cases' were not actually that at all, but faulty diagnoses, and that the stress factor in the condition was very important. Also, the dietary requirements typically laid down do not work with everybody; there are people who actually need the things they are told not to eat. It's very individual.

BS: MS is a disease of the central nervous system, attacking the spinal cord and the spinal system. It's a dysfunction of the connective impulses of the nervous system, affecting the skeleton of the structure. It shakes the whole system. It's at least worth having a look at the idea that someone who is affected may have a very rigid spine, a very rigid approach with a lot of straight-up-and-down lines laid down, and the whole system is shaking that. Ask whether it comes at a moment when their stereotype-structure is being smashed down. Perhaps it needs to smash down? Again, it picks the moment for, in its multiple form, this sclerosis is a hardening process; it may be the very moment that they need to break out.

Research into gluten-free diets in the treatment of multiple sclerosis is important, I know. But I wonder how far it's the self-clearing of going on a diet, the sudden interest in a new subject, the feeling that there is something that can help, which make the difference. The people you go and discuss these things with are there. Suddenly there is a response; you have an hour given to you, with its care and attention. The diet doesn't usually cure the blessed thing on its own. One of the reasons the symptoms emerge is to get this attention, which is in itself the cure.

### Tuberculosis

With respiratory troubles, the lungs; first, ask what it's like, why it's there, why it's taken this form, and set up a dialogue with it. Air is involved with chest ailments – lack of it, or too much of it. It can be the need for an expression of some kind. People who have these troubles quite often find they are related to their posture; it is frequently a caved-in stance that goes with the effect on the lungs. Pick up the posture in the moment, get into the feeling of 'What does it remind you of?' It often leads back to an environment somehow deprived of oxygen, or an airless ambience that arose at some particular moment, causing the pneuma of the lungs to begin to harden, or to be inflamed, whatever it is that is affecting their whole lung. On the other hand, where somebody is too much up in the air you may get an over-enlargement of the thorax to the detriment of the base of the body. Their legs get left out; you can almost see them groping into space.

So we look at the ailment, listen to the ailment, noting that anything to do with breathing is almost certainly to do with the element of Air, but taking in the rest of their body in relation to it. Inflamed lungs are obviously making a different statement from waterlogged lungs; as the imaging in dreams of a burned-out desert with a fiery sun overhead is very different from marshland. One has a Water basis and the other is

Earth, dried out by sun, by Fire. People may have a spatial displacement too that has to be taken into account. Just setting up a dialogue with it may very well tell you what it's about. Check it; it makes such an accurate statement.

## High blood pressure

*A participant*: I work with mathematical, social and political trends, and I have become attuned to the idea of counselling the collective. I've been trying to work out the somatic *reaction* to the *action* of the collective psyche. I propose that it is the economy: money is the somatic, bodily function. Inflation, I suggest, is equivalent to high blood pressure, a fever, a galloping disease.

*BS*: I would say this makes sense if one thinks of the economy as the use of energy. In dreams, money often comes up as libido, life force; what is happening to it is a measure of the energy level within the corpus. Currency is energy. Map that, yes, and ask what high blood pressure is. It's the dysfunction of the interaction of the heart, isn't it? The rate of putting *in* is out of sync with the rate of putting *out* of the energy, of the flow of the blood – and up goes the blood pressure. Then the walls of the arteries, the channels, containers of the flow of life, are under too much pressure.[83]

## Rheumatoid arthritis and back trouble

*IGB*: Rheumatoid arthritis is still at a much earlier stage of studying than the other kinds of rheumatism. There is a distinction made here between men and women, you'll be glad to know. It's suggested that women who have a tendency for the symptom of their 'dis-ease' to come in this form are typically 'nervous, tense, worried, moody, depressed.... ' While the men are 'self-sacrificing, masochistic, conforming, self-conscious, shy, inhibited, perfectionist' and an odd one, 'interested in sport' (I suspect that all this is going to be very, very heavily shot down). They could well be, as it were, holding everything in.

*BS*: Yes, it's the same thing, retention; very often you also find constipation, which is one of the symptoms of rheumatoid arthritis.

*A participant*: I've been working with someone who's had arthritis of the neck and a lot of back trouble; she was on her back for six months some years ago. A lot of things have emerged from this: she

---

83 Calcification and build-up of plaque results and hardening follows.

once accused her parents of 'breaking her brother's back', and what emerged was that she felt as though they'd broken *her* back. It led to an image she'd had for her feeling of depression and chaos: she'd called herself 'a floating jelly baby' with no shape at all. Her backbone, her structure, had been diminished, broken in the beginning. The presenting problem was that her life was diffused, chaotic and un-focused. It all seems to tie in together.

*BS*: Rheumatoid arthritis is inflammation of the connective padding tissue around usually several joints, where the two ends interact with each other, while osteo-arthritis has to do with the degeneration of the actual cartilage, probably of a single joint. It's always useful to look up the etymology of the name and the history of the case itself. It's highly symbolic language. A hardening of the cartilages may be to do with that calcification of the stereotype or whatever that has been put on the person and is taking out the life, the very marrow of the bones. That will already begin to tell you something.

Any arthritis involves inflammation of the joints; but ask what kind of rheumatoid arthritis it is. Look at it with the people and you can see what happens. Very often it's the energy of locked direction. Fire is wanting to go somewhere and the feet are being put in the wrong direction. Some rheumatism is about the grip on the ground; the feet go claw-like. When somebody's trying to get a grip on their environment, the hands go claw-like. There can also be a disconnection of joints in the hands or the back or wherever; it's as if one part of the joint is repelling another. It is a disease which attacks the bone structure, the skeleton, the framework of somebody. Ask, what was their framework in the beginning? Why is it under attack?

*IGB*: So it's important to note whether it's hands or feet.

*BS*: Yes, within the skeleton. It tells you. You just look at the person standing there, and it will tell you. Things that push bones apart have a different energy from those which tighten them in, and the temperament usually goes with it. It's fascinating.

*A participant*: I have a woman client who has arthritis all over. She's all those things on that list you gave us: 'self-sacrificing, masochistic, conforming, self-conscious, shy, inhibited, perfectionist'. Yes. But you said those were for a man … ?

*BS*: How is she based in and balanced on her own feminine principle? Has she got a lot of masculine in her?

*Reply*: Yes.

*BS*: I would think that that's a good indicator....

*Reply*: ... And she was a great tennis player, interested in sport....

*BS*: Well, given the over-use of certain muscles in sport, it isn't in the least surprising, is it? It might well later come in as rheumatoid arthritis, the inflammation of the connective ends. There's usually a lot of anger. If people have done a lot of conforming, placating, serving and are all screwed up, they are going to have a great deal of unexpressed anger to balance it. As I said, wherever you get inflammation, watch for locked-up fire. It's very different from the crumbling of bone and cartilage – a different story.

## Migraine

*A participant*: I work with people with migraines, and it's astonishing the number who mention Saturday morning.

*BS*: 'Perfectionist' is a very valuable word to do with migraine.

*IGB*: A study has been done with males in working situations: they never get migraine during the week. It's only at the weekend that everything bottled up comes out. I had a friend who always got it on Saturday; he lay in bed most of the day with these terrible headaches. Tests have been done which suggest that sufferers have similarities to the Type A cardiovascular personality, but additionally that migraines afflict rather rigid, somewhat self-righteous, fanatical, self-sacrificing, trying-too-hard people. This would be descriptive of those who get it at weekends. It comes at the leisure moment.

*Another participant*: That's exactly what happens to me, that's when mine comes. It comes when I relax. But again it depends where the migraine starts.

*BS*: Yes indeed it does. And after all, Type A people, as defined there, wouldn't find it easy to relax. 'Relaxation' for them would be a tension and an anxiety and a threat, and their overwork might have to do with holding that anxiety at bay. We have to ask, 'What does Saturday mean to you?' For some people it's extra work, having to be back in the bosom of the family or whatever. What is it masking? Also, take it that there are a number of different types of migraine. Is it the kind involving blackout, or seeing rainbow zigzags? Is it half vision? If they say, 'I'm sick to the stomach, sick to the head, it's that split vision with black spots floating round,' we ask, 'What is it that you cannot stomach? What is it that is splitting your vision?'

*IGB*: One kind of migraine seems to be connected with bottling up, trying too hard, being fanatical – some of the Type A components. The other kind is more a way of coping with emotional pain or difficulty by taking it up into the head.

*BS*: And despair. There's fear of failure, the inability to go on, and often the need for a rest. It's the only time the true introvert can get into a darkened room and be left alone. It legitimises their need to withdraw. That's why you have to ask the individual. These tests use cover-words, I think, very important and valid – infinitely better, certainly, than fifty years ago when the psychic factor wasn't even taken into account – but still …

*IGB*: The important thing about these tests is that society generally is beginning to recognise and accept that certain personality types are prone to certain types of illness. Obviously, they are statistical studies with random samples, subject to all the variations of statistics. And certainly the characteristics of the individuals involved are lost in the mass. Even so, the studies are at the point where professionals cannot deny them. They have to start paying attention; they have to deal with them.

Thinking of research, I remember reading of some investigations which found that the body-chemistry of certain types of people was such that they suffered quite unpleasant headaches after sexual inter-course. Now, there may well have been a psychosomatic component in that – or not. But, thinking of Saturday, we may need to ask about the sexual patterns of the people involved …

*BS*: Is it that their sexuality, rather than releasing tension (which is what that research was about), is held up in the head? 'What does Saturday mean to you?' is a good question for the person to hear, because then they can bring up 'Well, every Friday night I try to make love.' What are their expectations of the weekend? What can they mask during the other five or six days, but cannot at that point? And you can carry that over to bank holidays, summer holidays, school holidays. To explore all these variants, and even to begin to befriend them, is to open up the language. Most people, if they are imaginative enough to have symptoms and sensitive enough to feel pain, can usually also be helped, through imaging, to discover what this is saying to them. This is one thing we all have in common.

It's a crucially important line, because it holds the difference between the expectation and the reality. You spend five days waiting for the weekend and what do you do when you've got the weekend? What happens to your energy? It's almost an echo, like waiting for the end of term at school; it produces so many physiological symptoms, so much unease in the body and confusions in the person who really wants to function – really does function – on Saturday mornings. What's Saturday morning all about anyway?

*A participant*: At a language class (not a counselling session) I'd said, 'Well OK, what colour would you give your days, your weekends?' and one Japanese lady coloured her weekend black. Some Japanese ladies are totally at the service of their husbands and their children. She had no space to herself at all and she could not say, 'Get your own breakfast'.

*Another participant*: There are huge numbers of people who find the weekend an absolute trial, purgatory; they have terrible trouble, a ghastly time, and long for Monday, back with colleagues and freedom and a different way of life. They dread every weekend.

*Another participant*: Single people have the loneliness of seeing everybody else doing things together. People you can contact during the week are obviously with their families at weekends. I have one client who finds weekends hellish; she makes very elaborate plans to avoid them.

*BS*: And it may not be the current Saturday mornings. It may be a memory-habit, a pattern, say, for coming back from school to home at the weekends or whatever. Therefore we follow the symptom and let it flip through the memory. It's extraordinary, but it has a tremendous bearing on how the person functions right now. It's about the five-day working-week, when you have to deal with all kinds of stresses. You may incorporate all kinds of attitudes into it and resist it in all kinds of ways. And the culmination of all that five-day effort is to produce the two-day weekend, which may completely fail. There is so much in it, it's quite astonishing.

# APPENDIX 5

## TOUCHED BY THE ARCHETYPE
## Barbara Somers and a Participant

*Participant*: I had the experience of being 'touched by the archetype' in adolescence. It was a great experience where I seemed to be lifted into the spiritual realm. I was full of joy and love, but later on I had to go back and it made a vertical split. Afterwards, I couldn't relate to my peer group so well. However, it did help me through adolescence, giving me a bit more clarity than I would have had. But it would have been a help to have been able to talk. And I did come back to the same stage much later on.

*BS*: Did you feel when you were young that you had a good understanding of the touching side, of touch? Or was that a confusion?

*Reply*: Yes, from my father's side. He was a very demonstrative, affectionate man early on. But not from my mother so much.

*BS*: That's very difficult for a girl; it shakes the taboo. The original touch from the mother is terribly important. Otherwise later, particularly around adolescence, you tend to get this split between god-immanent and god-transcendent, so that the spiritual can raise you above matter. If you'd had an adequate bonding of touch, it's quite possible that you'd have been able to hold the spiritual and the tangible together, but because this didn't happen you naturally went *up*, and had to come back.

*Reply*: I recognised it quite a bit afterwards. But I had to work at that side of it.

*BS*: We all get split. However, the early experience of bonding and rooting allows the spiritual not to split us apart, but to hold us together. The language of mystics of all kinds, who have supreme inner experience, practically always puts it in the language of touch, sensuality and sexuality. And the split.

*Reply*: The spiritual was a touching experience.

*BS*: The touching, to begin with, holds spirit and matter together, allowing the child to branch out and come back to its original wholeness. The lack of touch starts the whole search; the archetypes seem to come in to help force the split to become apparent, in order that we will come together in a new way.

# THE MAKING OF THE PICTURES

The pictures came from a conscious flow of creativity; they created the theme themselves. The information was in the flow of energy. I just relaxed, centred, emptied out and allowed the process to take me wherever it went, while my internal critic had to be put on hold.

When I started, I had a theme and layout in mind. However, when I tried to follow this plan, my mind would go blank and I came to a standstill, so I decided to put the plan aside and release all structure and expectations. As I relaxed and played with the materials, surprises and happy accidents began to occur and inspiration began to flow.

I was concerned that I now had no theme, but I continued in this unknowing way of working to see where it would lead. By now I was experimenting with methods and textures that I had not used before. A theme began to evolve as profiles emerged. A theme of unknown, unrecognisable people - symbols of humanity.

Then one morning, on waking, these words came to me:

*The experience of creativity is an entry into the mysterious. Techniques, expertise and knowledge are just tools. The key is to abandon oneself to the energy that fuels the birth of all things. The energy has no form or structure yet all the forms and structures come out of it.*

Since moving to Lyme Regis five years ago and allowing myself to be creative, I realise spirituality and creativity are one and the same. It is a connection to the Other, the muse, the flow, the Oneness.

Doing the pictures made me surrender to the process of manifestation and to follow that process wherever it led, becoming sensitive to what it needed of me on every level.

Love of the subject and admiration of Barbara is what has inspired this project. As Barbara says in the book: "our wound is our gift - and our talent".

Pamela Allsop
Transpersonal Psychotherapist UK reg.
Dorset, England

pamela.allsop@btinternet.com

# BIBLIOGRAPHY

Boswell, J., *Selections from the Works of Samuel Johnson*,
ed. C.G. Osgood. Henry Hott and Co: New York 1939.

Dychtwald, K., *Bodymind. Pantheon*. New York 1977.

Edinger, E., *Ego and Archetype*. Shambhala: Boston,
Massachusetts 1992.

Frankl, V.E., *Man's Search for Meaning*. Beacon Press: Boston,
Massachusetts 1959.

Frankl, V.E., *Man's Search for Ultimate Meaning*. Insight Books,
Plenum Press: New York 1997.

Fromm, E., *Escape from Freedom*. Unwin: London 1941.

Fromm, E., *The Art of Loving*. Unwin: London 1956.

Golding, W., *Lord of the Flies*. Faber & Faber: London 1954.

Gordon-Brown, I. and B. Somers, *The Raincloud of Knowable Things*.
Archive Publishing: Dorset 2008.

Jung, C.G., *Marriage as a Psychological Relationship*. CW 17,
Routledge and Kegan Paul: London 1909-10.

Jung, C.G., *Psychological Types*. CW 6, RKP: London 1921.

Jung C.G., *Individuation*. CW 7, RKP: London 1928.

Jung, C.G., *Commentary on 'The Secret of the Golden Flower'*. CW 13,
RKP: London 1929.

Jung, C.G., *Archetypes of the Collective Unconscious*. CW 9i,
RKP: London 1934.

Jung C.G., *'Wotan' in Civilisation in Transition*. CW 10,
RKP: London 1936.

Jung, C.G., *The Structure & Dynamics of the Psyche*. CW 8,
RKP: London 1960.

Jung, C.G., letter to Miguel Serrano, 14th September 1960, *Letters* Vol. 2,
RKP: London 1960.

Jung C.G., *Man and his Symbols*. Picador: London 1978.
Also as *Approaching the Unconscious*. Aldus Books: London 1964.
Also as *The Function of Religious Symbols*, CW 18,
Princeton University Press 1976.

Jung, C.G., *Memories, Dreams, Reflections*. Collins and RKP: London 1963; Fontana, Harper Collins 1995.

Keleman, S., *Your Body Speaks Its Mind*. Random House: London 1971.

Keleman, S., *Living Your Dying*. Random House: London 1974.

Keleman, S., *Human Ground: Sexuality, Self and Survival*. Random House: London 1975.

Laing, R.D., *The Divided Self*. Penguin Books: London 1960.

LeShan, L., R. Bolletino, M. Bobis & S. Koraleski, *Cancer as a Turning Point: A Handbook for People with Cancer, Their Families and Health Professionals*. Plume, Penguin Putnam: New York 1994.

Lowen, A., *Bioenergetics*. Arkana: London 1979.

Milne, A.A., *When We Were Very Young*. Methuen: London 1924.

Morris, J., *Conundrum*. Faber & Faber: London 1974.

Nixon, P., adapted from 'The Human Function Curve: with special reference to cardiovascular disorders'. In *Practitioner*, 217, 765, 935, Department of Medical Illustration and Teaching Services, Charing Cross Hospital and Medical School 1976. From *Counselling News*, 23, 8 1978.

Pelletier, K.R., *Mind as Healer, Mind as Slayer: A Holistic Approach to Preventing Stress Disorders*. Delacorte and Delta: New York 1992.

Rapoport, J., *The Boy Who Couldn't Stop Washing: The Experience & Treatment of Obsessive-Compulsive Disorder*. Collins: London 1990.

Reich, W., *The Function of the Orgasm*. Translated by T. Wolfe. Orgone Institute Press: New York 1942.

Rowe, D., *Depression: the Way Out of Your Prison*. Routledge and Kegan Paul: London 1983.

Serrano, M., *C.G. Jung & Hermann Hesse: a Record of Two Friendships*. Translated by F. MacShane. Schocken Books: New York 1966.

Simonton, C., J. Creighton & S. Matthews-Simonton, *Getting Well Again: a Step-by-Step Self-Help Guide to Overcoming Cancer for Patients and their Families*. Mass Market Paperback, Bantam Books: New York 1992.

Somers, B. and I. Gordon-Brown, *Journey in Depth*. Archive Publishing: Dorset 2002.

Storr, A., *The Art of Psychotherapy*. Seeker & Warburg: London 1979.

Truby King, F., *Feeding and Care of Baby*. Macmillan and Co Ltd: London 1924.

Wickes, F., *The Inner World of Childhood: A Study in Analytical Psychology*. Coventure: London 1977.

Wilhelm, R. & C.G. Jung, *The Secret of the Golden Flower: A Chinese Book of Life*. Routledge and Kegan Paul: London 1931.

Winnicott, D., 'Transitional objects and transitional phenomena', *International Journal of Psychoanalysis*, 34:89-97 1953.

# INDEX